Individual Differences and Processing Instruction

La vita é atroce, lo sappiamo, ma proprio perché mi aspetto tanto dalla condizione umana, i periodi di felicità, i progressi parziali, gli sforzi di ripresa e continuità mi sembrano altrettanti prodigi che compensano quasi la massa immensa dei mali, degli insucessi, dell'incuria e dell'errore. Sopraverrano le catastrofi e le rovine, trionferà il caos, ma di tanto in tanto verrà anche l'ordine. La pace si instaurerà di nuovo tra le guerre. Le parole umanità, libertà, giustizia ritroveranno qua e là il senso che noi abbiamo tentato d'infondergli. Non tutti i nostri libri periranno: si instaureranno le nostre statue infrante; altre cupole, altri frontoni sorgeranno dai nostril frontoni, dalle nostre cupole; vi saranno uomini che penseranno, lavoreranno e sentiranno come noi: oso contare su questi continuatori che seguiranno a intervalli regolari, lungo i secoli, su questa immortalità intermittente.

From *Memorie di Adriano*,
Marguerite Yourcenar, Einaudi 2005, p. 348

Individual Differences and Processing Instruction

Edited by James F. Lee and Alessandro G. Benati

SHEFFIELD UK BRISTOL CT

Published by Equinox Publishing Ltd.

UK: Kelham House, 3 Lancaster Street, Sheffield, S3 8AF
USA: ISD, 70 Enterprise Drive, Bristol, CT 06010

www.equinoxpub.com

ISBN-13 978 1 84553 343 4 (hardback)
978 1 84553 344 1 (paperback)

British Library Cataloguing-in-Publication Data

A catalogue record for this book is available from the British Library.

Library of Congress Cataloging-in-Publication Data
Individual differences and processing instruction / Edited by James F. Lee and Alessandro G. Benati.
pages cm.
Includes bibliographical references and index.
ISBN 978-1-84553-343-4 (hb) -- ISBN 978-1-84553-344-1 (pb)
1. Languages, Modern--Grammar--Study and teaching. 2. Grammar, Comparative and general. 3. Learning, Psychology of. I. Lee, James F., editor of compilation. II. Benati, Alessandro G.
P53.I44 2013
418.0071--dc23
2012049317

Typeset by ISB Typesetting, Sheffield, UK

Printed and bound in Great Britain by Lightning Source UK Ltd., Milton Keynes and Lightning Source Inc., La Vergne, TN

Contents

Acknowledgements

We would like to express our gratitude to all the contributors to this edited collection. A special thank you to our colleagues and reviewers who have provided valuable advice and suggestions to improve the content and style of the individual chapters in the book.

A special thank you also to Janet Joyce, Valerie Hall and Sarah Norman at Equinox for helping us in developing and producing this collection.

Preface

Input processing theory (VanPatten, 1996, 2004, 2007) and the overall results of the research conducted to support the principles and sub-principles of this theoretical framework provide the foundation on which the pedagogical model called processing instruction has been built (Lee and VanPatten 1995, 2003; VanPatten 1996). Processing instruction is an approach to grammar instruction; the aim of which is to help L2 learners circumvent the use of ineffective processing strategies when they process input and to instil appropriate processing strategies so that they deliver better intake from the input. The main purpose of this pedagogical model derived from VanPatten's model of input processing is to ensure that L2 learners process forms/structures correctly and efficiently in the input they receive.

Processing instruction research has consistently shown that it is an effective pedagogical intervention to alter processing strategies and ensure that L2 learners establish form-meaning connections and syntactic mappings correctly. As underscored by Wong (2004: 33), 'the goal of processing instruction is to help L2 learners derive richer intake from input by having them engage in structured input activities that push them away from the strategies they normally use'. Processing instruction is an instructional intervention that guides learners to focus on small parts/features of the targeted language when they process the input. The characteristics of processing instruction have been described in detail in previous literature (Benati and Lee 2008, 2010; Farley 2005; Lee and Benati 2007a, 2007b; Lee and Benati 2009; VanPatten 1996; Wong 2004, 2005).

Research on the effects of processing instruction has found that this new approach can affect the acquisition process and help L2 learners to deliver appropriate and accurate intake to the developing system. Processing instruction has been claimed to be an effective form of intervention in altering inappropriate processing strategies (e.g., primacy of meaning; lexical preference principle; preference for nonredundancy principle; first noun principle; and many other sub-principles) and instilling appropriate ones. Processing instruction has also been found to be an effective approach to grammar instruction as its main effects have been measured in different target languages (French, Italian, English, German, Japanese, Russian, and Spanish), different grammatical forms (past tense, present tense, gender morphology) and structures (word order, passive constructions). It is an effective form of instruction for learners from different proficiency levels, background and native languages (e.g. Italian, Chinese, English, Korean, Japanese: see Lee and Benati 2009 for a full review of PI studies). A more recent trend in research (Benati and Lee 2008) within the input processing theory and the processing instruction model has investigated possible secondary effects of this approach to grammar instruction.

One clear lacuna in the database is to measure the possible role that individual differences, such as age, gender, and native language background, might play in the results generated by processing instruction. The present collection of papers, brought together by James Lee and Alessandro Benati, offers a number of perspectives on the relative role of individual differences in processing instruction. The editors set the scene in Part I 'Theoretical Issues' by providing an overview of individual differences in second language acquisition and general findings from research on processing instruction. In Part II of the book, 'Empirical Studies', six studies investigating the role that individual differences might play in the results generated by processing instruction are presented and discussed.

References

Benati, A., and Lee, J. F. (2008). *Grammar Acquisition and Processing Instruction*: Clevedon: Multilingual Matters.

Benati, A., and Lee, J. F. (2010). *Processing Instruction and Discourse*. London: Continuum.

Farley, A. 2005. *Structured Input: Grammar Instruction for the Acquisition-Oriented Classroom*. New York: McGraw-Hill.

Lee, J. F., and Benati, A. (2007a). *Delivering Processing Instruction in Classrooms and Virtual Contexts: Research and Practice*. London: Equinox.

Lee, J. F., and Benati, A. (2007b). *Second Language Processing: An Analysis of Theory, Problems and Possible Solutions*. London: Continuum.

Lee, J. F., and Benati, A. (2009). *Research and Perspectives on Processing Instruction*. Berlin: Mouton de Gruyter.

Lee, J. F., and VanPatten, B. (1995). *Making Communicative Language Teaching Happen*. New York: McGraw-Hill.

Lee, J. F., and VanPatten, B. (2003). *Making Communicative Language Teaching Happen*, 2nd edn. New York: McGraw-Hill.

VanPatten, B. (1996). *Input Processing and Grammar Instruction: Theory and Research*. Norwood, NJ: Ablex.

VanPatten, B. (2004). Input processing in second language acquisition. In VanPatten, B. (ed.), *Processing Instruction: Theory, Research, and Commentary* (pp. 5–31). Mahwah, NJ: Lawrence Erlbaum Associates.

VanPatten, B. (2007). Input processing in adult second language acquisition. In VanPatten, B. and Williams, J (eds), *Theories in Second Language Acquisition* (pp. 115–35). Mahwah, NJ: Lawrence Erlbaum Associates.
Wong, W. (2004). The nature of processing instruction. In VanPatten, B. (ed.), *Processing Instruction: Theory, Research, and Commentary* (pp. 33–63). Mahwah, NJ: Lawrence Erlbaum Associates.
Wong, W. (2005). *Input Enhancement: From Theory and Research to the Classroom*. New York: McGraw-Hill.

Part 1

Theoretical Issues

1 Individual Differences in Instructed Second Language Learning: Working Memory, Aptitude and Age Differences

Alessandro G. Benati, University of Greenwich (UK)*

Introduction

In the last thirty years, findings from second language acquisition research have provided better insights into the processes and constraints implicated in the way languages are learned. Input has been one of the main focuses of attention in second language acquisition research. Krashen (1982) argues that input is a necessary ingredient in the acquisition of another language, as learners acquire a second language similar to the way they acquired their first language. VanPatten (1996) and Gass (1997) assign a key role to input and in particular to the amount of input that is actually processed by second language (L2) learners (this new construct is called *intake*). There is evidence that L2 learners follow developmental sequences (Pienemann, 1998) and learn morphemes in a similar order so that they might have access to innate knowledge (White, 2003). They analyse and process linguistic input relying on internal mechanisms (VanPatten, 2004).

* **Alessandro Benati** is Director of Research and Enterprise in the School of Humanities and Social Sciences at the University of Greenwich. He is an academic scholar in the area of second language acquisition. His research focuses on how language learners process incoming linguistic information at input level. He has worked extensively with James Lee on various projects. He has published books and journal papers in the areas of second language teaching and language acquisition. He is editor of an international book series in Instructed Second Language Research (Bloomsbury Publishing).

Despite the fact that these factors have a direct effect on the way languages are learned, it is also the case that 'learners are not all alike nor do they attain similar degrees of knowledge or proficiency over time. It is the study of individual differences that attempts to address variation in outcome over time' (VanPatten and Benati, 2010: 42).

Research on the effects of individual differences in second language acquisition has focused principally on constructs such as age and context differences, aptitude and working memory, intelligence, learning styles, and motivation. All these factors have been considered the main predictors of second language learning success (Dörnyei and Skehan, 2003).

In this chapter, three major areas of inquiry within the theoretical and empirical framework concerned with the effects of individual differences on second language learning will be briefly presented. We will examine working memory, language aptitude and age from a cognitive and psycholinguistic perspective. The concepts of working memory, aptitude and age differences will be explained and the relevance of these factors to second language acquisition highlighted.

Working Memory

The Concept of Working Memory

The role of memory has been debated in second language acquisition theory and research. Memory is the ability to encode, store and retrieve information. Three types of memory have been identified: sensory memory; short-term memory/working memory; long-term memory.

Sensory memory is responsible for receiving the information through different modalities. This information is subsequently processed and only a small proportion of the information enters short-term memory. Sensory memory and short-term memory are limited in their capacity to process and store information (Skehan, 1998).

Short-term memory receives input from the sensory system and then transfers information to long-term memory which is capable of storing information for a longer period of time. Baddeley and Hitch (1974, 1994) renamed short-term memory as 'working memory'. It can be defined as 'the ability to mentally maintain information in an active and accessible state, while concurrently and selectively processing new information' (Conway *et al.*, 2007: 3). A number of accounts have been put forward to describe the precise nature of working memory. However, the most prominent account is the model proposed by Baddley and Hitch (1974), which was subsequently revised by Baddeley (2000). According to their model, working memory consists of a limited capacity store and is supported by two systems: the phonological loop which is responsible for processing auditory information; and the visual-spatial sketchpad, which is responsible for processing visual information.

Long-term memory refers to a system for storing information, which can be retrieved at a later stage. The storage capacity is very difficult to quantify and many attempts have been made over the years to do so. It appears that items in long-term memory might be stocked in associative networks (VanPatten, 2003).

In all the memory models a central feature remains the purpose, capability and function of working memory. Working memory refers to the 'processing space in the mind/brain when a person holds and computes information' (VanPatten and Benati, 2010: 167). It is, however, possible that information entered in the working memory does not enter into long-term memory for processing because some parts of the input are selected for further processing and other parts are suppressed at the perception stage (Schmidt, 2001). As VanPatten and Benati (2010: 167) point out, 'there are multiple theories and models of working memory, but what they all have in common is the idea that working memory has a limited capacity. That is, a person can only process and store in working memory a limited amount of information before it must be disposed of so that the person can continue processing new incoming information'.

A range of empirical studies within a cognitive and psycholinguistic account of language acquisition have been conducted to investigate the role of working memory in second language acquisition. Some studies have investigated the possible relationship between individual differences in working memory and L2 performance, whereas others have addressed the role of various working memory components on language learning (e.g., Miyake and Shah (1999) who suggested that working memory is a component of aptitude). Overall these studies have provided empirical support for the view that working memory plays a direct role in the acquisition of an L2 under certain conditions of exposure: processing capacity; input; and task demands.

Information processing theory was applied to the input processing theoretical framework in the early 80s–90s (VanPatten, 1990a). Research conducted during this period focused on the various factors and processes responsible for how L2 learners process input and more importantly what part of that input becomes intake. From an information processing perspective it was assumed that individuals have a limited capacity for processing information. McLaughlin, Rossman and McLeod (1983) describe this 'limitation' along two dimensions: attention and information processing ability.

Attention, Information Processing Ability and Second Language Acquisition

Over the past few years, researchers and theorists have examined the role of attention and information processing in second language acquisition with the intention of shedding some light on how and when L2 learners focus their attention and select information. They have developed various opinions on the role and effects of attention in language learning. On one hand, Schmidt (1995; 2001) has argued that second language acquisition is driven by what L2 learners pay attention to and notice in the input. On the other hand, Gass (1997) maintains that attention is only one factor responsible for the acquisition of a second language. Attention can be defined as a cognitive process used by learners to selectively concentrate on one thing while ignoring other things. Three main concepts of attention have been discussed: selection, capacity and effort.

Many theorists have argued that L2 learners have limited capacity for processing information (e.g., Broadbent, 1958; Allport, 1988). This means that learners must select the incoming stimuli from several stimuli, otherwise activities that draw upon this limited supply of attention will interfere with each other. One of the questions addressed by research into the role of attention as selection is to establish what and how language learners initially select and process in the input.

Within this research and theoretical framework, theorists and researchers have investigated, parallel to the notion of attention, the role of awareness. Krashen has assigned a limited role to awareness, suggesting that conscious learning has no effects on the ability of L2 learners to acquire and use a second language in spontaneous communication. Schmidt (1990) has criticized Krashen's position, arguing that L2 learners require attention in order to successfully process forms in the input. Learners must pay attention to a form in the input and also notice it for that form to be processed and acquired. Schmidt's 'noticing hypothesis' suggests that noticing is necessary but it is not a sufficient condition for effective processing to take place. A degree of awareness is also crucial for L2 learners to incorporate the new language into their internal system. Therefore, for Schmidt, selection accompanied by noticing are the two main ingredients for learners to acquire a second language.

Broadbent (1958) suggests that L2 learners select information early in the processing of the information. According to his model, audio and visual information is first registered through the sensory system. After detection, selected information enters into the working memory system. The basic assumption in this model is that L2 learners cannot process more than one form at a time. In addition to this, simultaneous attention to form and meaning is not possible. In second language acquisition, the limited attentional capacity of the learner makes it unlikely for the learner to attend both to the message and formal features of a target language (VanPatten, 1990b). Tomlin and Villa (1994: 192) have characterized attention as comprising three components: alertness (learners' readiness to deal with incoming stimuli); orientation (ability to align attention to a stimulus); and detection (the process that selects a particular bit of information). Detection refers to the cognitive registration of the stimuli. It is the process responsible for selecting, engaging a specific piece of information and registering this information in memory. Detection, and not selection and noticing, is, according to Tomlin and Villa (1994), the key element for the derivation of intake from the L2 input. Detection is a crucial component for attention, as it constitutes the process used by learners to register data in working memory. Robinson (2003), incorporating Schmidt (2001) and Tomlin and Villa's model (1994), defined noticing as detection plus rehearsal in working memory before encoding in long-term memory. Robinson argued that both noticing and understanding are the result of rehearsal mechanisms, and the level of awareness is determined by the amount and rehearsal in the working memory.

From an input processing perspective, VanPatten (1996) has accepted the limited capacity model. He argued that the input gets 'hanged' when learners attend to too many stimuli, and therefore L2 learners filter the information utilizing internal strategies to cope with the amount of information they receive. The input processing capacity of L2 learners is limited and their internal processors might not detect all the linguistic data available. One of the key questions addressed by VanPatten is: what causes certain stimuli in the input to be detected and not others? According to VanPatten (1996), when learners process input, they filter the input, which is reduced and modified into a new entity called 'intake'. Only part of the input L2 learners receive is processed and becomes intake. This is mainly due to processing limitations, as our working memory does not have enough capacity to do much more than process content words.

In his model of input processing, VanPatten (1996, 2004, 2007) argues that input processing consists of two sub-processes: making form-meaning connections and parsing. VanPatten has identified a series of processing strategies/principles used by L2 learners when they process and filter linguistic data at input level. These strategies/principles allow learners to selectively attend to incoming stimuli without being overloaded with information. The two main principles in VanPatten's input processing theory are:

- Principle 1 (P1). The Primacy of Meaning Principle. Learners process input for meaning before they process it for form.
- Principle 2 (P2). The First Noun Principle. Learners tend to process the first noun or pronoun they encounter in a sentence as the subject /agent.

In the first principle, VanPatten (2004: 7) affirms that during input processing, L2 learners initially direct their attention towards the detection of content words to understand the main meaning of an utterance. Learners tend to focus their attention onto content words in order to understand the message of the input they are exposed to. In doing so, they do not process the grammatical form, and consequently fail to make form-meaning connections. The Primacy of Meaning Principle is further subdivided into six sub-principles (see Table 1.1) developed by VanPatten in order to examine the interplay between various linguistic and cognitive processes during language comprehension.

In the second principle, he states that L2 learners tend to process the first noun or pronoun they encounter in a sentence as the subject or agent (VanPatten, 2004: 15). This processing strategy would lead L2 learners to misinterpret the meaning of an utterance and cause delay in acquisition. VanPatten's First Noun Principle (2004) has three main associated sub-principles (see Table 1.2). These sub-principles attempt to identify other factors, which might influence the way L2 learners parse sentences correctly and attenuate their use of the First Noun Principle.

The second concept of attention is 'capacity'. The capacity of attention refers to the degree of attention allocated to the processing of information at any one time. Attention has a limited capacity as the sensory system of the brain is presented with a large amount of stimuli at any time, and due to working memory constraints it is impossible to process them all. Both the number of stimuli and the amount of attention paid to each of them is therefore restricted. Two of the theories often presented and examined are the single resource pool and the multiple resource pool (see Robinson, 2003). Kahneman (1973) has argued that there is a single resource pool of attentional supply that L2 learners allocate to tasks. This resource varies in terms of an individual's arousal state and the demands of the task. Complex tasks would demand more attention than simpler and automatized tasks such that

Principle 1. The Primacy of Meaning Principle: learners process input for meaning before they process it for form. (VanPatten, 2007: 117).
P 1a. The Primacy of Content Words Principle: learners process content words in the input before anything else (VanPatten, 2007: 117).
P 1b. The Lexical Preference Principle: if grammatical forms express a meaning that can also be encoded lexically (i.e., that grammatical marker is redundant), then learners will not initially process those grammatical forms until they have lexical forms to which they can match them (VanPatten, 2007: 118).
P 1c. The Preference for Non-Redundancy Principle: learners are more likely to process non-redundant meaningful grammatical markers before they process redundant meaningful markers (VanPatten, 2007: 119).
P 1d. The Meaning-Before-Non-Meaning Principle: learners are more likely to process meaningful grammatical markers before non-meaningful grammatical markers (VanPatten, 2007: 119).
P 1e. The Availability of Resources Principle: for learners to process either redundant meaningful grammatical forms or non-meaningful forms, the processing of overall sentential meaning must not drain available processing resources (VanPatten, 2007: 119).
P 1f. The Sentence Location Principle: learners tend to process items in sentence initial position before those in final position and those in medial position (VanPatten, 2007: 125).

Table 1.1 Summary of Principle 1 sub-principles (VanPatten, 2007)

Principle 2. The First Noun Principle: learners tend to process the first noun or pronoun they encounter in a sentence as the subject/agent.
P 2a. The Lexical Semantics Principle: learners may rely on lexical semantics, where possible, instead of the First Noun Principle to interpret sentences (VanPatten 2007: 124).
P 2b. The Event Probabilities Principle: learners may rely on event probabilities, where possible, instead of the First Noun Principle to interpret sentences (VanPatten 2007: 123).
P 2c. The Contextual Constraint Principle: learners may rely less on the First Noun Principle (or L1 transfer) if preceding context constrains the possible interpretation of a clause or sentence (VanPatten 2007: 124).

Table 1.2 Summary of Principle 2 sub-principles (VanPatten, 2004)

performing two tasks simultaneously is more demanding than one alone. Wickens (1980) has expanded this view and has proposed that two separate resource pools are responsible for allocation of attention to different task demands. These resources include: processing mechanisms (i.e. cognitive vs. response processes); processing modality (i.e. audio vs. visual perception); and processing codes (i.e. spatial vs. verbal activities).

The third concept related to the construct of attention refers to the learners' effort in processing information (Robinson, 2003). It is assumed that sustained attention to a stimulus is essential for carrying out a task. The degree of effortful attention to a task depends on the capacity demands of the task. If the task is high in capacity demands then more effortful attention is needed or the performance and processing might deteriorate. Less attention-demanding tasks would allow L2 learners to process more information and conduct a secondary task.

The relationship between working memory and second language acquisition is central to studies measuring language aptitude. It does play a central role in language processing for its role (ability to process symbols, store capacity and integrate information) in both comprehension and production of language.

Aptitude

The Concept of Language Aptitude

Carroll and Sapon (1959: 14) first defined language aptitude as a complex of 'basic abilities that are essential to facilitate foreign language learning'. Dornyei (2006: 45) refers to aptitude as the 'broader concept of human abilities, or intelligence, covering a variety of cognitively-based learner differences' that L2 learners bring to the task of acquisition. These cognitive abilities includes, among others, the following: learners' ability to perceive and encode sounds; working memory; and grammatical sensitivity (e.g., pattern recognition ability). VanPatten and Benati (2010) have defined language aptitude as a learner's propensity to learn another language.

Carroll (1981) proposed that language aptitude is comprised of four abilities:

- Phonemic coding ability. This is the learners' capacity to code sounds that can be retained. This is considered a unique auditory component of foreign language aptitude and is especially important in a language classroom which emphasizes spoken language.

- Grammatical sensitivity. This is the ability to recognize the functions of words in sentences. This component is relevant in language classes that emphasize an analytical approach to learning a foreign language.
- Inductive language learning ability. This is the capacity to infer and extrapolate rules to create new sentences. It is a kind of general memory, and learners seem to differ in the way they might apply and use their memory to the foreign language situation.
- Memory and learning. This is the capacity to form links in memory. This component, like the inductive learning ability, may vary according to an individual's ability.

Scholars have developed various component-based aptitude tests in order to measure aptitude abilities and capacities (e.g., MLAT, PLAB, CANAL-FT). The MLAT is probably the most influential aptitude test currently available. It consists of five subtests:

- Number learning test – measures associative memory.
- Phonetic script test – measures phonemic coding capacity.
- Spelling clues test – measures high speed language vocabulary and
- phonemic coding ability.
- Words in sentences test – measures grammatical sensitivity.
- Paired associated test – again, a test of associative memory.

Another broadly similar test battery is the PLAB (Pimsleur, 1966) which was developed specifically for high-school learners. This aptitude test placed greater emphasis on auditory factors rather than memory factors. More recently a new test battery has been developed, CANAL-F (Grigorenko, Sternberg and Ehrman, 2000), to measure human intelligence with the overall purpose of identifying learning difficulties, e.g. auditory.

Language Aptitude and Second Language Acquisition

Aptitude is an individual difference factor that was initially perceived as a self-contained factor largely unrelated to second language acquisition. However, in more recent years, the relation between aptitude and second language acquisition has received considerably more attention in second language acquisition theory and research. Skehan (1998) has argued that specific components of aptitude are related to stages of information processing. Dornyei and Skehan (2003) have attempted to make explicit links between stages of L2 processing and specific aptitude constructs (see Table 1.3).

Stages of L2 processing	Aptitude constructs
Input processing strategies	Attentional control, Working memory
Noticing	Phonetic coding ability, Working memory
Pattern identification	Phonetic coding ability, Working memory Grammatical sensitivity, Inductive language learning ability
Pattern restructuring and manipulation	Inductive language learning ability
Pattern control	Automatization, Integrative memory
Pattern integration	Chunking, Retrieval memory

Table 1.3 Stages of L2 processing and their related aptitude constructs

Dornyei and Skehan have suggested that it is possible that individual aptitude differences might have an effect on successful noticing and processing input. Individual phonetic coding ability and working memory capacity might therefore influence they way learners acquire a second language. Processing instruction, as described by VanPatten (1996), might be an effective focus on form technique to enhance L2 learners' grammatical sensitivity component.

Robinson (2001) has abandoned the concept of isolated aspects of aptitude and instead has developed a new concept, which involves what he called *aptitude complexes* (aptitude for focus on form; aptitude for incidental learning (oral and written); aptitude for explicit rule learning). In the Aptitude Complex Hypothesis, Robinson claims that learning draws on different combinations of cognitive abilities (aspects of aptitude) depending on the conditions of instructional exposure. Robinson makes an explicit call for more research to investigate the extent to which various instructional treatments (e.g., processing instruction; input enhancement) may or may not be sensitive to individual differences within these *aptitude complexes*.

Age Differences

The Concept of Age

Age is considered one of the major affective factors in second language acquisition research. A great variety of views have been expressed on the age question in children and adults who learn either the native language (L1) or the second language (L2) at different ages. A number of hypotheses have been proposed to account for the correlation of age and ultimate attainment in second language acquisition. Empirical studies have been designed to investigate the question of the optimal age to learn a second language. In the so-called 'Critical Period Hypothesis' (CPH), it is argued that there is a period of time during which a human displays a heightened sensitivity to certain environmental stimuli and therefore it is easier for them to acquire a second language (Richards and Schmidt, 2002; Larsen-Freeman, 2008). CPH for language learning is usually defined to last from the age of two to puberty. According to this theory, children are better second language learners than adults because their brains are specifically organized to learn language whereas adults' are not. One of the key arguments in this hypothesis is that a child's brain is more plastic compared with that of an adult. According to this hypothesis, a child can learn two or three languages with ease. Lenneberg (1967) asserted that language acquisition is mainly an innate process influenced by certain biological factors, which limit the critical period for acquisition of a language from two years of age to puberty. Lenneberg suggests that after lateralization (a process by which the two sides of the brain develop certain functions and normally completed at puberty), the brain loses plasticity, and it is, therefore, more difficult to acquire another language. Early exposure to a second language is therefore a potential advantage in acquiring a second language. Recent empirical evidence clearly indicates that earlier learners acquire an L2 more proficiently over a particular age range, i.e., from 5 to 15 years (Johnson and Newport, 1991; Birdsong and Molis, 2001). However, we must notice that despite the fact that the age effect is an established factor in second language acquisition, researchers have also found evidence that adults can achieve high levels of ultimate success in the acquisition of a second language. Adults are capable of high-order language functions and learning strategies.

Long (2007) and Eubank and Gregg (1999) have argued that there is not just a critical period, but multiple periods, which might constrain different aspects of language acquisition (for example the acquisition of phonology vs. the acquisition of syntax).

Another hypothesis related to the concept of age is the so-called Sensitive Period Hypothesis (SPH) which proposes a gradual deterioration in the process of language learning (cf. Robinson, 2002).

Age Differences and Second Language Acquisition

A number of views and interpretations have been expressed on the age question in children and adults. The common view is that children have an advantage over older learners in language learning (Ellis, 2008; Larsen-Freeman, 2008). The CPH states that a period between two and puberty exists during which learning a second language is accomplished more rapidly. In recent years a number of empirical studies have been undertaken to investigate whether or not age affects learning outcomes (Birdsong, 1999; Singleton 2001). Younger learners and adults have neurological, cognitive and psychological differences that come into play in second language acquisition. Children are usually considered to be better learners than adults. They tend to have fewer inhibitions than adults and have a desire to actively participate in the social life around them that helps them to learn new languages. They do not have analytical skills and tend to process languages generally through sensory experience, and language develops from exposure to simplified and concrete input. Adult language learners are, instead, notorious for their lack of ultimate mastery of language structure. However, older learners possess analytical ability and pragmatic skills. Adults are people with years of experience and real-world knowledge. They have established values, beliefs and opinions and relate new knowledge and information to previously learned information and experiences. This might help them to perform language tasks with much greater complexity. While younger learners normally achieve a higher level of ultimate attainment in a second language, adults have greater analytical capacity and pragmatic skills. Lightbown and Spada (2008) have argued that 'acquisition' is affected by factors such as learners' characteristics and the environment. Adults might be better at problem solving and have greater metalinguistic abilities than children. Adults find themselves in situations that demand more complex language and the ability to express more difficult concepts.

The most popular position related to age and second language acquisition is 'the younger = the better' hypothesis. This position is supported by a number of studies comparing pre-puberty groups vs. post-puberty groups that have indicated that pre-puberty groups are better at learning than post-puberty groups (Singleton, 2001). Research on second language acquisition among immigrants has shown that the younger the child the higher is the probability of a native-like accent (Lightbown and Spada, 2008). Johnson and Newport (1991) tested the acquisition of English morphology with two different age groups (3–15 years old and 17–30 years old). The results of this study showed that those who began learning later did not develop native-like language abilities.

A different hypothesis is that 'the older = the better'. Dekeyser (2000) replicated Johnson and Newport's experimental study with a group of immigrants. He obtained different results and concluded that adult learners were better than the younger ones. Classroom studies in the sixties and seventies had indicated that older learners are better than younger ones. Findings from these studies rejected the notion that 'the younger = the better' (see review of studies in Singleton, 2007).

Birdsong (2005; 2006) has argued that memory, learning conditions, and second language processing speed are factors connected to age. Cognitive processes are different in young learners and adult learners. Archibald (2005) has argued that it is difficult to support the view that a critical period truly exists as there is contradictory evidence investigating age as an indicator of successful language learning. He valued other factors as indicators of language learning. Factors related to age such as the motivation to learn, other individual differences, access to input and opportunities for interaction are important determining variables that might affect the rate and success of second language acquisition.

Muñoz (2006) showed that differences between younger and older learners disappear once, given the same time and exposure, they reach the same cognitive development.

Conclusion

Individual differences refer to a number of personal characteristics, which might affect human thinking and behaviour. However, individual differences have not consistently been found as a predictor of success in second language acquisition. In this chapter a brief overview of three individual differences (working memory, aptitude, age differences) has been provided.

A number of constructs have been related to the concept of aptitude. Broadly, the concept of language aptitude is related to the broader concept of human abilities covering a variety of cognitive-based learner differences (Dornyei, 2006). A number of aptitude language tests have been developed over the years, to predict the rate of progress and success under conditions such as motivation, opportunity to learn and quality of instruction. However, research on the role of aptitude in second language acquisition success has produced conflicting results. Research should look at the possible interaction between aptitude and variables such as different types of instructional treatments and instructional tasks.

Working memory 'is a psychological construct that refers to the processing space in the mind/brain when a person computes information' (VanPatten and Benati, 2010: 167). Working memory is an essential element (although it has a limited capacity in humans) in developing our ability to process linguistic data. The relationship between working memory and second language acquisition is central to studies measuring language aptitude. It does play a central role in language processing for its role (ability to process symbols, store capacity and integrate information) in both comprehension and production of language.

In examining the findings investigating the CPH we must conclude that conflicting results and views have undermined the original claim that a critical period exists in second language acquisition. The CPH fails to account for the numerous adult learners who appear to have achieved native-like proficiency (Singleton, 2007).

References

Allport, A. (1988). What concept of consciousness? In Marcel, A. G. and Bisiach, E. (eds), *Consciousness in Contemporary Science* (pp. 159–82). Oxford: Oxford University Press.

Archibald, J. (2005). Second language acquisition. In O'Grady, W., Archibald, J., Aronoff, M. and Reseller, J. (eds), *Contemporary Linguistics: An Introduction* (pp. 420–21). 5th edn. New York: Bedford.

Baddeley, A. D. (2000). The episodic buffer: A new component of working memory? *Trends in Cognitive Science*, 4, 417–23.

Baddeley, A. D., and Hitch, G. J. (1974). Working memory. In Bower, G. A. (ed.), *The Psychology of Learning and Motivation: Advances in Research and Theory* (pp. 47–89). New York: Academic Press.

Baddeley A. D., and Hitch, G. J. (1994). Developments in the concept of working memory. *Neuropsychology*, 8, 485–93.

Birdsong, D. (ed.) (1999). *Second Language Acquisition and the Critical Period Hypothesis*. Mahwah, NJ: Erlbaum.

Birdsong, D. (2005). Interpreting age effects in second language acquisition. In Kroll, J. and de Groot, A. M. B. (eds), *Handbook of Bilingualism: Psycholinguistic Approaches* (pp. 109–27). Oxford: Oxford University Press.

Birdsong, D. (2006). Age and second language acquisition and processing: A selective overview. *Language Learning*, 56, 9–49.

Birdsong, D., and Molis, M. (2001). On the evidence for maturational effects in second language acquisition. *Journal of Memory and Language*, 44, 235–49.

Broadbent, D. E. (1958). *Perception and Communication*. New York: Pergamon Press.

Carroll, J. (1981). Twenty-five years of research on foreign language aptitude. In Diller, K. C. (ed.), *Individual Differences and Universals in Language Learning Aptitude* (pp. 83–117). Rowley, MA: Newbury House.

Carroll, J. B., and Sapon, S. M. (1959). *Modern Language Aptitude Test (MLAT)*. San Antonio: Psychological Corporation.

Conway, A. R. A., Jarrold, C., Kane, M. J., Miyake, A., and Towse, J. N. (eds) (2007). *Variation in Working Memory*. New York: Oxford University Press.

DeKeyser, R. (2000). The robustness of critical period effects in second language learners. *Studies in Second Language Acquisition*, 22, 499–533.

Dornyei, Z. (2006). Individual differences in second language acquisition. In Bardovi- Harlig, K. and Dornyei, Z., *Themes in SLA Research* (pp. 42–68). AILA Review vol. 19. Amsterdam: John Benjamins Publishing.

Dornyei, Z., and Skehan, P. (2003). Individual differences in second language learning. In Doughty, C. J. and Long, M. H. (eds), *The Handbook of Second Language Acquisition* (pp. 589–630). Oxford: Blackwell.

Ellis, R. (2008). *SLA Research and Language Teaching*. New York: Oxford University Press.

Eubank, L., and Gregg, K. (1999). Critical periods and (second) language acquisition: Divide et Impera. In Birdsong, D. (ed.), *Second Language Acquisition and the Critical Period Hypothesis* (pp. 65–99). Mahwah, NJ: Lawrence Erlbaum Associates.

Gass, S. (1997). *Input, Interaction, and the Second Language Learner*. Mahwah, NJ: Lawrence Erlbaum Associates.

Grigorenko, E.L., Sternberg, R.J. and Ehrman, M. (2000). A theory-based approach to the measurement of foreign language aptitude: the CANAL-F theory and test. *Modern Language Journal*, 84, 390–405.

Johnson, J., and Newport, E. (1991). Critical period effects on universal properties of language: the status of subjacency in the acquisition of a second language. *Cognition*, 39, 215–58.

Kahneman, D. (1973) cited in Ruthruff, E., Van Selst, M., Johnston, J. C. and Remington, R. (2006). How does practice reduce dual-task interference: integration, automatization, or just stage-shortening? *Psychological Research*, 70, 125–42.

Krashen, S. (1982). *Principles and Practice in Second Language Acquisition*. London: Pergamon.

Larsen-Freeman, D. (2008). *Techniques and Principles in Teaching*. New York: Oxford University Press.

Lenneberg, E. H. (1967). *Biological Foundations of Language*. New York: Wiley.

Lightbown, P., and Spada, N. (2008). *How Languages are Learned*, 3rd edn. New York: Oxford University Press.

Long, M. (2007). *Problems in SLA*. New Jersey: LEA.

McLaughlin, B., Rossman, T., and McLeod, B. (1983). Second language learning: an information processing perspective. *Language Learning*, 33, 135–58.

Miyake, A., and Shah, P. (eds) (1999). *Models of Working Memory: Mechanisms of Active Maintenance and Executive Control*. New York: Cambridge University Press.

Muñoz, C. (2006). *Age and the Rate of Foreign Language Learning*. Clevedon: Multilingual Matters.

Pienemann, M. (1998). *Language Processing and L2 Development*. New York: Benjamins.

Pimsleur, P. (1966). *Pimsleur Language Aptitude Battery*. New York: Harcourt Brace Jovanovich.

Richards, J. C., and Schmidt, R. (2002). *Longman Dictionary of Language Teaching and Applied Linguistics*. London: Longman.

Robinson, P. (2001). Individual differences, cognitive abilities, aptitude complexes and learning conditions in second language acquisition. *Second Language Research*, 17, 368–92.
Robinson, P. (ed.) (2002). *Individual Differences and Instructed Language Learning*. Philadelphia/Amsterdam: John Benjamins.
Robinson, P. (2003). Attention and memory during SLA. In Doughty, C. and Long, M. (eds), *The Handbook of Second Language Acquisition* (pp. 631–79). Oxford: Blackwell.
Schmidt, R. (1990). The role of consciousness in second language learning. *Applied Linguistics*, 11, 129–58.
Schmidt, R. (ed.) (1995). *Attention and Awareness in Foreign Language Learning*. Manoa: University of Hawai'i.
Schmidt, R. (2001). Attention. In Robinson, P. (ed.), *Cognition and Second Language Instruction* (pp. 3–32). Cambridge: Cambridge University Press.
Singleton, D. (2001). Age and second language acquisition. *Annual Review of Applied Linguistics*, 21, 77–89.
Singleton, D. (2007). The critical period hypothesis: some problems. *Interlinguistica*, 17, 48–56.
Skehan, P. (1998). *A Cognitive Approach to Learning Language*. Oxford: Oxford University Press.
Tomlin, R., and Villa, V. (1994). Attention in cognitive science and second language acquisition. *Studies in Second Language Acquisition*, 16, 183–204.
VanPatten, B. (1990a). Attending to content and form in the input: an experiment in consciousness. *Studies in Second Language Acquisition*, 12, 287–301.
VanPatten, B. (1990b). Evaluating the role of consciousness in second language acquisition: terms, linguistic features, and research methodologies. In Hulstijn, J. and Schmidt, R. (eds), *Consciousness in Second Language Learning* (pp. 27–36). AILA Review vol. 11. Amsterdam: John Benjamins Publishing.
VanPatten, B. (1996). *Input Processing and Grammar Instruction: Theory and Research*. Norwood, NJ: Ablex.
VanPatten, B. (2003). *From Input to Output: A Teacher's Guide to Second Language Acquisition*. New York: McGraw-Hill.
VanPatten, B. (ed.). (2004). *Processing Instruction: Theory, Research, and Commentary*. Mahwah, NJ: Erlbaum.
VanPatten, B. (2007). Input processing in adult second language acquisition. In VanPatten, B. and Williams, J. (eds), *Theories in Second Language Acquisition* (pp. 115–35). Mahwah, NJ: Erlbaum.
VanPatten, B., and Williams, J. (eds) (2007). *Theories in Second Language Acquisition*. Mahwah, NJ: Erlbaum.
VanPatten, B., and Benati, A. (2010). *Key Terms in Second Language Acquisition*. London: Continuum.
White, L. (2003). *Second Language Acquisition and Universal Grammar*. Cambridge: Cambridge University Press.
Wickens, C. D. (1980). The structure of attentional resources. In Nickerson, R. (ed.), *Attention and Performance* (pp. 239–57). Hillsdale, NJ: Erlbaum.

2 Foci and General Findings of Research on Processing Instruction: Moving beyond Limitations

James F. Lee, University of New South Wales (Australia)*

Introduction

The purpose of this chapter is twofold: to review the existing research on PI and to provide a critical assessment of that research. I organize the review according to the different foci around which PI research has been conducted. I have identified seven. Organizing the research in this way establishes both the breadth and depth of the empirical work done to date. The critical assessment addresses the generalizability as well as the limitations of the existing research. A previous critical assessment (Lee, 2004) identified as limitations the fact that the target languages investigated were exclusively Romance languages, the learners investigated were exclusively native speakers of English almost all of whom were university-aged students, and the fact that individual differences in learners' characteristics had not been addressed. Do these limitations still apply?

This chapter is comprised of two distinct parts: a review of research findings on processing instruction and an assessment of the limitations of that research. First, I will review the existing research on PI, organized

* **James Lee** is Deputy Head of the School of Humanities and Languages at the University of New South Wales, Sydney, Australia where he teaches Spanish area studies and second language acquisition. His main research interest is second language input processing and, with Alessandro Benati, has co-authored several books on processing instruction. His most recent work is with Paul Malovrh, *The Developmental Dimension in Instructed Second Language Learning: The L2 Acquisition of Object Pronouns in Spanish* (Bloomsbury, 2013).

according to the seven different research foci that have guided the research; these are PI's research strands. In doing so, I aim to establish that the previous research has both breadth and depth. Two questions guide the review. What research has been carried out in each of these areas? What are the general findings of that research? The foci or research strands around which the review is organized are:

1. Comparing the effects of processing instruction to the effects of other types of instruction such as traditional instruction and meaning-based output instruction with the goal of determining whether processing instruction is effective or not.
2. Comparing the effects of full processing instruction, which consists of the combination of explicit information and structured input activities, with the effects of providing learners only with structured input activities or only with explicit information, in order to determine which component-element of processing instruction is the causative variable.
3. Comparing the effects of structured input to the effects of aurally and visually enhanced structured input with the goal of improving learning outcomes via such enhancements.
4. Comparing the effects of delivering processing instruction in classrooms to groups of learners to delivering it in computer laboratories to individuals in order to determine if one delivery format yields superior results.
5. Measuring the effects of processing instruction using discourse-level tasks to determine if the effects of processing instruction, which is typically sentence-oriented, extend to discourse-level tasks.
6. Measuring the effects of processing instruction over time to determine how durative and long-term they are.
7. Determining whether learners will transfer the processing strategy training via processing instruction they receive on one linguistic item to their processing of a different linguistic item.

Part I: The General Findings

Research focus (1): The effects of processing instruction compared to the effects of other types of instruction

VanPatten and Cadierno (1993), the first published investigation on processing instruction, aimed to demonstrate that PI was an effective type of instruction by comparing it to traditional instruction on Spanish direct object pronouns. The processing group in PI research never produces the target form; learners hear it and read it. Input is structured so that they use the form to interpret the meaning of a sentence. The traditional instruction was modelled on activities included in one of the most popular Spanish language textbooks in the United States. This instruction was output-oriented and contained a mix of mechanical and meaningful output practices. Learners in the traditional group were required to produce the target form in each item. VanPatten and Cadierno also included a control group who received no instruction on the target form and only completed the pre-tests and post-tests. They designed two types of assessments, one to measure interpretation of the target form and the other to measure form production. By statistically comparing the scores on the pre-tests they determined that there were no significant differences across the three groups prior to treatment meaning that all groups started with equivalent knowledge of the target form and that any difference found after treatment would be attributed to the effects of instruction. Immediately after instruction they administered the post-tests. Only the PI group showed significant improvement on the interpretation task. The interpretation task scores of the PI group were statistically significantly higher than those of the traditional instruction and control groups; there was no statistical difference between the scores of the traditional instruction and control groups on the interpretation task. Both the PI and traditional groups showed significant improvement on the form production task. The form production scores of the PI and traditional groups were not statistically different from each other and both groups' scores were significantly higher than the control group's score. Many other studies emerged from this study and from these results many similar if not identical findings were gathered.

Cadierno (1995) had identical results on Spanish third person past tense as did Cheng (2002) for Spanish copula choice with past participles. These were also the results in Benati (2009) for the Japanese affirmative and negative present tense markers. In two investigations, the traditional instruction group improved on the interpretation post-test, but not as much as the PI group did. The PI group's scores were statistically significantly higher than the traditional group's scores. These were the results in Benati (2001) for the Italian future tense and VanPatten and Wong (2004) for the French causative constructions with the verb *faire*. In these two investigations the form production results were identical to those found by VanPatten and Cadierno (1993); both PI and traditional instruction groups improved significantly and equally and both outperformed the control group. The results on interpretation and production were stable in delayed post-testing (Benati, 2001; Cadierno 1995; Cheng, 2002; VanPatten and Cadierno, 1993).

In two studies, structured input activities alone with no explicit information were given to one group of learners whereas a second group received traditional instruction (Lee and Benati, 2007a: ch. 3). The forms investigated were Japanese affirmative and negative present tense markers and the Japanese past tense marker. In both studies the group receiving structured input activities significantly outperformed the traditional group on the interpretation test. The two groups performed equally well on the production test in both experiments.

One difference between PI's structured input activities and traditional instruction is the meaningfulness of the items in PI because all the items in the PI activities require learners to work with meaning. As only some of the traditional output activities were meaningful research was undertaken to compare the results of PI with those of meaning-based output instruction (MOI), in which all the production practices involved meaning. The PI group has been found to significantly outperform the MOI group on interpretation tasks on the English simple past tense (Benati, 2005), the Italian and French subjunctive (Lee and Benati, 2007a), the Spanish subjunctive (Farley, 2001a), and Spanish direct object pronouns (VanPatten, Farmer and Clardy, 2009). The interpretation scores of the two treatment groups have also been shown to improve equally on the Spanish subjunctive (Farley, 2001b; 2004a) and Spanish direct object pronouns (Keating and Farley, 2008; Morgan-Short and Bowden, 2006). The results are mostly consistent for production measures in that both PI and MOI groups improved significantly and equally (Benati, 2005; Farley, 2001a; 2001b; 2004a; Lee and Benati, 2007a; Morgan-Short and Bowden, 2006; VanPatten, Farmer and Clardy, 2009). Only Keating and Farley (2008) found that the MOI group and another output group called meaning-based drills instruction significantly outperformed the PI group on the production task.[1] Benati (2005) compared the performance of three groups of learners who received instruction on the English simple past tense. One group received PI, another traditional instruction and the third MOI. The PI group significantly outperformed the other two groups on the interpretation task; there was no statistically significant difference between the scores of the traditional and MOI groups. The three groups improved significantly and equally on the production task. Toth (2006) found equal improvement for PI and a communicative task group on grammaticality judgments on the anti-causative clitic *se* in Spanish.

Is processing instruction an effective type of explicit (grammar) instruction? All the studies cited in this section indicate that it is. Is processing instruction more effective than traditional instruction? It is more effective in that learners who receive PI show improvement in both processing and production assessments whereas learners who receive traditional instruction typically only show improvement in production assessments. Is processing instruction more effective than meaning-based output instruction? The results of the research on this question are divided but the number of studies indicating that PI is more effective than meaning-based output instruction is greater than the number indicating that they are equally effective. As VanPatten, Farmer and Clardy (2009: 125) point out, different researchers have interpreted and designed MOI differently. Meaningful comparisons between PI and MOI can only be carried out if the implementation of MOI remains constant just as it has for PI.

Research focus (2): The effects of full processing instruction compared to the effects of structured input activities and explicit information

What I call *full* PI consists of two elements: explicit information (EI) and structured input (SI) activities. The explicit information provides learners with an explanation of the target form (morphosyntactic characteristics) and its function emphasizing the connection between form and meaning. Additionally, learners receive information about the processing strategies they use erroneously or inefficiently and the one they should use instead (e.g., VanPatten, 1996: 62). Structured input activities manipulate the input so that learners must attend to the target form and use it to make meaning (e.g., Wong, 2004a). An issue that emerged in the professional discussion after VanPatten and Cadierno had published their study was the question of which aspect of processing instruction was responsible for the changes in learners' performance. The explicit information being provided to learners was, at the time, quite different to textbook explanations of form that the learners were exposed to and structured input activities were also, at the time, not found in the textbook practices the learners were exposed to. What was the causative variable, explicit information or structured input practices?

VanPatten and Oikennon (1996) were the first to address the issue of which component of PI is the causative one. They had three treatment groups and targeted Spanish direct object pronouns. They used the same materials as VanPatten and Cadierno (1993) had. One group received full PI consisting of the combination of EI and SI. A second group received only SI (no explanation) and a third only EI (no practice). These latter two groupings served to isolate the components of PI. VanPatten and Oikennon found that the PI and SI groups improved significantly on the interpretation and production tasks and that there was no statistically significant difference between the two groups' scores on either task. Both groups, however, significantly outperformed the EI group on both tasks. Learners who carried out structured input activities in the absence of explicit information performed just as well as learners who carried out structured input activities after having received explicit information about the target form. That is, adding EI to SI did not improve learners' performance. VanPatten and Oikennon concluded, therefore, that the causative variable in PI was performing structured input activities.

Benati found identical results with the Italian future tense (Benati, 2004a) and Italian noun-adjective agreement (Benati, 2004b) and thus reached the same conclusion as VanPatten and Oikennon (1996) had. Wong (2004b) found for the French negative + indefinite article construction that the PI and SI groups' scores were not statistically different from each other as measured by interpretation and production measures. The control group and the group that had received only explicit information performed identically. The PI and SI groups performed equally well on the interpretation task and both significantly outperformed the EI and control groups. Whereas the PI group significantly outperformed the EI group on the production task, the scores of the EI and SI groups were not statistically different. As noted above, Lee and Benati (2007a) found that an SI group significantly outperformed a traditional instruction (TI) group that had received explicit information on both interpretation and production measures of the Japanese past tense marker and affirmative/negative present tense markers. Only one study has shown that a full PI group significantly outperformed an SI group on interpretation and production on the Spanish subjunctive (Farley, 2004a).

Sanz and Morgan-Short (2004) examined the effects of positive evidence versus explicit information and explicit negative feedback on Spanish object pronouns. They created four groups around the variables +/– explicit information and +/– negative feedback. They found that all four groups improved significantly and equally as measured by a sentence interpretation task, a sentence production task and a video retelling. In other words, the –explicit information/–negative feedback group performed as well as the +explicit information/+negative feedback group. Sanz and Morgran-Short argued that the task-essential nature of structured input activities was sufficient to bring about changes in the learners' performance.

Several studies have examined the effects of explicit information in processing instruction not in terms of final outcomes, that is, accuracy scores on post-tests, but on aspects of the learning process. Fernández (2008) compared the effects of full PI to SI with Spanish direct object pronouns and the Spanish subjunctive. She hypothesized that due to the explicit information they received, learners receiving full PI would process items accurately sooner and faster than the learners receiving SI only. Her research introduced a new dependent variable to processing instruction research, trials to criterion. She created assessment tasks that contained target items and distracter items such that in a set of four items there were three target and one distracter item. She set the criterion as correctly answering three target items and one distracter item in a row. She then counted how many items a learner answered (trials) before reaching the criterion.

Fernández measured four aspects of performance: trials to criterion, response time, accuracy after criterion, and the proportion of participants who reached criterion. She found different results for the two target items investigated. For Spanish direct object pronouns, she found no significant differences between the PI and SI groups on any of the four measures. For the Spanish subjunctive, she found that the PI group significantly outperformed the SI group on all four measures. She concluded that the benefits of explicit information depended on the nature of the task or the aspect of performance measured and the processing problems presented by specific linguistic items.

Henry, Culman and VanPatten (2009) examined the role of explicit information in PI by comparing the effects of full PI to SI with German accusative case markings on articles in two word order patterns, SVO and OVS (subject–verb–object and object–verb–subject). Like Fernández (2008), they measured how many participants in each group reached the criterion and how many trials to criterion each group required. They found that significantly more learners in the full PI group (+explicit information) reached the criterion and that they required significantly fewer trials to criterion than the SI group did. They attributed their findings not only to explicit information but to the interaction between explicit information, linguistic structure and the processing problem it presents to learners.

Culman, Henry and VanPatten (2009) also compared the effects of full PI to SI with German accusative case markings on articles but focused on OVS word order although the materials did contain SVO and distracter sentences. They also included the level of the learner (first versus third semester) as a variable. They provided learners with 30 items to process and examined performance (accuracy) at four points: (1) items 1–3; (2) items 8–10; (3) items 15–17; and (4) items 28–30. The three items in each set consisted of two distracter and one target item. In terms of accuracy, they found a significant effect for treatment group with the first three items in that the

PI group significantly outperformed the SI group. At all other points, there were no significant differences between the two groups. They then extracted from the four sets of items the four target OVS sentences and compared the two groups' performances on just these four sentences. Focusing on these sentences, they found that the PI group had significantly outperformed the SI group on each of the four sentences. Level of the learner was never a significant factor affecting performance.

VanPatten and Borst (2012a) also examined the effects of explicit information with German accusative case markings on articles and OVS word order. They also included the variable of grammatical sensitivity, which I take up in the section on individual differences. They found that the group receiving explicit information (full PI) required significantly fewer trials to reach the criterion than the group who did not receive explicit information (5 versus 24). VanPatten and Borst's analysis of the two groups' post-test scores revealed a significant interaction between Time and Treatment that revealed that both groups improved significantly and that the group receiving explicit information showed a tendency to outperform the group that had not received explicit information ($p < .07$). VanPatten and Price (2012) found the same result for the French causative with *faire* construction. That is, learners who received explicit information began processing correctly significantly faster than those learners who had not received explicit information but that in the final outcome (accuracy) both groups of learners reach the same level. VanPatten and Borst (2012b) conducted a similar experiment that targeted Spanish object pronouns in pre-verbal position, that is, OVS word order. The results of this study showed that there was no effect for explicit information on trials to criterion nor on post-test scores.

VanPatten *et al.* (2013) performed four experiments on four languages but examined linguistic structures that are affected by learners use of the first noun strategy during processing. One purpose of the study was to examine the effects of explicit information on trials to criterion and on learning outcomes for Spanish object pronouns in OVS sentence patterns, German accusative-case markings on definite articles in OVS sentence patterns, Russian accusative/nominative case inflections on nouns in OVS sentence patterns, and French causative construction with *faire*. Across the four experiments receiving explicit information or not did not have a significant effect on learning outcomes. Both groups performed with equal accuracy by the end of the treatment. Receiving explicit information or not did not have a significant effect on trials to criterion for Spanish and Russian but receiving explicit information significantly speeded up correct processing for German and French. VanPatten *et al.* state:

> Thus, EI may or may not be beneficial or useful for learners in real time processing, and by beneficial we specifically mean when learners begin to process correctly....the noted beneficial effects seem to depend on the nature of the explicit information and whether it is easy enough and portable to use during real time comprehension (VanPatten *et al.*, 2013: 519).

Taken together, these findings strongly point to the causative component of processing instruction, that is, the element that is responsible for improved learner performance being the structured input activities not explicit information when learning outcome is measured (accuracy on posttests). The linguistic structure investigated may be supported by explicit information particulary when learning process (trials to criterion) is measured. Structured input activities provide learners with the task-essential practice needed to promote acquisition. The question of when explicit information is *critical* seems to be a function of the linguistic item. The question of when explicit information is beneficial appears to be a more complex one and is just beginning to be explored and understood (Sanz and Morgan-Short, 2004).

Research focus (3): The effects of structured input compared to the effects of aurally or visually enhanced structured input

Lee and Benati (2007b) pursued a line of investigation that sought to determine if the effects of processing instruction and/or structured input activities could be made greater when the input was enhanced aurally or visually compared to its normal unenhanced presentation. In a series of investigations, they found that enhancing the target form did not result in statistically significantly higher scores compared to unenhanced forms. They found no differences on either interpretation or production measures of Italian noun-adjective agreement, the Italian future tense, and Japanese past tense markers. In a study on the Italian subjunctive, they found no differences in interpretation and production scores between a group that received PI, a group that received PI with enhancements and was taught in a classroom, and a group that received PI with enhancements and performed the activities individually in a computer laboratory. Agiasophiti (Chapter 7, this volume) compared colour-enhanced and unenhanced version of PI on German accusative-case definite articles in OVS word order patterns. She found no effect for enhancement on the immediate and delayed administrations of an interpretation test. She did find a significant effect for enhancement on the immediate production posttest but not on the delayed administration of the production posttest. These findings are rather consistent, indicating that enhanced structured input is no more effective than unenhanced structured input for improving learners' performance. To echo Sanz and Morgan-Short (2004), the task-essential nature of structured input activities is not affected by aural and visual enhancements.

Research focus (4): The effects of delivering processing instruction in classrooms to groups of learners compared to delivering it in computer laboratories to individuals

It was perhaps inevitable that research would be undertaken to examine the effectiveness of delivering processing instruction via computer, as educational practice is continually exploring the use of technology to enhance learning. Processing instruction was designed for classroom use and the instructional materials were delivered as packets in classrooms to each student enrolled in that class. VanPatten (1996: 71–82) provides a sample lesson based on the materials used in VanPatten and Cadierno (1993). Several studies have compared classroom and computer-delivered PI. The mode of delivering PI was not a statistically significant variable in any of the studies. In other words, processing instruction was delivered equally successfully in a classroom to a collective of students as on computers in a laboratory to individuals. The studies examining the mode of delivering PI focused on several linguistic structures and the effects were measured with a variety of tasks:

a) a form recognition test with the Spanish preterite/imperfect aspectual distinction (Lee and Benati with Aguilar-Sánchez and McNulty, 2007)
b) a contextualized preference task with Spanish negative informal commands (Lee and Benati with Aguilar-Sánchez and McNulty, 2007)
c) interpretation and production tasks with the French and Italian subjunctive (Lee and Benati, 2007a; 2007b).

This line of investigation has also found that PI delivered in either a classroom or on computer yielded statistically higher results than MOI delivered in either a classroom or on a computer as measured by an interpretation task for Italian and French subjunctive (Lee and Benati, 2007a). The four groups improved equally on a production task (Lee and Benati, 2007a).

Research focus (5): The effects of processing instruction as measured by discourse-level assessment tasks

By 2004, the research base included studies that had incorporated not only sentence-level assessments but also discourse-level ones. VanPatten and Sanz (1995) and Sanz (1997) demonstrated that PI on Spanish direct object pronouns led to improved scores on oral and written video-based retellings. Sanz (2004) and Sanz and Morgan-Short (2004), again with PI on Spanish direct object pronouns, found positive effects on oral video retellings. Cheng (2002; 2004) found positive effects for PI on Spanish copular verbs using a picture-based guided composition. Benati (2001) used a five-picture story sequence and asked learners to produce one sentence per picture using the Italian future tense. Post 2004, we also find the use of discourse-level production tasks. Marsden (2006) included a discourse-level speaking task among her assessments of learners' acquisition of present indicative verb morphology in French. She found that the PI learners improved significantly on this task. Benati and Lee with McNulty (2010) used a guided composition and found a positive effect for PI on the Spanish subjunctive after *cuando*.

VanPatten, Inclezan, Salazar and Farley (2009) compared the effects of processing instruction and dictogloss training (DG) on object pronouns in Spanish. They also had a control group. They used three assessment tasks: interpretation, sentence production and reconstruction (dictogloss). The latter task required learners to listen to discourse-level input and to produce written discourse-level output. For the reconstruction task, learners heard a 40-word text twice. They were not allowed to take notes as they listened. Working individually, they had to reconstruct the text in Spanish as closely as possible to the original. The text contained five instances of object pronouns. The researchers conducted an immediate post-test and a delayed post-test six weeks later. VanPatten *et al.*'s statistical results are quite complicated and I only include certain results here. At both immediate and delayed administrations they found that the PI group significantly outperformed both the DG and control groups on the interpretation task and that there were no significant differences between the DG and control groups' performance. They found that the PI group significantly outperformed the control group on the immediate production post-test but that there were no significant differences in scores between the PI and DG groups nor between the DG and control groups. At the delayed post-test, there were no significant differences between the three groups. The PI and DG groups performed equally well on the immediate administration of the reconstruction task and both significantly outperformed the control group. The delayed administration yielded no statistically significant differences between the three groups. The researchers analysed each group's performance over time separately. No group showed a significant difference from the pre-test to the immediate post-test to the delayed post-test although the PI and DG groups' scores approached significance. VanPatten *et al.* attributed the results on the reconstruction task to its difficulty. Another plausible explanation for their complicated findings may be that they used half the number of practice items as did VanPatten and Cadierno (1993) on a target item that is acquired late (Malovrh and Lee, 2010; 2013).

One limitation of the PI database noted in 2004 was the absence of discourse-level interpretation tasks to assess the effects of PI (Lee, 2004: 319). Discourse-level tasks would confirm the broader effects of PI on interpretation and might potentially demonstrate further limitations of traditional instruction. That limitation no longer applies. Benati and Lee with Hikima (2010) used two discourse-level interpretation tasks, originally developed by Hikima (2011), to measure the effects of processing instruction on the Japanese passive construction. One was a story the learners heard and the other was a dialogue also delivered aurally. Both were delivered in segments with questions posed after learners heard each segment. Learners' performance on the two discourse-level tasks improved significantly after having received PI whereas the control group showed no improvement. Benati and Lee (2010) used a discourse-level interpretation task in their study of the English past tense marker *–ed*. The learners listened to a dialogue. Afterwards, they turned to a list of the verbs used in the dialogue and ticked them to indicate whether the verb listed referred to present or past events that they had heard in the dialogue. Learners who had received PI significantly outperformed the learners who had received TI and also the learners from the control group. The scores of the latter two groups were not significantly different from each other.

Now that results using discourse-level interpretation in addition to production tasks have been accumulated, we have evidence in favour of '*The Discourse Hypothesis*: PI will yield significant improvement on discourse-level tasks' (Benati and Lee, 2008: 173). The effects of PI have been successfully measured on oral and written video retellings, guided compositions, reconstructions to some extent, aurally delivered dialogues, and aurally delivered stories.

Research focus (6): The effects of processing instruction measured over time

The effectiveness of an instructional intervention should not only be determined immediately after the instructional treatment but at later points in time as well. Are the effects of instruction sustained? Is learning retained? I refer to the effects of instruction as 'durative' when they are measured in the shorter term of a month after instruction. I refer to the effects measured in the longer term of beyond one month as 'long-term' effects. It is fair to say that few studies of PI have been undertaken to examine long-term effects. VanPatten and Fernández (2004) provided learners with processing instruction on Spanish direct object pronouns and then controlled the curriculum so that the learners received no further instruction or practice with direct object pronouns. Groups whose instructors inadvertently provided a review of object pronouns or any additional practice to learners were not included in the long-term analyses. VanPatten and Fernández measured the effectiveness of PI immediately after instruction and again eight months later. The learners' scores on the immediate post-test showed statistically significant improvement from the pre-test. Their scores eight months later also showed statistically significant improvement from the pre-test. These scores did, however, significantly diminish from those on the immediate post-test. VanPatten and Fernández demonstrated that PI does have long-term effects on learners' performance but, importantly, there was still an effect for instruction eight months later. Diminished but still significant effects of instruction after twelve to fourteen weeks are documented for German accusative-case definite articles in OVS word order patterns (Agiasophiti, Chapter 7, this volume). Diminished but still significant long-term effects were also found six weeks after processing instruction on Spanish direct object pronouns by VanPatten, Inclezan, Salazar and Farley (2009) and by VanPatten, Farmer and Clardy (2009). The first of these studies compared the effects of PI to dictogloss. The second compared PI to MOI. Marsden (2006) compared the effects of PI to that of enriched input and measured those effects on listening, reading, writing, speaking sentences and speaking at the discourse-level. The target linguistic structure was French present tense verb morphology. In addition to immediate post-testing, she carried out a post-test fourteen weeks after instruction. Marsden found that the effects of PI were stable (sustained) at the delayed post-test and were stable on all the assessments she carried out. The evidence is mounting to support the claim that the effects of processing instruction are long-term.

Many other studies have included delayed post-testing that I consider to demonstrate the durative effects of processing instruction, be the post-testing one week after instruction (Cadierno, 1995; Lee and Benati, 2007b; Lee and Benati with Aguilar-Sánchez and McNulty, 2007; Morgan-Short and Bowden, 2006; VanPatten and Cadierno, 1993), two weeks (Farley, 2001a; 2001b; 2004a; 2004b; Lee, 2013), three weeks (Benati, 2001; Cheng, 2002; 2004), twenty four days (Toth, 2006), or four weeks later (Benati, 2004a; Cadierno, 1995; Keating and Farley, 2008; VanPatten and Cadierno, 1993). The primary question under investigation in most of this research was a comparison of instructional types (Benati, 2001; Cadierno, 1995; Cheng, 2002; 2004; Farley, 2001a; 2001b; 2004a; Keating and Farley, 2008; Morgan-Short and Bowden, 2006; VanPatten and Cadierno, 1993). All studies that included delayed post-testing found statistically significant improvement for the PI group from the pre-test to the delayed post-test. The effects were measured using a variety of tasks: aural interpretation, oral or written production, form selection, and grammaticality judgments. In only two studies the scores on the delayed post-test were significantly lower than those on the immediate posttest but remained significantly higher than those on the pretest (Cheng, 2002; Lee, 2013).

These data very strongly support the conclusion that the effects of processing instruction are both durative and long-term. Because this research focus has so strongly supported the durative effects of PI, it is not always necessary for each new study on the effects of processing instruction to examine durative effects although it is still desirable. That is, I believe the database is strong enough for us to assume that PI will show durative effects. Long-term effects are still in need of further research and documentation with a variety of linguistic structures in different language families.

Research focus (7): Transfer-of-training effects

The research up until 2004 only examined, and appropriately so for a fairly new line of research, the direct or primary effects of instruction on a target form or structure. That is, in each investigation the learners were taught to use a target-language appropriate processing strategy on a targeted linguistic form. The researchers then assessed whether learners used that processing strategy on the targeted form. I suggested that 'PI researchers might move one step away from assessing direct/primary effects and determine whether secondary effects develop in learners as a result of receiving PI. Do learners who receive PI transfer that training to other forms?' (Lee 2004: 319). To establish transfer-of-training effects would demonstrate what

VanPatten queried, 'Does processing instruction actually affect the acquired system, what is called in the general model, the developing system?' (VanPatten, 1996: 154). The database now includes several studies that have indeed established transfer-of-training effects with PI. Benati and Lee with Houghton (2008) found that training on the English past tense marker *–ed* transferred to the third-person singular present tense marker *–s*. They found statistically significant improvement with the present tense form on both interpretation and form production tasks. The successful transfer-of-training took place across similar forms, that is, from word-final verb morphology to word-final verb morphology. Benati and Lee (2008) provided training to learners on Italian noun-adjective gender agreement and found that it transferred to the future tense. Again, they found statistically significant transfer effects on both interpretation and form production tests. The successful transfer-of-training took place from word-final nominal morphology to word-final verb morphology. Benati and Lee with Laval (2008) trained learners to process imperfective verb morphology in French and found that it transferred to subjunctive forms. Statistically significant transfer effects were found on both interpretation and production tasks. Both forms are word-final verb morphemes but the imperfective occurs in a main clause whereas the subjunctive occurs in a subordinate clause. Benati (2009) also found transfer-of-training effects. He trained learners to process the Japanese affirmative/negative present tense markers and found that it transferred to the past tense marker. Statistically significant transfer effects were found on both interpretation and production tasks. Both forms are word-final as well as sentence-final verb morphemes. We can conclude from these results that if learners are taught to process one type of word-final morphology they transfer it to other word-final morphology and can do so across word class and clause boundaries. Leeser and DeMil (in press) found transfer-of-training effects from accusative case object pronouns in Spanish to dative case object pronouns, both in OVS sentence patterns, but only on an interpretation task, not on a production task.

Benati and Lee with Laval (2008) added another dimension to their research by examining whether the training with imperfective verb morphology would transfer to a syntactic construction, the causative with *faire*. They found that it did and, once again, statistically significant effects were found on both interpretation and production tasks.

Three of these studies compared the effects of PI to those of traditional instruction in the assessment of both primary and transfer-of-training effects. Benati and Lee with Laval (2008) found that the PI group significantly outperformed the TI and control groups on the transfer-of-training assessments. The TI and control groups did not improve on either the interpretation or production assessments and there were no statistically significant differences between their scores. Benati and Lee (2008) found for Italian morphology that the TI group's score on the transfer-of-training production assessment was statistically significantly higher after training than before. There was no effect noted in the interpretation assessment for the TI group. Benati (2009) found similar results for Japanese. The PI group transferred their training as measured by interpretation and production tasks whereas the TI group only showed a significant difference in performance on the production assessment.

The transfer-of-training research allows us to begin to propose that PI affects a learner's developing system in that it changes the way they process input. To stimulate further research Benati and Lee (2008) developed two relevant hypotheses.

> *The Secondary Transfer-of-Training Hypothesis*: learners who receive training on one type of processing strategy for one specific form will appropriately transfer the use of that strategy to other forms without further instruction in PI. *The Cumulative Transfer-of-Training Hypothesis*: learners who receive training on one type of processing strategy will begin to work differently with primary linguistic data (Benati and Lee, 2008: 174).

Part II: Moving beyond Limitations

The second part of this chapter is a critical assessment of the research done on PI. This assessment will address the generalizability as well as the limitations of the findings from the existing research base. In a previous critical assessment, Lee (2004) noted that the following issues, among others, limited the generalizability of the research findings up to that time: a focus on Romance languages, the use of native speakers of English enrolled in university courses as research participants, and no consideration of the effects of individual differences on outcomes.

VanPatten and Cadierno (1993), the first empirical investigation of processing instruction, targeted direct object pronouns in Spanish. Many other studies of Spanish followed with additional research emerging on Italian and French. As of 2004, PI research was limited to investigations of one language family, Romance languages. Has the research moved beyond Romance languages? Important in this type of empirical investigation is that all studies sought to create homogeneous groups of research participants. In the studies up to 2004, the researchers investigated native speakers of English and with one exception (VanPatten and Oikennon, 1996) the participants were university-aged students. This homogeneity in the characteristics of the participants can also be viewed as a limitation. Has subsequent research investigated speakers of other languages? Has research on the effects of PI on younger learners been conducted? Finally, the research up to 2004 had not examined whether there were any individual differences among the learners that influenced, positively or negatively, their interaction with processing instruction. Has subsequent research investigated individual differences?

Beyond Romance Languages

As noted in Lee (2004) the then extant research on processing instruction had examined only Spanish, French and Italian as second languages. I stated that 'I am confident regarding the generalizability of processing instruction to Romance languages but reasonable questions could be posed regarding the generalizability of processing instruction beyond Romance languages' (Lee, 2004: 315). Since 2004, significant work has been carried out investigating English, German, and Japanese as second languages. These languages are typologically distinct from the Romance languages.

Culman, Henry and VanPatten (2009), Henry, Culman and VanPatten (2009) and VanPatten and Borst (2012a) have all examined the effects of explicit information on the German accusative-case definite articles and word order. These works were presented in detail in reference to the research focus on the causative component in processing instruction.

Benati (2005) compared the effects of processing instruction, traditional instruction (TI) with its focus on language production, and meaning-based output instruction (MOI) on the English simple past tense marker *–ed* with university-aged adults. He found that the PI group significantly outperformed the other two groups who performed equally on a sentence-level interpretation task. He also found that all three groups improved significantly and improved equally on a sentence-level form production task. Benati and Lee with Houghton (2008) compared the effects of PI and TI on the English simple past tense marker *–ed* with middle-school-aged native speakers of Korean. They found that the PI group significantly outperformed the TI group on the sentence-level interpretation task but that the two groups improved significantly on the sentence-level production task and performed equally. Benati and Lee (2010) once again examined the English simple past tense marker. They compared the effects of PI and TI with a control group. In this study they assessed the effects of instruction using a sentence-level interpretation task and a discourse-level interpretation task. They presented the latter to the learners as a dialogue, which had been recorded and then played to the learners. They listened to the entire dialogue, once only. Afterwards, they were given a list of 20 verbs that had occurred in the dialogue and had to indicate whether the verb had referred to a past or present event. On both assessment tasks, the PI group significantly outperformed the TI and control groups. There were no significant differences in the scores for the TI and control groups.

Benati (2009) examined the effects of processing instruction versus traditional instruction on the affirmative and negative present tense verb markers of Japanese, *–masu* and *–masen*, respectively. He also included a control group. He found that the PI group significantly outperformed the TI and the control groups on a sentence-level interpretation task. The latter two groups did not improve and their scores showed no statistically significant difference. He found that both PI and TI groups improved significantly and equally on a sentence-level form production task. Both groups significantly outperformed the control group. Lee and Benati (2007a) examined the effects of structured input activities (SI) versus traditional output-oriented instruction on the Japanese affirmative and negative present tense verb markers. They found that the SI group significantly outperformed the TI group on a sentence-level interpretation task. They found that both groups improved significantly and equally on a sentence-level form production task. They also conducted another comparison of structured input and traditional instruction on the Japanese past tense verb marker (*–mashita*). The results were identical to those for the affirmative/negative markers. That is, they found that the SI group significantly outperformed the TI group on a sentence-level interpretation task. They found that both groups improved significantly and improved equally on a sentence-level form production task. Lee and Benati (2007b) followed up this work by examining the effects of enhancing the target form (*–mashita*) aurally and visually in structured input activities. They compared the performance of three groups. One group received structured input activities delivered with aural (loudness, vocal tension) and visual (bold) enhancements on the target form. Another group received the same activities but without the enhancements which is the typical presentation of structured input activities. A third group acted as a control; they received no activities but performed the assessments. Both structured input groups improved significantly from pre-test to post-test on both the interpretation and production tasks. There were no statistical differences between the two groups on either task; they performed equally. The control group's scores did not improve from pre-test to post-test. The researchers also performed a delayed post-test one week after instruction. The results they obtained on the immediate post-tests had held steady. Benati and Lee with Hikima (2010) examined whether learners who received processing instruction on the Japanese passive construction would improve not only on sentence-level interpretation and production tasks but also on two discourse-level interpretation tasks. They presented the discourse-level tasks as a story and as a dialogue. They compared the performance of a PI group to that of a control group who received no instruction. The PI group significantly outperformed the control group on all four assessment tasks.

Any concern about the generalizability of PI beyond Romance languages has been addressed by the numerous studies on English, German and Japanese as second languages. Processing instruction and its associated structured input activities focus on a target-language specific processing problem and trains learners to use a target-language specific processing strategy. These findings contribute positive evidence to the Target Language Hypothesis. '*The Target Language Hypothesis*: PI can help learners of any target language develop an appropriate, target-language specific processing strategy to address a target-language specific processing problem' (Benati and Lee, 2008: 169).

Beyond Native Speakers of English

In 2004, Lee noted the homogeneity of the participants on whom processing instruction research had been conducted. 'The PI research has examined three target languages, Spanish, French and Italian, but only one native language, English... Is processing instruction effective across a variety of native languages?' (Lee 2004: 318). Subsequent to 2004, several studies have emerged in which the participants were not native speakers of English.

All the research on English as a second language examined non-native speakers of English. Benati (2005) examined native speakers of Chinese and Greek whereas Lee and Benati with Houghton (2008) examined native speakers of Korean. Benati and Lee (2010) examined native speakers of Chinese. Most of the research on Japanese as a second language examined native speakers of Italian studying Japanese at a private language school in Italy (Benati, 2009; Lee and Benati, 2007a; 2007b). Benati (Chapter 5, this volume) investigates native speakers of Turkish as did Uludag and VanPatten (2012). Angelovska and Benati (Chapter 7, this volume) investigate native speakers of German. In their work on the effects of processing instruction as measured by discourse-level tasks on the Spanish subjunctive after the adverb *cuando*, Benati and Lee with McNulty (2010) and Lee and

McNulty (Chapter 3, this volume) examined the learners' language background as a variable. One of their groups consisted of non-native speakers of English for whom Spanish was a third or subsequent language. They found positive effects for processing instruction with (individual) native speakers of German, Polish and Russian as well as Italian, Cantonese and Mandarin. It is important for the generalizability of processing instruction that we now have a more varied participant pool. These findings across different groups of native speakers of languages other than English provide positive evidence to support the Native Language Hypothesis. '*The Native Language Hypothesis*: PI will be effective for instilling target-language specific processing strategies, no matter the native language of the learners' (Benati and Lee, 2008: 169).

Beyond University-aged Participants

In 2004, all but one study had examined adult, university-level second language learners. VanPatten and Oikennon (1996) examined American high-school students. Subsequently, research has established the positive effects of processing instruction with 12–13-year-old Chinese and Greek children (Benati, 2005), middle-school-aged Korean children (Benati and Lee with Houghton, 2008), primary-school-aged Chinese children (Benati and Lee, 2010) and 10-year-old native speakers of German (Angelovska and Benati, Chapter 6, this volume) learning the English simple past tense marker –*ed.* Marsden (2006) found positive effects for PI on French present indicative verb morphology with 13–14-year-old adolescents. Benati (Chapter 4, this volume) found positive effects for PI on the English passive with 13–14-year-old native speakers of Turkish. Laval (Chapter 5, this volume) found positive primary and secondary effects for PI on the French imperfect, subjunctive and causative with 9–10-year-old native speakers of English. Mavrantoni and Benati (Chapter 8, this volume) found positive effects for PI on the English third person simple present tense marker with 8–10-year-old and 15–17-year-old native speakers of Greek. The subject pool now includes primary-, middle- and high-school learners. The results conclusively point to PI being effective instruction no matter the age of the learner. These findings provide positive evidence to support the Age Hypothesis. '*The Age Hypothesis*: PI will be just as effective as an intervention with younger learners as it is with older learners' (Benati and Lee, 2008: 168). Only the studies in this volume include the age of the learners as a variable in the research design. We have evidence that PI is effective with younger learners, but are there differential effects due to the age of the learner?

Beyond Homogeneity and Toward Individual Differences

Lee (2004) noted that the PI research to date had presented results only in aggregate terms. 'A lacuna in the database is, therefore, a consideration of individual differences. What are the characteristics of the learners who benefit the most from PI? What are the characteristics of the learners who benefit the least, if indeed there are learners who make no significant improvement after instruction?' (Lee, 2004: 318). Some work subsequent to 2004 has considered that individual differences might affect results.

Lee and Benati with Aguilar-Sánchez and McNulty (2007) compared computer versus classroom delivery of processing instruction on Spanish past aspectual distinction and Spanish negative informal commands. After reporting the positive effects of PI for both linguistic targets, they considered individual differences in performance. They documented the following individual differences in performance among the 25 learners who participated in the study and concluded that some learners benefited more than others from instruction.

1. 64% of learners improved on aspectual distinction while 88% did on commands as measured by the immediate post-test.
2. Nine learners did not benefit from instruction on aspectual distinction while three did not on commands (immediate post-test).
3. Six learners significantly improved on both linguistic targets (immediate post-test) and the same six learners' performance remained constant from the immediate to the delayed post-test. The other 19 learners' performance vacillated.
4. The pre-test scores could be grouped as high, medium or low for both target structures.
5. Learners who scored high on the two pre-tests did not improve significantly on the immediate post-test. Only learners who scored medium or low improved significantly from pre-test to post-test.

VanPatten *et al.* (2009) compared processing instruction to dictogloss on Spanish direct object pronouns. They drew attention to certain participants in their data set. The reconstruction task they used proved difficult for learners. They indicated that in their PI group 32% of learners scored zero on all three administrations of the test (pre-test, immediate post-test, delayed post-test) whereas 37% of participants in the dictogloss group scored zero on all three tests. The majority of learners did not score zero. They were able to demonstrate the benefits of instruction on the reconstruction task. It is, however, clear that some learners had not benefited from instruction sufficiently to demonstrate it on the reconstruction task. What were the characteristics of the (un)successful learners?

Benati and Lee with McNulty (2010) and Lee and McNulty (Chapter 3, this volume) treated language background as a variable in their research on the effects of processing instruction on the Spanish subjunctive after the adverb *cuando*. They examined native speakers of English who had studied only Spanish as a second language, native speakers of English who were studying Spanish as a third or subsequent language, and non-native speakers of English studying Spanish as a third or subsequent language. The pre-test scores of the learners showed no statistically significant differences across the groups for accurate sentence interpretation, accurate form production in sentences, and accurate form production in a guided composition. After receiving processing instruction, the three groups improved significantly and equally. There were no statistically significant differences in post-test scores across the three groups. In other words, language background did not affect performance as measured by accuracy. One aspect of the non-native English speakers' performance on the guided composition pre-test did stand out. Specifically, this group generated significantly more contexts in their guided compositions in which a subjunctive form after *cuando* should have been used than the other two groups did. There was a difference between the groups going into instruction. This difference, however, disappeared after instruction. There was no statistically significant difference between the groups' performance on the post-test composition in the number of contexts generated for using the subjunctive forms. The two groups of native English speakers benefited from instruction in that they learned the forms and they learned to create contexts in which to use the forms. The non-native speakers benefited from instruction in that they learned to use the correct forms in contexts that they were already generating. What appeared to be an advantage prior to instruction was equalized through instruction. They concluded that all their learners benefited from processing instruction but there were differential benefits.

VanPatten and his colleagues have recently published numerous studies that explore the variable of grammatical sensitivity, a component of language aptitude, in relation to the effects of explicit information. As the results of this research related to explicit information were presented above in the section on Research focus 2, I focus here on the results related to grammatical sensitivity. VanPatten and Borst (2012a) provided learners with processing instruction on German accusative-case definite articles in OVS word order patterns. Grammatical sensitivity was weakly correlated with trials to criterion and did reach a level of statistical significance as a covariate, although it accounted for very little of the variance. It was also weakly correlated with post-test scores. VanPatten and Borst (2012b) provided learners processing instruction on Spanish object pronouns in OVS word-order patterns. They found no effects for grammatical sensitivity on trials to criterion or post-test scores. VanPatten *et al.* (2013) conducted four experiments on four languages but with linguistic structures that are all affected by learners' use of the first noun strategy during processing. They found no significant correlation between grammatical sensitivity and learning outcome scores for Spanish object pronouns in OVS word order patterns, German accusative case definite articles in OVS word order patterns, Russian accusative/nominative noun inflections in OVS word order patterns, and the French causative construction with *faire*. They found no significant correlation between grammatical senstivity and trials to criterion for Spanish object pronouns in OVS word order patterns, Russian accusative/nominative noun inflections in OVS word order patterns, and the French causative construction with *faire*. They did find a significant correlation between grammatical sensitivity and trials to criterion for German accusative case definite articles in OVS word order patterns but the significant correlation was attributed to just the group who received explicit information. Given all their other findings, VanPatten *et al.* assert that the finding for German is an anomoly (VanPatten *et al.*, 2013: 521). They explain the lack of a role for grammatical sensitivity in processing instruction as due to the fact that processing instruction is not an intervention that tries to help learners internalize rules. 'Previous research has clearly demonstrated aptitude as an important variable in *rule learning*. The present study is the first to examine its relevance in *acquisition as processing*' (VanPatten *et al.*, 2013: 521, emphasis original).

VanPatten, Inclezan, Salazar and Farley (2009) compared the effects of processing instruction and dictogloss training (DG) to a control group on object pronouns in Spanish. They used three assessment tasks: interpretation, sentence production and reconstruction. I focus here only on the results from the reconstruction task which proved difficult for learners. This study is the only one, to my knowledge, to use a dictogloss-like reconstruction task to measure learners' performance, rightfully so because the task reflects the training of the dictogloss comparison group. They required learners to listen to discourse-level input, in this case they heard a 40-word text twice. They were not allowed to take notes as they listened. They then had to produce written discourse-level output. Working individually, the learners had to reconstruct the text in Spanish as closely as possible to the original.

The input text contained five instances of object pronouns. VanPatten *et al.* conducted an immediate post-test and a delayed post-test six weeks later. The statistical analyses of the learners' performance on the reconstruction task are complicated and so the researchers analysed each group's performance over time separately. No group showed a significant difference from the pre-test to the immediate post-test to the delayed post-test although the PI and DG groups' scores approached significance. VanPatten *et al.* attributed the results on the reconstruction task to its difficulty. The rationale for discussing VanPatten *et al.*'s finding under the heading of individual differences is that they drew attention to the performance of certain participants in their data set. They indicated that in their PI group 32% of learners scored zero on all three administrations of the test (pre-test, immediate post-test, delayed post-test) whereas 37% of participants in the dictogloss group scored zero on all three tests. In other words, some learners either had not benefited from processing instruction and dictogloss training at all or had not benefited sufficiently to demonstrate it on the reconstruction task. Their purpose in pointing out these learners is to underscore the difficulty of the reconstruction task. The majority of learners did not, however, score zero. They were able to demonstrate the benefits of instruction on the reconstruction task. There are individual differences in results but they were impossible to explore in the context of VanPatten *et al.*'s study. What, then, were the characteristics of the (un)successful learners? Who benefits the most? Who benefits the least?

The findings from these studies provide evidence that individual differences may be at play in the results of processing instruction. Clearly, more research is needed to address the Individual Difference Hypothesis. '*The Individual Difference Hypothesis*: some learners benefit more from PI than do others' (Benati and Lee, 2008: 172). An important question for future research to consider is: What are the differences that matter? How do we uncover the different ways in which instruction is differentially beneficial?

Conclusion

The purpose of this chapter was twofold: to review the existing research on processing instruction (PI) and to provide a critical assessment of that research. Significant numbers of studies have investigated the seven research foci identified. The current research base for processing instruction can be characterized as having both breadth and depth. A previous critical assessment (Lee, 2004) identified as limitations the fact that the target languages investigated were exclusively Romance languages, the learners investigated were exclusively native speakers of English, that almost all were university-aged students, and the fact that individual differences in learners' characteristics had not been addressed. The critical assessment offered here has demonstrated that the research on processing instruction conducted since 2004, including the works in this volume, has moved this area of research beyond those limitations.

Notes

1. VanPatten, Farmer and Clardy (2009) is a replication of Keating and Farley (2008). VanPatten *et al.* identified several items in Keating and Farley's MOI materials that pushed learners to process input and not just produce output. When they corrected for these types of items, VanPatten *et al.* found that PI was superior to MOI.

References

Benati, A. (2001). A comparative study of the effects of processing instruction and output-based instruction on the acquisition of the Italian future tense. *Language Teaching Research*, 5, 95–127.

Benati, A. (2004a). The effects of structured input and explicit information on the acquisition of Italian future tense. In VanPatten, B. (ed.), *Processing Instruction: Theory, Research, and Commentary* (pp. 207–55). Mahwah, NJ: Erlbaum.

Benati, A. (2004b). The effects of processing instruction and its components on the acquisition of gender agreement in Italian. *Language Awareness*, 13, 67–80.

Benati, A. (2005). The effects of PI, TI and MOI in the acquisition of English simple past tense. *Language Teaching Research*, 9, 67–113.

Benati, A. (2009). *Japanese Language Teaching: A Communicative Approach*. London: Continuum.

Benati, A., and Lee, J. F. (2008). *Grammar Acquisition and Processing Instruction: Secondary and Cumulative Effects*. Bristol: Multilingual Matters.

Benati, A., and Lee, J. F. (2010). *Processing Instruction and Discourse*. London: Continuum.

Benati, A., and Lee, J. F. with Hikima, N. (2010). Chapter 5: Exploring the effects of processing instruction on discourse-level interpretation tasks with the Japanese passive construction. In Benati, A. and Lee, J. F., *Processing Instruction and Discourse* (pp. 148–77). London: Continuum.

Benati, A., and Lee, J. F. with Houghton, S. D. (2008). Chapter 4: From processing instruction on the acquisition of English past tense to secondary transfer-of-training effects on English third person singular present tense. In Benati, A. and Lee, J. F., *Grammar Acquisition and Processing Instruction: Secondary and Cumulative Effects* (pp. 88–120). Bristol: Multilingual Matters.

Benati, A., and Lee, J. F. with Laval, C. (2008). Chapter 5: From processing instruction on the acquisition of French *imparfait* to secondary transfer-of-training effects on French subjunctive and to cumulative transfer-of-training effects with French causative constructions. In Benati, A. and Lee, J. F., *Grammar Acquisition and Processing Instruction: Secondary and Cumulative Effects* (pp. 121–57). Bristol: Multilingual Matters.

Benati, A., and Lee, J. F. with McNulty, E. (2010). Chapter 4: Exploring the effects of processing instruction on a discourse-level guided composition with the Spanish subjunctive after the adverb *cuando*. In Benati, A. and Lee, J. F., *Processing Instruction and Discourse* (pp. 97–147). London: Continuum.

Cadierno, T. (1995). Formal instruction from a processing perspective: an investigation into the Spanish past tense. *Modern Language Journal*, 79, 179–93.

Cheng, A. (2002). The effects of processing instruction on the acquisition of *ser* and *estar*. *Hispania*, 85, 308–323.

Cheng, A. (2004). Processing instruction and Spanish *ser* and *estar*: forms with semantic-aspectual value. In VanPatten, B. (ed.). *Processing Instruction: Theory, Research, and Commentary* (pp. 119–41). Mahwah, NJ: Erlbaum.

Culman, H., Henry, N., and VanPatten, B. (2009). The role of explicit information in instructed SLA: an on-line study with processing instruction and German accusative case inflections. *Die Unterrichtspraxis*, 42, 19–31.

Farley, A. P. (2001a). The effects of processing instruction and meaning-based output instruction. *Spanish Applied Linguistics*, 5, 57–94.

Farley, A. P. (2001b). Authentic processing instruction and the Spanish subjunctive. *Hispania*, 84, 289–99.

Farley, A. (2004a). The relative effects of processing instruction and meaning-based output instruction. In B. VanPatten (ed.), *Processing Instruction: Theory, Research, and Commentary* (pp. 143–68). Mahwah, NJ: Erlbaum.

Farley, A. (2004b). Processing instruction and the Spanish subjunctive: is explicit information needed? In VanPatten, B. (ed.), *Processing Instruction: Theory, Research, and Commentary* (pp. 227–39). Mahwah, NJ: Erlbaum.

Fernández, C. (2008). Reexamining the role of explicit information in processing instruction. *Studies in Second Language Acquisition*, 30, 277–305.

Henry, N., Culman, H., and VanPatten, B. (2009). More on the effects of explicit information in instructed SLA: a partial replication and a response to Fernández (2008). *Studies in Second Language Acquisition*, 31, 559–75.

Hikima, N. (2011). The effects of processing instruction and re-exposure on interpretation discourse level tasks: the case of Japanese passive forms. Unpublished doctoral dissertation. University of Greenwich, Greenwich, UK.

Keating, G., and Farley A. (2008). Processing instruction, meaning-based output instruction, and meaning-based drills: impacts on classroom L2 acquisition of Spanish object pronouns. *Hispania*, 19, 639–50.

Lee, J. F. (2004). On the generalizability, limits, and potential future directions of processing instruction research. In VanPatten, B. (ed.), *Processing Instruction: Theory, Research, and Commentary* (pp. 311–23). Mahwah, NJ: Erlbaum.

Lee, J. F. (2013). The relationship between learning rate and learning outcome for processing instruction on the Spanish passive voice. In Benati, A., Laval, C. and Arche, M. (eds), *The Grammar Dimension in Instructed Second Language Learning*. London: Bloomsbury.

Lee, J. F., and Benati, A. (2007a). *Delivering Processing Instruction in Classrooms and Virtual Contexts: Research and Practice*. London: Equinox.

Lee, J. F., and Benati, A. (2007b). *Second Language Processing: An Analysis of Theory, Problems and Possible Solutions*. London: Continuum.

Lee, J. F., and Benati, A., with Aguilar-Sánchez, J. and McNulty, E. M. (2007). Chapter 4: Comparing three modes of delivering processing instruction on preterite/imperfect distinction and negative informal commands in Spanish. In Lee, J. F. and Benati, A., *Delivering Processing Instruction in Classrooms and Virtual Contexts: Research and Practice* (pp. 73–98). London: Equinox.

Leeser, M. J., and DeMil, A. J. (in press). Investigating the secondary effects of processing instruction in Spanish: From instruction on accusative clitics to transfer-of-training on dative clitics.

Malovrh, P. A., and Lee, J. F. (2010). Connections between processing, production and placement: Acquiring object pronouns in Spanish as a second language. In VanPatten, B. and Jegerski, J. (eds), *Research in Second Language Processing and Parsing* (pp. 231–55). Amsterdam: John Benjamins.

Malovrh, P. A., and Lee, J. F. (2013). *The Developmental Dimension in Instructed Second Language Learning: The L2 Acquisition of Object Pronouns in Spanish*. London: Bloomsbury.

Marsden, E. (2006). Exploring input processing in the classroom: an experimental comparison of processing instruction and enriched input. *Language Learning*, 56, 507–566.

Morgan-Short, K., and Bowden, H. W. (2006). Processing instruction and meaningful output-based instruction: effects on second language development. *Studies in Second Language Acquisition*, 28, 31–65.

Sanz, C. (1997). Experimental tasks in SLA research: amount of production, modality, memory, and production processes. In Pérez-Leroux, A.T. and Glass, W. R. (eds), *Contemporary Perspectives on the Acquisition of Spanish: Vol. 2 Production, Processing and Comprehension* (pp. 41–56). Somerville, MA: Cascadilla Press.

Sanz, C. (2004). Computer delivered implicit versus explicit feedback in processing instruction. In VanPatten, B. (ed.). *Processing Instruction: Theory, Research, and Commentary* (pp. 241–55). Mahwah, NJ: Erlbaum.

Sanz, C., and Morgan-Short, K. (2004). Positive evidence versus explicit rule presentation and explicit negative feedback: a computer-assisted study. *Language Learning*, 54, 35–78.

Toth, P. D. (2006). Processing instruction and a role for output in second language acquisition. *Language Learning*, 56, 319–85.

Uludag, O., and VanPatten, B. (2012). The comparative effects of processing instruction and dictogloss on the acquisition of the English passive by speakers of Turkish. *International Review of Applied Linguistics in Language Teaching*, 50, 189–212.

VanPatten, B. (1996). *Input Processing and Grammar Instruction: Theory and Research.* Norwood, NJ: Ablex.

VanPatten, B., and Borst, S. (2012a). The roles of explicit information and grammatical sensitivity in processing instruction: nominative-accusative case marking and word order in German L2. *Foreign Language Annals*, 45, 92–109.

VanPatten, B., and Borst, S. (2012b). The roles of explicit information and grammatical sensitivity in the processing of clitic object pronouns and word order in L2 Spanish. *Hispania*, 95, 270–84.

VanPatten, B., and Cadierno, T. (1993). Explicit instruction and input processing. *Studies in Second Language Acquisition*, 15, 225–43.

VanPatten, B., Collopy, E., Price, J., Borst, S., and Qualin, A. (2013). Explicit information, grammatical sensitivity, and the First-noun Principle: a cross-linguistic study in processing instruction. *Modern Language Journal*, 97, 504–525.

VanPatten, B., Farmer, J., and Clardy, C. (2009). Processing instruction and meaning-based output instruction: a response to Keating and Farley (2008). *Hispania*, 92, 116–26.

VanPatten, B., and Fernández, C. (2004). The long-term effects of processing instruction. In VanPatten, B. (ed.), *Processing Instruction: Theory, Research, and Commentary* (pp. 273–89). Mahwah, NJ: Erlbaum.

VanPatten, B., Inclezan, D., Salazar, H., and Farley, A. (2009). Processing instruction and dictogloss: a study on object pronouns and word order in Spanish. *Foreign Language Annals*, 42, 557–75.

VanPatten, B., and Oikennon, S. (1996). Explanation vs. structured input in processing instruction. *Studies in Second Language Acquisition*, 18, 495–510.

VanPatten, B., and Price, J. (2012). What does explanation do for the language learner? An experiment in processing instruction with the causative *faire*. *The French Review*, 86, 96–107.

VanPatten, B., and Sanz, C. (1995). From input to output: processing instruction and communicative tasks. In Eckman, F.R., Highland, D., Lee, P. W., Mileham, J. and Weber, R. R. (eds), *Second Language Acquisition Theory and Pedagogy* (pp. 169–85). Mahwah, NJ: Erlbaum.

VanPatten, B., and Wong, W. (2004). Processing instruction and the French causative: another replication. In VanPatten, B. (ed.), *Processing Instruction: Theory, Research, and Commentary* (pp. 97–118). Mahwah, NJ: Erlbaum.

Wong, W. (2004a). The nature of processing instruction. In VanPatten, B. (ed.), *Processing Instruction: Theory, Research, and Commentary* (pp. 33–63). Mahwah, NJ: Erlbaum.

Wong. W. (2004b). Processing instruction in French: the roles of explicit information and structured input. In VanPatten, B. (ed.), *Processing Instruction: Theory, Research, and Commentary* (pp. 187–205). Mahwah, NJ: Erlbaum.

Part 2

Empirical Studies

3 The Effects of Language Background on the Results of Processing Instruction on the Spanish Subjunctive/Indicative Contrast after the Adverb *cuando*

James F. Lee, University of New South Wales (Australia)*
and Erin M. McNulty, Dickinson College (USA)**

Introduction

Several investigations on the effects of processing instruction on second language development have examined subjunctive mood verbal morphology.

* **James Lee** is Deputy Head of the School of Humanities and Languages at the University of New South Wales, Sydney, Australia where he teaches Spanish area studies and second language acquisition. His main research interest is second language input processing and, with Alessandro Benati, has co-authored several books on processing instruction. His most recent work is with Paul Malovrh, *The Developmental Dimension in Instructed Second Language Learning: The L2 Acquisition of Object Pronouns in Spanish* (Bloomsbury, 2013).

** **Erin M. McNulty** is an Assistant Professor since 2009 at Dickinson College in Carlisle, Pennsylvania where she coordinates the language program and teaches Spanish language and linguistics. She earned a doctorate in Hispanic Linguistics from Indiana University, Bloomington where she won the prestigious Lieber Award, an eight campus-wide award recognizing outstanding teaching. Her research areas of interest are second language acquisition and pedagogy, while specifically focusing on input processing. She co-authored a chapter about her research in delivering instruction in virtual contexts, and she translated a bilingual book of poetry written by Claudia Aburto Guzmán, *La lente y la ciudad/The lens and the city*.

Principally, they have examined what is popularly termed in pedagogical grammars the subjunctive of doubt (Farley, 2001a; 2001b; 2004a; 2004b; Fernández, 2008; Lee and Benati, 2007a; 2007b). Complex sentences contain independent and dependent clauses or main and subordinate clauses in which there are grammatical interrelationships. For Spanish and other Romance languages (e.g., Italian, French) when the semantic intent of the independent clause expresses doubt, disbelief, uncertainty or, in some languages, opinion, then the verb in the dependent clause, when the grammatical subjects are not co-referential, must be in the subjunctive mood. In other words, the semantics of the independent clause triggers the form of the verb in the dependent clause. The morphological form of the subjunctive itself does not express the concept of doubt. The semantics of the verb phrase in the main clause is where one finds the expression of doubt, disbelief, uncertainty or opinion. Travis (2003) argues, therefore, that the subjunctive form in these conditions is a semantic agreement marker, an apt description. The example in (1) contrasts with the example in (2) that together illustrate that doubt is expressed in the main clause and it triggers semantic agreement in the dependent clause. If the semantic intent of the independent clause expresses knowledge or certainty, affirms or asserts belief, then the verb in the dependent clause must be in the indicative mood. The subjunctive mood is encoded morphologically and is distinct in form from the indicative mood as seen in the forms of the italicized verbs in (1) and (2). As the English translations show, *venga* and *viene* mean the same thing.

(1) Dudo que Juan *venga.*
I doubt that Juan is coming.
(2) Sé que Juan *viene.*
I know that Juan is coming.

Other uses of the subjunctive are, arguably, more meaningful. In Spanish, we find a possible subjunctive/indicative contrast after the temporal adverb *cuando* 'when/whenever'. Although this adverb is one of several in which the contrast can occur, the present study focuses only on *cuando.* The use of *cuando* plus subjunctive indicates that the event, action or state is something that the speaker is anticipating will happen at some undetermined point in the future or that it might not ever happen. The semantics are [+futurity, +uncertainty]. The subjunctive morphology is underlined in sentence (3). The verb form in the main clause is a future form and so the subjunctive form is, again, a semantic agreement marker. But the subjunctive form also indicates an uncertain time. When will Carlos return home?

(3) Más tarde, Carlos va a tomar una copa de vino cuando regres_e_ a casa.
Later, when he returns home, Carlos is going to have a glass of wine.

The present indicative is also possible in Spanish after the adverb *cuando* as in (4) where the reading of the events is that of habitual actions.

(4) Todos los días, Carlos toma una copa de vino cuando regres_a_ a casa.
Every day, when he returns home, Carlos has a glass of wine.

The English translation of *regrese* and *regresa* is the same, 'returns', and does not offer the same insights into the events as Spanish morphology does. Spanish provides a more nuanced reading of the events. In the present study, we focus on the idea that the subjunctive form expresses uncertainty as to when an action or event will occur whereas the indicative form expresses a habitual event or action.

Several processing problems affect L2 learners' processing of the subjunctive/indicative contrast after *cuando* to indicate uncertainty of time or habit. More so than the subjunctive of doubt, the subjunctive/indicative contrast after *cuando* is potentially affected by the Lexical Preference Principle. The lexical temporal adverbs *más tarde* and *todos los días* in (3) and (4) co-occur with subjunctive and indicative verb morphology. When such lexical indicators are in the input, learners might prefer to use or attend to them rather than the verb morphology to interpret the sentences correctly (Lee, 1999; Rossomondo, 2007). Learners' preference for finding meaning in lexical items is captured in VanPatten's Lexical Preference Principle.

> Lexical Preference Principle. If grammatical forms express a meaning that can also be encoded lexically (i.e., that grammatical marker is redundant), then learners will not initially process those grammatical forms until they have lexical forms to which they can match them (VanPatten, 2007: 118).

Subjunctive verb morphology generally occurs in an unfavourable processing position. Barcroft and VanPatten (1997) have shown that grammatical items in sentence-initial and sentence-final position are processed more easily than items in sentence-medial position. Other studies support this finding (Klein, 1986; Rosa and O'Neill, 1998). VanPatten (2002; 2004) hypothesizes that a sentence location is favoured or disfavoured due to processing resources. Elements at the beginning are, by definition, the first on which available resources are applied to process an input string. If the resources are constrained then that means the resources may be gobbled up to process that initial item(s) and may not be available for medial items. As the learner approaches the end of the input string (i.e., once again redirects attention to processing the string), the resources may now be available and thus an element in final position gets processed or has chances of being processed (VanPatten, 2004: 13).

The position of the subjunctive verb form in the dependent clauses in (3) is such that processing resources might not be available. VanPatten (2004) has captured this processing problem in his Sentence Location Principle.

> The Sentence Location Principle: learners tend to process items in sentence initial position before those in final position and those in medial position (VanPatten, 2004: 14).

Previous Processing Instruction Research on the Subjunctive

In all but one previous investigation of the effects of processing instruction (PI) on the acquisition of subjunctive verb morphology the target of investigation was the use of the subjunctive in Romance languages termed, in pedagogical grammars, the subjunctive of doubt. The results generated by this research are consistent. All investigations have demonstrated that PI brings about significant improvement in learners' performance on interpretation and production tasks (Benati and Lee with Laval, 2008; Farley, 2001a, 2001b, 2004a, 2004b; Fernández, 2008; Lee and Benati, 2007a, 2007b). All but one of the studies (Fernández, 2008) uses a pre-test + treatment + post-test design and employs the repeated measures Analysis of Variance (ANOVA) as the principal statistical procedure to evaluate results. In each of these works, the pre-tests indicated that the various treatment groups had equivalent knowledge of the target form so that any differences found after receiving treatments were interpreted as an effect of the treatment. We now review each of these studies.

Farley (2001a) compared the effects of PI and meaning-based output instruction (MOI) on the Spanish subjunctive of doubt. He found that the PI group significantly outperformed the MOI group on the interpretation test, but that the two groups performed equally well on the production test. This finding is the prototypical one in PI research (see the review in Lee and Benati, 2009). Farley (2001b; 2004a) replicated his 2001 study but with a greater number of participants, 67 instead of 29. This time he found no differences between the scores of the PI and MOI groups on either the interpretation or production task. Both groups improved significantly and performed equally well. This finding with the MOI group is unique among the other studies of the subjunctive that examine MOI (Lee and Benati, 2007a). Farley (2004b) examined the relative effects of full PI (explicit information plus structured input practices) and structured input practices (SI) on the acquisition of Spanish subjunctive. Both groups made significant improvement on the interpretation and production tasks, but the full PI group made greater gains than the SI group. This finding is unique among the other PI studies that have found equally positive effects for full PI and SI (Benati, 2004a, 2004b; VanPatten and Oikennon, 1996; Wong, 2004).

Fernández (2008) investigated the effects of explicit information with the Spanish subjunctive of doubt. One group received full PI that included explicit information; the other group did not receive explicit information but only carried out structured input activities. She measured the effects of explicit information in four ways. First, she established a criterion level of correctly answering three target items and one distracter item consecutively. She found that not all participants reached the criterion and that significantly more learners in the group that received explicit information reached the criterion than in the structured input only group. She found that the explicit information group required significantly fewer trials to reach the criterion than did the structured input only group. She also found that the explicit information group responded to items significantly faster (response time) than the structured input group and that the explicit information group responded significantly more accurately after reaching the criterion than the structured input group. She also performed the same experiment with direct object pronoun in OVS (object–verb–subject) sentence pattern in Spanish and found none of the significant differences she did with the subjunctive. She concluded that the structure of the target linguistic item may be critical in determining the effects of explicit information. (See Lee, Chapter 2, this volume for a review of the role of explicit information in the effects of PI.)

Lee and Benati (2007a) investigated the effects of PI and MOI, delivered either in classrooms or on computers, on the acquisition of Italian and French subjunctive of doubt/opinion. The significant main effects and significant interactions for the two languages were identical. Those learners who received PI performed significantly better than those who received MOI on the interpretation test. Both treatment groups performed equally well on the production test. They found no significant differences between those who received classroom instruction and those who received individualized computer-delivered instruction on either the interpretation or production tasks.

The post hoc analyses showed that the PI classroom groups for Italian and French performed equally as well as the PI computer groups on the interpretation and production tasks. These analyses revealed that the MOI classroom group performed significantly better than the MOI computer group on the interpretation task but equally well on the production task. The French MOI groups performed equally well on both interpretation and production tasks. Lee and Benati (2007a) concluded that PI was a more effective instructional treatment than MOI given the differences on the interpretation test. They also concluded that computer delivery of PI was an effective way in which to deliver instruction in that computer delivery in laboratories yielded the same results as instructor-delivery in classrooms.

Lee and Benati (2007b) investigated the effects of PI and enhanced PI on the acquisition of Italian subjunctive of doubt/opinion. Additionally, the enhanced PI material was delivered either in a classroom or via computer in a laboratory. The target forms received acoustic enhancement (louder and tenser) if the input was aural or textual enhancement (bold typeface) if the input was written. They found no statistically significant differences across the three treatment groups on either production or interpretation tests. All three groups improved significantly from pre- to post-test and improved equally. All three types of PI were equally effective at improving learners' interpretation and production of Italian subjunctive forms. Lee and Benati (2007b) concluded that structured input could not be effectively enhanced any more than it was by virtue of being structured input. That is, structuring the input makes the form as salient to the learner as the form can be. Additionally, they concluded that computers could deliver PI in laboratories to individual learners just as effectively as classroom teachers could to groups of learners – a conclusion that echoes their previous work (Lee and Benati, 2007a).

Benati and Lee with Laval (2008) examined learners' progress with French subjunctive of doubt as a side effect of being instructed on French past imperfective verb morphology. That is, they sought to find any secondary, transfer-of-training effects of PI. The learners took interpretation and production pre-tests on the two verb forms, subjunctive and imperfect. Then, learners received a treatment, either PI, traditional instruction focused on form production (TI) or the control group who received no treatment on French past imperfect. The treatments were followed immediately by post-testing on the two verb forms. They found that the PI group significantly outperformed the TI and control groups on the interpretation test for past imperfect verb morphology. They found that the PI and TI groups improved equally on the production of past imperfect verb morphology and that both groups significantly outperformed the control group. They found that the PI group significantly outperformed the TI and control groups on both the interpretation and production post-tests for the subjunctive. They concluded that PI was a superior type of intervention in that it yielded both interpretation and production differences on the primary target (past imperfect) as well as the same differences on the secondary target (subjunctive). They do note that direct PI on the French subjunctive yields higher post-test scores than those obtained measuring secondary effects. Nonetheless, that PI has been shown to produce secondary effects corroborates VanPatten's (1996: 8) assertion that PI affects learners' developing systems.

All the studies reviewed above examined one particular use of subjunctive verb morphology albeit across three Romance languages, Italian, Spanish and French. Benati and Lee with McNulty (2010) examined a different use of the subjunctive, the subjunctive/indicative contrast after the adverb *cuando*, and used, not only sentence-level assessment tasks, but a discourse-level production task to assess the effects of PI. As they went through the process of screening research participants they found that they had few participants who fit the criteria of having completed all the pre- and post-testing plus having been present for the two phases of instruction plus being native speakers of English for whom Spanish was their only subsequent language. They decided, therefore, to include language background as a variable in the design and identified three groups. One group matched the prototypical PI research group: native speakers of English for whom the target language is their only additional language. The other two groups were native and non-native speakers of English. The second group consisted of native speakers of English for whom Spanish was not their only additional language. Previously, Lee and Benati with Aguilar-Sánchez and McNulty (2007) had found that a small group of learners (n = 5) who were native speakers of English for whom Spanish was not their only additional language did not perform differently than the prototypical group (n = 20) who were native speakers of English for whom Spanish was uniquely their second language. The third group consisted of non-native speakers of English studying Spanish. They were minimally trilingual: native language + English + Spanish.

Benati and Lee with McNulty (2010) found no significant differences in accuracy scores on the various pre-tests across the three language background groups. They did find that the non-native speakers of English generated more contexts for using a subjunctive form after *cuando* in the composition pre-test than the other groups. They were not producing subjunctive forms but they were generating more contexts in which to do so. After receiving instruction, Benati and Lee with McNulty (2010) found that language background was not a significant factor affecting post-treatment performance in terms of accuracy and in terms of contexts generated. All learners of varying language backgrounds improved significantly and, ultimately, equally on a sentence-level interpretation test, a sentence-level form production test, and a discourse-level guided composition as a result of receiving PI. The discourse-level guided composition the learners wrote showed that after instruction all the learners' accuracy was significantly higher but also that they all generated significantly more contexts for using the subjunctive after *cuando*. After instruction no language background group produced more contexts than any other language group.

The present study follows from the research presented in Benati and Lee with McNulty (2010). We continue to examine language background but with one fewer participant. We expand our focus in the present study to more closely examine the tasks the learners performed as pre-tests and post-tests. In addition to the sentence-level interpretation task, we examine performance separately on three production tasks: a sentence-level fill-in-the-blank form-production task, a sentence-fragment task for which the learners heard the stimuli and then wrote an ending for the sentence, and a guided composition task. Benati and Lee with McNulty (2010) did not analyse performance on the two sentence-level tasks separately. Additionally, we examine the effects of PI instruction not only on changes in subjunctive use, but also changes in indicative use to determine if learners overgeneralize instruction. Benati and Lee with McNulty (2010) only analysed subjunctive use. Finally, and importantly, we employ a concept-oriented approach (Bardovi-Harlig, 2007) to document the forms learners use to express the semantic concepts of [+futurity, +uncertainty] before instruction on the subjunctive after *cuando* and then again after instruction.

Research Questions

Previous research has consistently demonstrated the positive effects of PI with Spanish, Italian and French subjunctive used in the context of expressions of doubt/uncertainty in the main clause. Recent work has also shown positive effects of PI with the Spanish subjunctive after the adverb *cuando*. In the present study we examine only PI and do not examine other interventions. As Collentine (2004: 180) stated, in determining whether PI retrains, redirects or re-tunes learners' processing mechanisms it may not be necessary to compare it to other types of instruction. So, for the present study, we focus only on the effects of PI to address whether it brings about changes in the developing systems of learners with differing language backgrounds. We address the following research questions.

1. Are there positive effects for processing instruction on the Spanish subjunctive after the adverb *cuando* for learners of different language backgrounds as measured by a sentence-level interpretation task, a sentence-level, fill-in-the-blank form-production task, a sentence-level, sentence-fragment production task, and a discourse-level guided composition task?
2. Do learners of different language backgrounds overgeneralize instruction on the subjunctive and produce subjunctive forms in non-subjunctive (indicative) contexts as measured by a sentence-level, fill-in-the-blank form-production task and a sentence-level, sentence-fragment production task?
3. What forms do learners of different language backgrounds produce to express the concepts of [+futurity, +uncertainty] encoded by the Spanish subjunctive after the adverb *cuando*, before and after receiving processing instruction, on a sentence-level, fill-in-the-blank form-production task, a sentence-level, sentence-fragment production task, and a discourse-level guided composition task?

Method

Participants

All participants were enrolled in the first semester of an intermediate-level Spanish language class at the University of New South Wales, Sydney. The lecturer for this course was one of the researchers, who delivered the explicit grammatical information in the form of a lecture, one hour of processing instruction in the lecture, as well as carried out the pre- and post-testing in the regularly scheduled weekly lecture. The tutor for this course was not one of the researchers and she delivered an hour of structured input practices in the tutorial. The original data pool consisted of 93 possible subjects. As the present study explores further the work presented in Benati and Lee with McNulty (2010), we have the same set of subjects minus one participant who withdrew consent. They represent three language background groups: those whose native language is English and who studied no other language than beginner-level Spanish (n = 15); those whose native language was English and had studied languages in addition to Spanish (n = 13); and those whose native language was not English and so were minimally trilingual (n = 7). The term 'English' refers to those learners whose native language is English and who indicated that Spanish was the only other language they had studied or knew (n = 15). We use 'English+' to refer to those native speakers of English who had studied or knew languages in addition to Spanish (n = 13). We use 'Other' to refer to those participants whose native language is not English (n = 7). All but one of these participants reported studying or knowing languages other than English and Spanish in addition to their native language. All participants had completed all elements of the pre- and post-testing as well as the instructional treatment (lecture and tutorial phases). Language profiles of the participants are provided in Benati and Lee with McNulty (2010: 129). No participant reported a hearing impairment. All participants included in the final data analyses scored 50% or less on all the different pre-test tasks.

The target grammatical item was the use of the Spanish subjunctive or indicative after the adverb *cuando*. Subjunctive forms had not been presented in the course prior to the research nor had any other use of the subjunctive been introduced. Most of the participants had studied beginner-level Spanish at the same university although a few had been placed directly into intermediate Spanish. Because the materials from the previous semester of beginner-level Spanish do not include the subjunctive, this treatment represents their first formal exposure to the Spanish subjunctive.

Procedures

The instructional format for the class in which the participants were enrolled consisted of a two-hour lecture to all students enrolled in the class in combination with smaller breakout tutorials of two consecutive hours for a total of four contact hours per week. The lecture took place on Wednesdays. The lecture focused on grammatical explanation that would then be practised the following week in the tutorials. The tutorials were scheduled for Mondays and Wednesdays. We presented the target grammatical item, subjunctive/indicative contrast after the adverb *cuando*, around the usual presentation and practice timetable for the class.

All participants received the same instruction beginning with the presentation of explicit information in the large lecture format as well as the practices in the lecture format and in the smaller group tutorials. The instruction lasted two days for a total of approximately three hours with the practices spread out over the two days. Given syllabus/course programme constraints, the post-testing took place seven to nine days after the in-class practices took place. The constraint was that other required course material had to be covered such that 45 minutes of testing could not take place at that time. We could, in a sense, call this delayed post-testing since it did not take place immediately after instruction. We do not feel that the learners' performance on the post-test was at all affected by the one-week delay in post-testing because previous PI research has revealed no diminished effects after one week, two weeks or even one month following instruction (see Lee, Chapter 2, this volume for a review of the durative effects of PI). We present in Table 3.1 an overview of the timeline of the experimental procedures.

Week 1	**Week 2**	**Week 3**	**Week 4**
Pre-testing in lecture 1. interpretation 2. production 3. composition (45 mins)	Instruction in lecture Explicit information (1 hr) plus practice (1 hr)	Practice in tutorials (1 hr)	Post-testing in lecture 1. interpretation 2. production 3. composition (45 mins)

Table 3.1 Overview of the experimental procedures

Materials

We adapted all the materials used in the present study, except the guided composition, from those McNulty developed (McNulty, 2011). The guided composition was developed for Benati and Lee with McNulty (2010). McNulty prepared her instructional materials following the guidelines set forth in Lee and VanPatten (1995; 2003) and Farley (2005) for developing structured input activities. The grammatical explanation (explicit information) used in the present study was also adapted from McNulty (2011). Her computer-delivered explanation was transformed into a lecture-based presentation by creating 19 PowerPoint slides; the content of each is provided in Benati and Lee with McNulty (2010: 130–33). Ten slides provide information about the function of the subjunctive and indicative after the adverb *cuando*. Six slides provide information about forming the subjunctive. Two slides provide information about processing the subjunctive and indicative forms. The learners were told explicitly that we wanted them to learn to detect the difference between an *–e* and an *–a* in an unstressed final syllable. The difference in vowel signalled the difference in meaning we provided in the initial part of the explanation, that is, the difference between uncertain future time and habitual actions or events. The other slide was the title slide. It took approximately an hour to make this presentation.

During the second hour of the two-hour lecture period, the participants carried out four referential activities, two provided written input and two aural input. Each activity contained eight items for a total of 32 practice items. Due to the lecture format, we presented each item individually on a PowerPoint slide and provided explicit feedback after each item. That is, a learner volunteered the answer and was told if it was correct or not. A sample of a referential activity is given in Appendix A. We provided the learners a work sheet on which to record their answers. These worksheets were collected at the end of the lecture. Participants who did not fill out the worksheet were not included in the analyses.

The following week learners received a packet of materials in their tutorial groups (two tutorials on Monday and the third on Wednesday). They were told that the materials were designed to follow up the lecture from the previous week. This arrangement is typical for the course. The lecture previews the material practised in the tutorial a week later. The packet contained 12 activities. The first four activities were of the referential type and contained eight items each giving a total of 32 referential items. These activities were quite similar to the ones they had performed after we presented the explicit information. The following eight activities were of the affective type and contained six items each giving a total of 48 affective items. Although the materials were based on McNulty's we had more class time available to us in the present study than she did in hers. We were able, therefore, to add another step to most of the affective activities that helped promote the meaningfulness or communicativeness of the activity. This second step is one that we found in Benati (2004a: 222) and Wong (2004: 202). We asked the learners to evaluate or provide some sort of perspective on the information included in the activity. A sample of an affective activity is provided in Appendix B.

Assessment Instruments and Scoring

Each of the pre-tests and post-tests consisted of two listening, two reading and two composition tasks, presented in that order. The assessment tasks are provided in Appendix C. One listening and one reading task assessed interpretation whereas the other listening and reading tasks evaluated form production. Each of these tasks contained six items; three required the subjunctive and three required the indicative. The total number of items was 24, that is, 12 interpretation items and 12 form-production items. The composition tasks evaluated discourse-level form/function production. Cheng (2002; 2004) used a guided composition to assess the effects of processing instruction on the Spanish copula with predicate adjectives. Her task consisted of a series of pictures that learners had to describe. We were unable to develop a picture-based composition for the present study because we could not devise a simple visual means of expressing contingencies in future or habitual actions. We did develop a guided composition in which we asked learners to consider future actions and the possible circumstances that might bring them about. We asked learners first to write about themselves and then to change perspectives and write about their best friend. We provided a set of six circumstances for the learners to consider in each composition.

We used the same tasks and items in both the pre-test and post-test. An important difference between the pre-test and post-test items was that for the interpretation and form-production tests, any item that was subjunctive or required a subjunctive form on the pre-test was changed to indicative on the post-test and vice versa. In the present study we analyse the two form-production tasks separately as the task demands are different and this study explores in more depth the types of forms produced prior to instruction. The results of the two interpretation tasks are pooled into one score. The results of the two composition tasks are also pooled into one score because the task demands are identical.

To address the first research question about the effects of instruction, we scored the pre-tests and post-tests for correct use of the subjunctive items. There were six target items across the two interpretation tasks and six across the two form-production tasks. The highest score possible for interpretation was six. The fill-in-the blank form-production task had three target items as did the sentence-fragment form-production test. The highest possible score on each of these was three. Pre-test scores for the form-production tasks are extremely low. The mean is 0 for the fill-in-the-blank task and .09 for the sentence-fragment task. We scored the combined guided compositions for the number of correct subjunctive forms used after the adverb *cuando*. Because learners varied in how many contexts they created for using the subjunctive, we converted the composition scores to percentages and report them as such. The low means scores on the pre-test, .71%, demonstrate that learners simply did not know the subjunctive forms prior to instruction. We also tallied the number of times a participant created a context with *cuando* that required a subjunctive form.

Results

The Effects of Instruction

The means scores, expressed as raw scores for all tasks except the guided composition, and standard deviations are provided in Table 3.2. We conducted a series of one-way ANOVAs on the various pre-test scores in order to determine that the three language background groups all started the treatment with equivalent knowledge of the target structure. If groups have the same or equivalent knowledge prior to treatment but emerge after the treatment with different levels of knowledge then we can attribute those changes to the treatments. We present a summary of the F statistics and p values that resulted from the one-way ANOVAs on pre-test scores in Table 3.3. No ANOVA was generated for fill-in-the-blank form production task because the pre-test means scores for each of the language groups was 0. As can be seen in the table, the participants forming the three groups showed no statistically significant differences in their pre-test scores on four of the five scores assessed. The pre-test scores between language groups were equivalent for interpretation, fill-in-the-blank form production, sentence-fragment form production, and for the number of correct subjunctive forms produced after *cuando* on the guided composition. The one pre-test score in which we found a trend towards significance was in the number of contexts generated when using a subjunctive form after *cuando* (p = .0526). A student's t test of the means demonstrated that the non-native speakers of English (Other) generated significantly more contexts for using a subjunctive form after *cuando* than did the English group (p = .0264) and the English+ group (p = .0273). They did not, however, produce more correct forms than the other two groups. Despite this one significant difference and because of the lack of significant differences in form-production scores, we continued to pursue language background as a variable in the statistical analyses.

		English N = 15		**English+** N = 13		**Other** N = 7	
		Pre	*Post*	*Pre*	*Post*	*Pre*	*Post*
Interpretation	M	2.13	5.13	2.15	5.69	1.71	4.86
	SD	1.13	1.06	.80	.85	.76	1.68
Fill-in-the-blank	M	0	2.73	0	2.77	0	2.86
form production	SD	0	.80	0	.83	0	.38
Sentence-fragment	M	.06	2.33	0	2.15	.29	2.43
form production	SD	.26	.90	0	1.07	.49	.79
Composition –	M	0%	78.90%	1.92%	94.92%	0%	88.86%
form production	SD	0	31.76	6.93	12.39	0	19.34
Composition –	M	4.20	8.60	4.15	9.23	6.86	10.71
contexts generated	SD	1.93	2.87	1.77	3.79	4.26	3.99

Table 3.2 Means and standard deviations on the pre-tests and post-tests by language background

Pre-test	*F* statistic	*p* value
Interpretation	.5720	.5701
Fill-in-the-blank form production	--	--
Sentence-fragment form production	2.5806	.0914
Composition: form production	.8381	.4418
Composition: contexts	3.2325	.0526

Table 3.3 Summary of the *F* statistics and *p* values contrasting pre-test scores across the three Language Background groups

Sentence-level Interpretation Task

Having determined that there were no statistically significant differences between the three groups of learners on the sentence-level interpretation pre-test, we submitted the data to a repeated measures ANOVA. The repeated measure was Time (pre-test versus post-test) and the between group factor was Language Background. The results of the ANOVA revealed a significant main effect for Time (F (1, 32) = 127.5545, p = .0001), but no main effect for Language Background (F (2, 32) = 2.0695, p = .1428) and no significant interaction (F (2, 32) = .4061, p = .6696). After receiving processing instruction on the Spanish subjunctive/indicative contrast after the adverb *cuando*, all three language background groups improved significantly and equally on the interpretation task. The average increase after treatment was 54%.

Fill-in-the-Blank Form-Production Task

Having established that there were no statistically significant differences between the three groups of learners on the pre-test scores for the fill-in-the-blank form-production task, we submitted the data to a repeated measures ANOVA. The repeated measure in the ANOVA was Time (pre-test versus post-test) and the between group factor was Language Background. The results of the ANOVA revealed a significant main effect for Time (F (1, 32) = 431.3734, p = .0001), but no main effect for Language Background (F (2, 32) = .0648, p = .9374) and no significant interaction (F (2, 32) = .0648, p = .9474). After receiving processing instruction on the subjunctive/indicative contrast after *cuando* all three language background groups produced significantly more correct forms than they did prior to the treatment with no difference in the number of correct forms produced across groups. The post-test scores for fill-in-the-blank form production increased, on average, by 92% from the pre-test scores.

Sentence-Fragment Form-Production Task

Having established that there were no statistically significant differences between the three groups of learners on the pre-test scores for the sentence-fragment form-production task, we submitted the data to a repeated measures ANOVA. The repeated measure in the ANOVA was Time (pre-test versus post-test) and the between group factor was Language Background. The results of the ANOVA revealed a significant main effect for Time (F (1, 32) = 175.1052, p = .0001), but no main effect for Language Background (F (2, 32) = .6684, p = .5195) and no significant interaction (F (2, 32) = .0682, p = .9342). After receiving processing instruction all three language background groups produced significantly more correct forms than they did prior to the treatment with no difference between the groups in the number of correct forms produced. The post-test scores for sentence-fragment form production increased, on average, by 73% from the pre-test scores.

Discourse-level Guided Composition Task: Correct Forms Produced

Having established that there were no statistically significant differences between the three groups of learners on the pre-test scores for the number of correct subjunctive forms produced on the guided compositions, we submitted the data to a repeated measures ANOVA. We used percentages in the ANOVA because different learners generated different numbers of contexts for using a subjunctive form. Even though we provided 12 stimuli and 12 was the maximum number of contexts generated on the pre-test, 14 was the maximum number generated on the post-test. (Benati and Lee with McNulty (2010) used raw scores.) The repeated measure in the ANOVA was Time (pre-test versus post-test) and the between group factor was Language Background. The results of the ANOVA revealed a significant main effect for Time (F (1, 32) = 409.8582, p = .0001), but no main effect for Language Background (F (2, 32) = 1.8972, p = .1665) and no significant interaction (F (2, 32) = .1.2516, p = .2997). After receiving processing instruction, these learners produced a significantly greater number of correct subjunctive forms after *cuando* than they did prior to the treatment. The average increase from pre-test to post-test was 86%.

Discourse-level Guided Composition Task: Contexts Generated for Using the Subjunctive after Cuando

Having found a statistically significant difference between the group of non-native speakers of English and the other two groups on the pre-test, we approached our analyses of the post-tests with due caution. We found that, prior to treatment, the non-native speakers of English generated more contexts for using the subjunctive after *cuando* than did the other two groups but they did not produce more correct forms than the other groups. We attribute this difference to this group's broader language learning experiences but not to any language in particular. The repeated measure in the ANOVA was Time (pre-test versus post-test) and the between group factor was Language Background. The results of the ANOVA revealed a significant main effect for Time ($F\,(1, 32) = 54.3608$, $p = .0001$), but no main effect for Language Background ($F\,(2, 32) = 2.3179$, $p = .1148$) and no significant interaction ($F\,(2, 32) = .3199$, $p = .7285$). After receiving processing instruction, all the learners generated a significantly greater number of contexts for using subjunctive forms after *cuando* than they did prior to the treatment. Having found that the non-native speakers of English created more contexts for using the subjunctive on the pre-test, we decided to compare their performance on the post-test to that of the other groups, even though Language Background was not a significant factor. The student's t test revealed that on the post-test, none of the three scores were significantly different from each other. All three groups improved and reached a similar level on the post-test. Prior to the treatment, the learners on average generated 4.71 contexts for using the subjunctive. After treatment the figure almost doubles to 9.24 contexts.

Overgeneralization of Instruction

Our second research questions addresses whether learners of different language backgrounds overgeneralize instruction on the subjunctive and thereby produce subjunctive forms in non-subjunctive (indicative) contexts on the sentence-level form production tasks: a sentence-level, fill-in-the-blank form-production task and a sentence-level, sentence-fragment production task. We do not include in this analysis the discourse-level guided composition task because it was designed only to elicit use of the subjunctive after *cuando*. Our analyses revealed that only four learners produced a subjunctive form in an indicative context and that these learners represented each of the three language backgrounds. Interestingly, each of the learners, on the task(s) in which they overgeneralized, overgeneralized completely. That is, they produced subjunctive forms on all three of the indicative items. Two participants representing the group who were native speakers of English who studied only Spanish as a second language overgeneralized on the fill-in-the blank form-production task. They did not do so on the sentence-fragment task. One participant representing the group of native speakers of English for whom Spanish was a third or subsequent language overgeneralized subjunctive forms on both form-production tasks. One participant representing the group who were not native speakers of English overgeneralized subjunctive forms on the fill-in-the blank task but not on the sentence-fragment task. Given these results, we did not pursue any statistical analyses. Overgeneralization of instruction happened rarely and was limited to certain individuals.

Forms Produced before and after Instruction

Our third research question addresses the forms learners of different language backgrounds produce to express the concepts of [+futurity, +uncertainty] encoded by the Spanish subjunctive after the adverb *cuando*, before and after receiving processing instruction. We will examine the forms they produced on all three production tasks: on a sentence-level, fill-in-the-blank form-production task, a sentence-level, sentence-fragment production task, and a discourse-level guided composition task. We present an analysis of the forms produced on the pre-tests in Table 3.4. As expected from the presentation of means in Table 3.2, the number of subjunctive forms produced in the pre-tests is only four and they were produced by four different learners. We found two types of future forms, the simple morphological future and the periphrastic future with learners preferring the morphological future. The future forms are produced in all three tasks by several different learners indicating that some learners are interpreting these contexts as [+future]. A very large percentage of the forms produced are present indicative, between 44% and 64%. We have combined preterite, imperfect, present perfect, present progressive, infinitives, and items omitted in the category of other forms. Individually the forms just mentioned occurred rarely. We do, however, note that on the sentence-fragment pre-test these other forms represent 37% of the data. The data suggest that prior to instruction, learners are not processing the [+futurity] element of the context. Moreover, language background does not appear to advantage any of the groups. Members of each

Form		**Fill in blank max = 105**	**Sentence fragment max = 105**	**Composition max = 165**
Subjunctive	total number of forms	0	3	1
	% of max	0	2.86	.61
	E	0	1	0
	E+	0	0	1
	O	0	2	0
	total number of learners	0	3	1
Future	total number of forms	21	14	33
	% of max	20.00	13.33	20.00
	E	3	2	6
	E+	4	5	6
	O	2	1	3
	total number of learners	9	8	15
Periphrastic future	total number of forms	7	3	7
	% of max	6.67	2.86	4.24
	E	2	1	1
	E+	1	2	3
	O	0	0	1
	total number of learners	3	3	5
Present indicative	total number of forms	63	46	106
	% of max	60.00	43.81	64.24
	E	9	7	10
	E+	9	10	9
	O	3	4	6
	total number of learners	21	21	25
Other forms	total number of forms	14	39	18
	% of max	13.33	37.14	10.91
	E	4	9	8
	E+	1	2	2
	O	1	4	0
	total number of learners	6	15	10

Table 3.4 Forms used on the pre-tests in contexts that require the subjunctive after the adverb *cuando*

language background group produced non-subjunctive forms in at least one of the three tasks analysed.

We present an analysis of the forms learners produced in contexts that require the subjunctive after *cuando* on the post-tests in Table 3.5. As expected from the means presented in Table 3.2, processing instruction is quite effective in that a great percentage of the forms produced after instruction are correct subjunctive forms (79% to 92%). Learners still use a variety of forms when they do not use a subjunctive form but the incidence of such forms has decreased dramatically. Language background never reached a level of statistical significance in the repeated measures ANOVAs presented previously indicating that it did not provide learners any advantage. Language background does not appear to offer any advantages or disadvantages in terms of the forms produced after instruction. Members of each group produced a variety of non-subjunctive forms with the exception that no non-native speaker of English produced a periphrastic future form.

Discussion and Conclusion

The goal of the present study was to explore the effects of language background on the results of processing instruction and to measure learners' performance on a discourse-level guided composition in addition to the more traditional sentence-level interpretation and form-production tasks associated with PI research. We also sought to determine whether instruction on the subjunctive is overgeneralized by any of the language background groups and to analyse the forms learners produced prior to and after instruction.

Language background in the present study refers both to the learners' native languages as well as to their experiences with languages other than Spanish. The statistical findings are perfectly consistent across the four different assessment tasks when we scored for correct interpretation or production of a subjunctive form. We found a significant effect for Time but no significant effect for Language Background and no significant interaction between Time and Language Background for each task. These results indicate that all three language background groups improved from pre-test to post-test and improved equally. In other words, the various language backgrounds of the participants neither hindered nor enhanced their performance. Processing instruction has never failed to deliver positive effects on sentence-level tasks either interpretation or form production. The finding related to form production has always generated the most debate because

Form		**Fill in blank max = 105**	**Sentence fragment max = 105**	**Composition max = 324**
Subjunctive	total number of forms	97	83	292
	% of max	92.38	79.05	90.12
	E	14	14	14
	E+	12	12	13
	O	7	7	7
	total number of learners	33	33	34
Future	total number of forms	0	2	6
	% of max	0	1.91	1.85
	E	0	0	2
	E+	0	1	0
	O	0	0	1
	total number of learners	0	1	3
Periphrastic future	total number of forms	1	0	12
	% of max	.95	0	3.70
	E	0	0	1
	E+	1	0	1
	O	0	0	0
	total number of learners	1	0	2
Present indicative	total number of forms	4	13	8
	% of max	3.81	12.38	2.47
	E	2	2	4
	E+	0	3	1
	O	0	2	1
	total number of learners	2	7	6
Other	total number of forms	1	7	6
	% of max	.95	6.67	1.85
	E	0	3	2
	E+	0	1	0
	O	1	0	0
	total number of learners	1	3	2

Table 3.5 Forms used on the post-tests in contexts that require the subjunctive after the adverb *cuando*

during PI treatment the learners perform only structured input activities that never require the learners to produce the target form. They hear the target form and they read it, but do not say or write it. Yet, after treatment, learners in PI groups are always able to produce the target form. Processing the form creates grammatically richer intake for the developing system. Once the form is in the developing system, learners can access it for production. As the results of the present study indicate, the forms can be accessed for use in isolated sentences and also for use in creating discourse-level contexts.

The most interesting effect for Language Background was revealed on the pre-test administration of the guided composition. The non-native speakers of English, the plurilinguals, created significantly more contexts that required the subjunctive after *cuando* on the pre-test than the other two groups did even though they used no subjunctive forms on the pre-test. We thought that this advantage would continue to the post-test but it did not. Although this group had the highest mean on the post-test, it was not significantly higher than the other groups. Everyone improved significantly and reached an equivalent level of creating from 8.6 to 10.7 contexts for using the subjunctive after *cuando*. This finding echoes that of Lee and Benati with Aguilar-Sánchez and McNulty (2007) who examined the effects of PI on the Spanish imperfect. They performed several analyses on their data such that they distinguished between high and low scores on the pre-tests. They found that learners who scored lower on the pre-test improved more than the high scorers such that the two groups' scores on the post-test were not significantly different from each other. The low scorers closed the gap suggesting that they benefited perhaps not more from PI than the high scorers but differently. One potential effect of instruction is that it closes the gap between groups. Everyone performed at an equivalent level once everyone received processing instruction in the present study.

Our second research question addressed whether learners of different language backgrounds would overgeneralize instruction. Overgeneralization, as an acquisitional process, refers to the tendency among first and second language learners to extend the use of a form into contexts, linguistic or pragmatic, in which it is not used accurately. Classroom learners are noted for extending the use of a newly learned form into linguistic contexts where it does not belong (e.g., Lightbown, 1983). In the present study, we taught the use of both subjunctive and indicative forms after the adverb *cuando*. The subjunctive forms were, however, the marked, novel forms and so we focused on the possible extension of those forms into indicative contexts that require the use of the indicative. Our two form-production tasks contained three items that required subjunctive use, [+futurity, +uncertainty], and three that required the indicative, [+habitual]. Our analyses revealed that only five of the 35 participants produced subjunctive forms in contexts that required the indicative. Moreover, the five learners represent all three language background groups suggesting that this aspect of their performance is not related to language background. This small number who overgeneralized, in and of itself, would allow us to conclude that overgeneralization occurs rarely. But there is another aspect of learner performance that indicates to us that overgeneralization, as an acquisitional process, is not occurring but that these five learners developed a test-taking strategy. All five learners used subjunctive forms on all six items of both tasks; they did not use an indicative form on any of the items.

Two previous studies of processing instruction have revealed that some learners adopt a test-taking strategy. Both VanPatten and Wong (2004) and Leeser and Demil (in press) examined a word-order-based processing problem in which the agent of the action of the verb occurs in post-verbal position. In VanPatten's (2004) model, this phenomenon is captured in the First Noun Principle which states that learners tend to assign subject or agent status to the first noun or pronoun they encounter in an utterance even if the second noun or pronoun is actually the agent/subject. These researchers trained learners to process the agent in second position at the same time as having learners process the agent in pre-verbal position. The novel element of the training was to attend to the second noun in the input as an agent. In both studies, they found that a subset of learners adopted a 'second noun strategy' by assigning agent status to the second noun in the utterance whether or not this second noun was the agent. Because our five participants produced subjunctive forms in all items that should have indicative, we assert that they have adopted a test-taking strategy. They are not attending to the meaning of [+futurity, +uncertainty] but are simply producing subjunctive forms everywhere. Because only five learners do this and that they do so in all contexts, we conclude that the larger poulation of learners we examined do not overgeneralize subjunctive forms in indicative contexts. Rather, we conclude that a very small subset of learners adopted a test-taking strategy: use the novel form in all contexts. Perhaps learners who engage in such test-taking strategies should be removed from the data pool in future research.

Our third research question examines learners' performance from a language development perspective. We know from the results of all PI research that after instruction learners produce the target forms correctly. So we posed the question: what forms are learners using before they receive instruction? The question is especially interesting when the target form occurs in a semantic context [+futurity, +uncertainty] that can be analysed. The data suggest that prior to instruction, learners are not regularly encoding the [+futurity] element of the context. Future forms account for 16%–26% of the forms produced. The present indicative appears to be the default form used in this context, accounting for 43%–64% of forms produced. A possible contributing factor is that Spanish uses two different forms, subjunctive in the context of [+futurity, +uncertainty] and present indicative in the context of [+habitual] whereas English uses only one for both contexts. Language background may be a contributor to form choice prior to instruction. Language background does not, however, appear to hinder nor enhance the performance of any of the groups after instruction. Members of each language background group produce non-subjunctive forms in at least one of the three tasks analysed. The groups are on equal footing as language learners when it comes to producing forms. Instruction was extremely successful in getting learners to produce correct forms with accuracy rates ranging from 79% to 92%.

Future Research

Many factors are included under the heading of individual differences as the other research in this volume demonstrates. Our examination of the effects of language background on learning the Spanish subjunctive after the adverb *cuando* did not reveal that language background differentially affected the outcomes. We measured outcome via sentence interpretation and various production measures, at both sentence- and discourse-level. Future research on the effects of language background and processing instruction could focus on the learning process itself. For example, a number of studies have emerged that measure not only learning outcomes but also an aspect of the learning process (e.g., Fernández, 2008; Henry, Culman and VanPatten, 2009; VanPatten and Borst 2012a; 2012b). These researchers measured trials to criterion, defined as the number of items attempted before a learner begins to process the target form correctly and consistently. Language background might be a factor in trials to criterion. Plurilinguals may have a learning rate advantage over those who are studying their second language. Native speakers of Romance languages may have a learning advantage for Spanish compared to native speakers of Asian languages. Future research could also focus on language background as one of several individual differences measured. For example, language background, language aptitude and working memory together may affect learning outcomes as well as learning rate.

In one other PI study, the investigators included a small group of learners in the data pool who had additional language experience (Lee, Benati,

Águilar-Sánchez and McNulty 2007). Given all the restrictions on selecting participants (e.g., pre-test scores for two linguistic forms, attendance for instruction on two linguistic forms, delayed post-testing on two linguistic forms) they experienced a very high attrition rate of 83%. They ended up with a group of 19 participants who were native speakers of English who had studied only Spanish. They had a group of six more who had also studied French. They analysed the data statistically separating the two groups and found no statistically significant differences between the two. We are not advocating that PI researchers no longer screen for language background but, where possible, language background could be included as a variable in the research.

Authors' Note

This research was funded in part by a Research Promotion Grant from the Faculty of Arts and Social Sciences at the University of New South Wales to James F. Lee.

References

Barcroft, J., and VanPatten, B. (1997). Acoustic salience of grammatical forms: the effect of location stress, and boundedness on Spanish L2 input processing. In Glass, W. R. and Pérez-Leroux, A. T. (eds), *Contemporary Perspectives on the Acquisition of Spanish: Production, Processing, and Comprehension* (pp. 109–121). Sommerville, MA: Cascadilla Press.

Bardovi-Harlig, K. (2007). One functional approach to second language acquisition: the concept-oriented approach. In VanPatten, B. and Williams, J. (eds), *Theories of Second Language Acquisition: An Introduction* (pp. 97–113). Mahwah, NJ: Erlbaum.

Benati, A. G. (2004a). The effects of structured input and explicit information on the acquisition of Italian future tense. In VanPatten, B. (ed.), *Processing Instruction: Theory, Research, and Commentary* (pp. 207–255). Mahwah, NJ: Erlbaum.

Benati, A. G. (2004b). The effects of processing instruction and its components on the acquisition of gender agreement in Italian. *Language Awareness*, 13, 67–80.

Benati, A. G., Lee, J. F. with Laval, C. (2008). From processing instruction on the acquisition of French imparfait to secondary transfer-of-training effects on French subjunctive and to cumulative transfer-of-training effects with French causative constructions. In Benati, A. and Lee, J. F., *Grammar Acquisition and Processing Instruction: Secondary and Cumulative Effects* (pp. 121–57). Bristol: Multilingual Matters.

Benati, A. G., Lee, J. F. with McNulty, E. (2010). Exploring the effects of processing

instruction on a discourse-level guided composition with the Spanish subjunctive after the adverb *cuando*. In Benati, A. and Lee, J. F., *Processing Instruction and Discourse* (pp. 97–147). London: Continuum.
Cheng, A. (2002). The effects of processing instruction on the acquisition of *ser* and *estar*. *Hispania*, 85, 308–323.
Cheng, A. (2004). Processing instruction and Spanish *ser* and *estar*: forms with semantic-aspectual value. In VanPatten, B. (ed.), *Processing Instruction: Theory, Research, and Commentary* (pp. 119–41). Mahwah, NJ: Erlbaum.
Collentine, J. G. (2004). Commentary: where PI research has been and where it should be going. In VanPatten, B. (ed.), *Processing Instruction: Theory, Research, and Commentary* (pp. 169–81). Mahwah, NJ: Erlbaum.
Farley, A. P. (2001a). The effects of processing instruction and meaning-based output instruction. *Spanish Applied Linguistics*, 5, 57–94.
Farley, A. P. (2001b). Authentic processing instruction and the Spanish subjunctive. *Hispania*, 84, 289–99.
Farley, A. (2004a). The relative effects of processing instruction and meaning-based output instruction. In VanPatten, B. (ed.), *Processing Instruction: Theory, Research, and Commentary* (pp. 143–68). Mahwah, NJ: Erlbaum.
Farley, A. (2004b). Processing instruction and the Spanish subjunctive: is explicit information needed? In VanPatten, B. (ed.), *Processing Instruction: Theory, Research, and Commentary* (pp. 227–39). Mahwah, NJ: Erlbaum.
Farley A. (2005). *Structured Input: Grammar Instruction for the Acquisition-Oriented Classroom*. New York: McGraw-Hill.
Fernández, C. (2008). Reexamining the role of explicit information in processing instruction. *Studies in Second Language Acquisition*, 30, 277–305.
Henry, N., Culman, H., and VanPatten, B. (2009). More on the effects of explicit information in instructed SLA: a partial replication and a response to Fernández (2008). *Studies in Second Language Acquisition*, 31, 559–75.
Klein, W. (1986). *Second Language Acquisition*. Cambridge: Cambridge University Press.
Lee, J. F. (1999). On levels of processing and levels of comprehension. In Gutiérrez-Rexach, J. and Martínez-Gil, F. (eds), *Advances in Hispanic Linguistics: Papers from the 2nd Hispanic Linguistics Symposium* (pp. 42–59). Somerville, MA: Cascadilla Press.
Lee, J. F., and Benati, A. (2007a). *Delivering Processing Instruction in Classrooms and Virtual Contexts: Research and Practice*. London: Equinox.
Lee, J. F., and Benati, A. (2007b). *Second Language Processing: An Analysis of Theory, Problems and Solutions*. London: Continuum.
Lee, J. F., and Benati, A. (2009). *Research and Perspectives on Processing Instruction*. Berlin: Mouton de Gruyter.
Lee, J. F., Benati, A. with Aguilar-Sánchez, J., and McNulty, E. M. (2007). Comparing three modes of delivering processing instruction on preterite/imperfect distinction and negative informal commands in Spanish. In Lee, J. F. and Benati, A., *Delivering Processing Instruction in Classrooms and Virtual Contexts: Research and Practice* (pp. 73–98). London: Equinox.
Lee, J. F., and VanPatten, B. (1995). *Making Communicative Language Teaching Happen*. New York: McGraw-Hill.

Lee, J. F., and VanPatten, B. (2003). *Making Communicative Language Teaching Happen*, 2nd edn. New York: McGraw-Hill.

Leeser, M. J., and DeMil, A. J. (in press). Investigating the secondary effects of processing instruction in Spanish: from instruction on accusative clitics to transfer-of-training on dative clitics. *Hispania.*

Lightbown, P. (1983). Exploring relationships between developmental and instructional sequences in L2 acquisition. In Seliger, H. W. and Long, M. H. (eds), *Classroom Oriented Research in Second Language Acquisition* (pp. 217–43). Rowley, MA: Newbury House.

McNulty, E. M. (2011). The effects of processing instruction on the acquisition of the Spanish subjunctive/indicative contrast after *cuando*. Doctoral dissertation. Indiana University, Bloomington.

Rosa, E., and O'Neill, M. (1998). Effects of stress and location on acoustic salience at the initial stages of Spanish L2 input processing. *Spanish Applied Linguistics*, 2, 24–52.

Rossomondo, A. E. (2007). The role of lexical temporal indicators and test interaction format on the incidental acquisition of Spanish future tense morphology. *Studies in Second Language Acquisition*, 29, 39–66.

Travis, C. (2003). The semantics of the Spanish subjunctive: its use in the natural semantic metalanguage. *Cognitive Linguistics*, 14, 47–69.

VanPatten, B. (1996). *Input Processing and Grammar Instruction: Theory and Research.* Norwood, NJ: Ablex.

VanPatten, B. (2002). Processing instruction: an update. *Language Learning*, 52, 755–803.

VanPatten, B. (2004). Input processing in second language acquisition. In VanPatten, B. (ed.), *Processing Instruction: Theory, Research, and Commentary* (pp. 5–31). Mahwah, NJ: Erlbaum.

VanPatten, B. (2007). Input processing in adult second language acquisition. In VanPatten, B. and Williams, J. (eds), *Theories in Second Language Acquisition* (pp. 115–35). Mahwah, NJ: Erlbaum.

VanPatten, B., and Borst, S. (2012a). The roles of explicit information and grammatical sensitivity in processing instruction: nominative-accusative case marking and word order in German L2. *Foreign Language Annals*, 45, 92–109.

VanPatten, B., and Borst, S. (2012b). The roles of explicit information and grammatical sensitivity in the processing of clitic object pronouns and word order in L2 Spanish. *Hispania*, 95, 270–84.

VanPatten, B., and Oikennon, S. (1996). Explanation vs. structured input in processing instruction. *Studies in Second Language Acquisition*, 18, 495–510.

VanPatten, B., and Wong, W. (2004). Processing instruction and the French causative: another replication. In VanPatten, B. (ed.), *Processing Instruction: Theory, Research, and Commentary* (pp. 97–118). Mahwah, NJ: Erlbaum.

Wong, W. (2004). Processing instruction in French: the roles of explicit information and structured input. In VanPatten, B. (ed.), *Processing Instruction: Theory, Research, and Commentary* (pp. 187–205). Mahwah, NJ: Erlbaum.

Appendix A

Sample of a referential activity from the lecture

Activity A. Choose the correct interpretation for each sentence. Remember, the form of the verb clues you into whether the time is uncertain or not. Since all the verbs are *–ar* verbs, an *–e* signals uncertainty whereas an *–a* signals certainty.

1. Cuando Juan toca la guitarra…
    a. We don't know when Juan will play the guitar.
    b. Juan plays the guitar all the time.
2. Cuando Rosa cante con música…
    a. We don't know when Rosa will sing with music.
    b. Rosa always sings with music.

Sample of a referential activity carried out in the tutorial.

Activity B. Similar to the previous activity, you will now hear part of a sentence. Choose the correct interpretation for each sentence. Remember, the form of the verb clues you in to whether the time is uncertain or not. Since all the verbs are *-ar* verbs, an *-e* signals uncertainty whereas an *-a* signals certainty.

1.
    a. We don't know when the professor will explain the homework.
    b. The professor normally explains the homework.
2.
    a. We don't know when the student will walk on campus.
    b. The student walks on campus all the time.

Sentence fragments learners heard:

1. Cuando el profesor explica la tarea...
2. Cuando el estudiante ande por el campus...

Appendix B

Sample of an affective activity

Step 1. Indicate whether, in your opinion, your instructor will do the following things. Note that opinion activities do not have a right or wrong answer. Keep in mind that the form of the verbs following *cuando* in 1–6 encodes the uncertainty of the time.

1. Cuando regrese a casa, tu instructor(a) va a tomar una copa de vino.
   ☐ sí ☐ no
2. Cuando lo necesite, tu instructor(a) va a limpiar su piso.
   ☐ sí ☐ no

Step 2. Based on your answers, how similar are you to your instructor? Indicate your response on the following scale.

1.	2.	3.	4.	5.
not at all similar		somewhat similar		completely similar

Appendix C

Activity 1 Interpretation

You will hear the first part of a sentence. Listen carefully and select the appropriate phrase that correctly completes each sentence.

1. a. se pierde (gets lost).
   b. va a perderse (gets lost).
2. a. da un paseo.
   b. va a dar un paseo.
3. a. busca otro trabajo.
   b. va a buscar otro trabajo.
4. a. tiene que cocinar.
   b. va a tener que cocinar.
5. a. se siente mejor.
   b. va a sentirse mejor.
6. a. pierde mucho peso.
   b. va a perder mucho peso.

Sentence fragments heard by learners for the pre-test. The items with subjunctive forms are ticked for the convenience of the reader.

1. *Cuando Carmen ande por la ciudad…* √
2. *Cuando Pilar termina su lectura…*
3. *Cuando Juan regresa de España…*
4. *Cuando Marta regrese de clase…* √
5. *Cuando Carmen se duche…* √
6. *Cuando Jorge practica un deporte…*

Activity 2 Form production

You will hear the beginning of a sentence. Please write your ending to the sentence using the verb provided.

1. … Jorge (regresar)______________________________.
2. … él (escuchar)______________________________.
3. … ella (necesitar)______________________________.
4. … ella (estudiar)______________________________.
5. … él (celebrar)______________________________.
6. … él (pagar)______________________________.

Sentence fragments heard by learners for the pre-test. The items requiring subjunctive forms are ticked for the convenience of the reader.

1. *Mi madre le va a ayudar a Jorge cuando...* √
2. *Juana saca el perro cuando...*
3. *Lola va a obtener un préstamo cuando...* √
4. *Lucía va a la biblioteca cuando...*
5. *Jorge sale con sus amigo cuando...*
6. *David va a tener poco dinero cuando...* √

Activity 3 Interpretation

The items with subjunctive forms are ticked for the convenience of the reader.

Select the appropriate phrase that correctly completes each sentence.

1. Cuando el niño esté enfermo ... √
   a. llora.
   b. va a llorar.
2. Cuando Clara lleve su pesada mochila (backpack)... √
   a. la espalda (back) le duele.
   b. la espalda (back) va a dolerle.
3. Cuando Jorge mira un paisaje (landscape) bonito...
   a. saca una foto.
   b. va a sacar una foto.
4. Cuando Lucía está aburrida...
   a. escucha la radio.
   b. va a escuchar la radio.
5. Cuando Julia maneje rápidamente... √
   a. recibe una multa (ticket).
   b. va a recibir una multa (ticket).
6. uando David admira a alguien...
   a. no habla mucho.
   b. no va a hablar mucho.

Activity 4 Form production

Conjugate the verb in parenthesis to correctly complete the sentence. (Items that require a subjunctive form are ticked for the convenience of the reader.)

1. Pilar va a pagar $50 cuando ____________ (comprar) su libro. √
2. David va a ganar mucho dinero cuando ____________ (trabajar) allí. √

3. Cuando Carla ____________ (tomar) mucho café, no puede dormir bien.
4. Joaquín va a comprar un coche cuando ____________ (ahorrar; 'save') dinero. √
5. Cuando Jorge ____________ (cocinar) algo con chocolate, le sale bien.
6. Cuando David ____________ (hablar) con sus amigos, se siente mejor.

Guided Composition 1

Use the following scenarios and circumstances to create a short composition about yourself and your future. You can invent other scenarios and circumstances to fit your life, but try to incorporate the ones provided.

What might you do in the future when the circumstances are right?

Circunstancias	*Escenarios*
cuando + …tener más dinero …tener más tiempo …tener empleo seguro …graduarse …aprender a ___ …conocer a ___	viajar por el mundo (travel the world) trabajar en el extranjero (work abroad) estudiar en el extranjero (study abroad) llegar a ser cocinero (become a chef) comprar ropa nueva (buy new clothes) comprar un coche (buy a new car) casarse (get married) tener hijos (have children)

En el futuro, cuando… ____

Guided Composition 2

Now write a similar paragraph, but this time do it with reference to your BEST FRIEND. What might he or she do in the future when the circumstances are right?

Circunstancias	*Escenarios*
cuando + …tener más dinero …tener más tiempo …tener empleo seguro …graduarse …aprender a ___ …conocer a ___	viajar por el mundo (travel the world) trabajar en el extranjero (work abroad) estudiar en el extranjero (study abroad) llegar a ser cocinero (become a chef) comprar ropa nueva (buy new clothes) comprar un coche (buy a new car) casarse (get married) tener hijos (have children)

En el futuro, cuando… ____________________________________

4 Age and the Effects of Processing Instruction on the Acquisition of English Passive Constructions among School Children and Adult Native Speakers of Turkish

Alessandro G. Benati, University of Greenwich (UK)*

Introduction

The effects of processing instruction have been measured in a series of classroom-based empirical studies (for a full review see Lee and Benati, 2009). Processing instruction has been compared to other types of form-focused interventions (e.g. traditional instruction, meaning-based instruction, and dictogloss) utilizing different types of assessment tasks and modes: interpretation tasks with aural modes, and production tasks with oral and written modes. These tasks measured learners' performance at sentence and discourse level (Benati and Lee, 2010). The overall findings from studies conducted to measure the effects of processing instruction have clearly indicated that processing instruction helps L2 learners process certain grammatical forms or structures that are affected by various processing problems (e.g., syntactic, perceptual, and semantic processing problems).The majority

* **Alessandro Benati** is Director of Research and Enterprise in the School of Humanities and Social Sciences at the University of Greenwich. He is an academic scholar in the area of second language acquisition. His research focuses on how language learners process incoming linguistic information at input level. He has worked extensively with James Lee on various projects. He has published books and journal papers in the areas of second language teaching and language acquisition. He is editor of an international book series in Instructed Second Language Research (Continuum Publishing).

of studies investigating the effectiveness of processing instruction have utilized adult learners with few exceptions where the population used was school-age learners (Benati, 2005; Benati, Lee and Houghton, 2008; VanPatten and Oikennon, 1996). Based on these empirical findings Benati and Lee (2008) formulated the Age Hypothesis:

> *The Age Hypothesis*. PI will be just as effective as an intervention with younger learners as it is with older learners (Benati and Lee, 2008: 168).

The majority of studies measuring the effectiveness of processing instruction have focused on native speakers of English learning Romance languages, especially Spanish (see Lee, 2004). However, the database has recently expanded to include native speakers of Chinese and Greek (Benati, 2005), Italian (Lee and Benati, 2007), and Korean (Benati, Lee and Houghton, 2008). Based on this set of findings Benati and Lee (2008) proposed the Native Language Hypothesis:

> *The Native Language Hypothesis*. PI will be effective for instilling target-language specific strategies, no matter the native language of the learners (Benati and Lee, 2008: 169).

In this chapter we will provide further evidence in support of the *Age Hypothesis* and the *Native Language Hypothesis* by measuring the effects of processing instruction on the acquisition of English passive constructions among school-age and adult native speakers of Turkish. Processing instruction was used in this study to alter one of the processing strategies captured by VanPatten's (1996) First Noun Principle (P2).

Previous Processing Instruction Research

Studies in Support of the Age Hypothesis

Studies that support the Age Hypothesis are those that have examined the effects of processing instruction on school-age children. What this partial review of the literature will show is that there has been no direct comparison of the effects of processing instruction on school-age children and adults. VanPatten and Oikennon (1996) carried out a study to investigate the effects of explicit information and structured input practice on the acquisition of Spanish direct object pronouns. The main purpose of this study was to establish which factor is the most effective component in the processing instruction approach. Fifty-nine English native speakers participated in this study.

They were high-school aged learners and were studying Spanish in their second year. The item investigated was, as in the case of VanPatten and Cadierno (1993), object pronouns in Spanish. A pre-test and immediate post-test design was adopted in this experiment. Participants were randomly assigned to three groups: the regular processing instruction group; the explicit information only group; and the structured input practice only group. The materials, assessment tasks and scoring procedures that VanPatten and Cadierno (1993) produced and used for their investigation were also utilized in this experimental study. Two assessment tasks were used (interpretation and production sentence-level tasks). The results of the interpretation task revealed that the processing instruction group and the structured input practice only group performed better than the explicit information only group. The findings from the production task also showed that the processing instruction group and the structured input practice only group performed better than the explicit information only group. The overall outcome of this study was that structured input practice was found to be the causative variable for learners' gains in interpretation and production sentence-level tasks.

Benati, Lee and Houghton (2008) examined whether learners who received processing instruction on the past tense in English can transfer this instructional training to the acquisition of the third person singular present tense (secondary effects). Twenty-six subjects participated in this classroom experiment. They were all Korean native speakers and they were studying beginner-level English in a middle school in Korea. These middle-school-aged learners were randomly assigned to one of two groups, the processing instruction group and the traditional instruction group. A pre-test/post-test procedure was used in this study with two different assessment tasks (interpretation and production sentence-level tasks). The overall outcomes of this study indicated that processing instruction not only provided learners with the primary benefit of learning to process and produce the morphological form on which they received instruction, but also a secondary benefit in that they transferred that training to processing and producing another morphological form on which they had received no instruction. These two studies (and others) are indicative of the positive effects of processing instruction with children. The question remains whether there are differential effects of processing instruction when children and adults are compared directly.

Studies in Support of the Native Language Hypothesis

Studies that support the Native Language Hypothesis are those that have expanded the processing instruction database by examining native speakers of languages other than English and second languages other than Romance languages. Benati (2005) investigated the effects of processing instruction, traditional instruction and meaningful output-based instruction on the acquisition of the English simple past tense. The relevant processing principle in this case was the Lexical Preference Principle. The subjects involved in Benati's study were forty-seven Chinese and thirty Greek school-age learners of English residing in their respective countries. The participants in both schools were divided into three groups: processing instruction, traditional instruction, and meaningful output-based instruction. One interpretation and one production measure were used in a pre-test/post-test design. The results from both studies were similar and revealed that processing instruction had positive effects on the processing and acquisition of the target feature. In both studies the processing instruction group performed better than the traditional and meaning output-based groups in the interpretation task and the three groups made equal gains in the production task. The two groups' performance was not compared directly but made very similar gains in interpretation and production.

Lee and Benati (2007) established that performing structured input activities is an effective treatment for helping learners make grammatical gains with the Japanese past tense marker. They examined the performance of 26 adults, native speakers of Italian, who were enrolled in a beginner-level Japanese language course at a private language school in Italy. Specifically, they compared the results of structured input practice with no explanation with those of traditional output instruction. The structured input group outperformed the traditional instruction group on the interpretation post-test whereas both groups made equal gains on the production post-test. The two studies reviewed in this section are indicative of a growing body of processing instruction research that has moved beyond the limitation first noted by Lee (2004), that of investigating native speakers of English learning Romance languages.

Research Questions

Within the processing instruction research framework, there is some evidence (see Introduction) to support the view that the effects of processing instruction are not restricted to adult native speakers of English. The main contributions of the research reported in this chapter to the ongoing debate on the effects of processing instruction on L2 acquisition are the following:

- to provide further evidence of the positive effects of processing instruction by directly comparing the performance of school-aged and adult learners whose native language (Turkish) has not yet been examined in the processing instruction database;[1]
- to provide new evidence of the effectiveness of processing instruction on the acquisition of a different linguistic item of the English grammatical system (English passive constructions);
- to offer further evidence of the effectiveness of processing instruction at altering the First Noun Principle used by L2 learners when processing input and helping learners to produce sentences containing the target feature;
- to further demonstrate that the positive effects of processing instruction are durable.

Based on the research aims and with the specific intent to measure the effects of processing instruction on the acquisition of English passive constructions, three research questions were formulated:

1. Would the two processing groups (children and adults) make equal gains in the correct interpretation of passive sentences in English?
2. Would the two processing groups (children and adults) make equal gains in the correct production of passive sentences in English?
3. Would the possible positive effects for instruction be retained over time by the two age groups (children and adults)?

Based on the results of previous research the following hypotheses were formulated:

- Children and adults will make similar gains from pre-test to post-test in both the interpretation and the production tasks.
- The results from both assessment tasks should also suggest that the earlier findings can be generalized for another structure (passive constructions) for learners with a different native-language background (Turkish).
- The two groups receiving processing instruction should equally retain the positive effects of instruction for both tasks over a delayed post-test administered three weeks after instruction.

Method

Participants

Participants were drawn from a group of students enrolled in an intermediate-level English class at a secondary school in Turkey and in a private university in Istanbul. The children-group were all 13–14 years old and were all Turkish native speakers. The adults-group were all between 19–21 years old and were also all Turkish native speakers. Both groups' learning of English was limited to classroom instruction, and they had no previous classroom exposure to the target form. Three main considerations were taken into account when deciding to select intermediate students: level of proficiency; vocabulary familiarity; and no previous exposure to the English passive construction. The original data pool consisted of 30 children and 16 adults. All participants completed the pre-tests and needed to score 50% or less on the two sentence-level tasks (interpretation and production) to be included in the final pool. The participants in the final pool (n = 17 children-group; n = 12 adults-group) received the same instructional treatment. The participants included in the final data analysis also completed the two post-tests (immediate and delayed).

Procedures

Figure 4.1 provides an overview of the experimental procedures. A pre-test battery was administered to all participants one week before the beginning of the experiment. Both instructional groups were taught for a total of four hours over a two-day period. The groups were taught by the regular classroom instructors, who acted as facilitator during the experiment and made all possible efforts to pay the same amount of attention and show the same enthusiasm across the different treatment conditions.

Materials

The English passive construction was selected for the instructional treatment for one main reason. This feature is affected by the First Noun Principle which has been investigated in other processing instruction studies. VanPatten (1996) has argued that learners tend to process the first noun or pronoun they encounter in a sentence as the subject or agent. In the sentence 'Chris was hit by Maria', learners might process Chris as the subject of the

PRE-TESTS (1 WEEK BEFORE) Interpretation and Production Tasks Final pool = 29 participants
↓↓ PI (Children-group – 17) PI (Adults-group – 12)
INSTRUCTIONAL PERIOD ↓ 2 CONSECUTIVE DAYS 2 HOURS' INSTRUCTION PER DAY
IMMEDIATE POST-TESTS DELAYED POST-TESTS (THREE WEEKS LATER) Interpretation and Production Tasks

Figure 4.1 Overview of the experiment

sentence and this will lead to a misinterpretation of the meaning of the sentence with a consequent delay in the ability of L2 learners to accurately map syntactic structure in the utterance. This sentence might be interpreted by L2 learners as if it was Chris who hit Maria as L2 learners would process the first item in the utterance as the agent (subject) of the sentence. VanPatten (1996) argues that when L2 learners process sentences containing a subject–verb–object (SVO) order, they do not encounter any problem in making correct syntactic mapping. However, in the case of linguistic structure such as English passive construction, the order of the sentence object–verb–subject (OVS) can cause a problem to L2 learners. The First Noun Principle is well documented by empirical studies investigating second language acquisition in children (Bever, 1970; Nam, 1975; Plèh, 1989) and adults (Ervin-Tripp, 1974; VanPatten, 1984; LoCoco, 1987; Lee, 1987).

One set of instructional materials was produced for the present study. The materials contained explicit information and structured input activities. The two processing instruction groups were asked to pay attention to the English passive construction in the input (see Figure 4.2) and were then given structured input practice (see sample items of a structured input activity in Figure 4.3). The two groups received the same amount and type of explicit information and structured input practice to help participants alter their reliance on word order (First Noun Principle) so that they would process English passive constructions accurately and efficiently. The groups were exposed to four hours' instruction. During the instructional period, feedback on performance was limited to telling participants when their

The main purpose of passive construction is to change the focus of attention of the sentence. MAKE SURE YOU UNDERSTAND WHO OR WHAT IS THE OBEJCT AND THE SUBJECT OF THE SENTENCE!

Active: Sally kissed John
Passive: John was kissed by Sally

THE TWO SENTENCES HAVE THE SAME MEANING BUT THE OBJECT AND THE SUBJECT OF THE SENTENCE ARE IN DIFFERENT POSITIONS

Figure 4.2 Explicit information related to processing word order

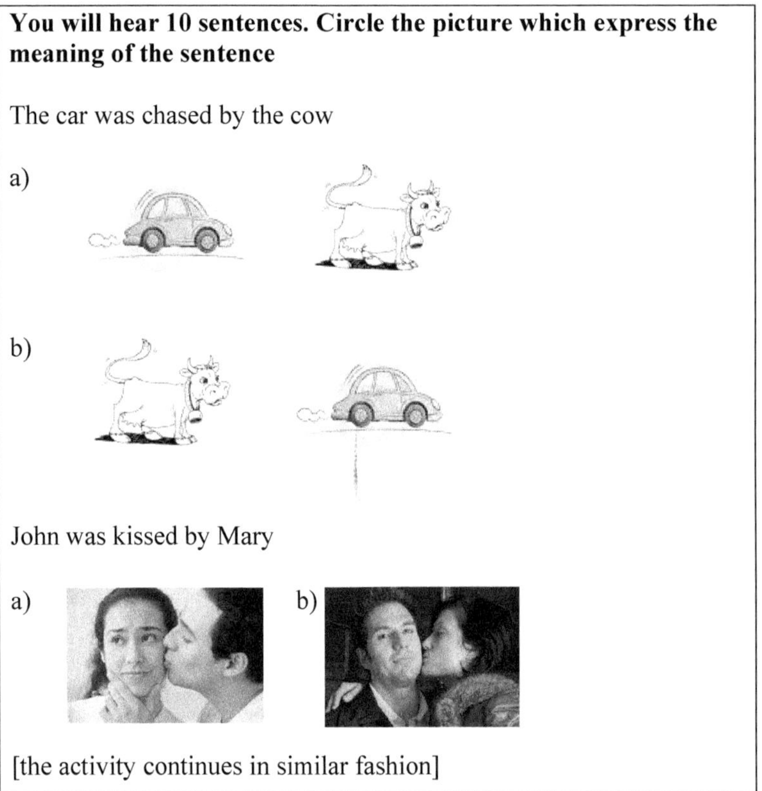

You will hear 10 sentences. Circle the picture which express the meaning of the sentence

The car was chased by the cow

a)

b)

John was kissed by Mary

a) b)

[the activity continues in similar fashion]

Figure 4.3 Sample items from a referential structured-input activity

interpretations were right or wrong, but did not receive any clarification as to why. No other feedback was provided.

The structured input activities (see more samples in Appendix A) included an equal number of referential and affective activities (20 in total). These activities were constructed following processing instruction guidelines (Farley, 2005; Lee and VanPatten, 1995; 2003). The activity in Figure 4.3 is an example of a referential activity. It is termed 'referential' because it has a right or a wrong answer. In this activity learners must attend to the grammatical markers of a passive construction (verb form and preposition) in order to establish who is doing the action (they need to establish who the agent is and who the patient is in the sentence) and understand the meaning of the sentence.

Affective activities have no correct or incorrect answer but rather learners' attention is directed to the passive construction through a task in which the form must be attended. Affective activities provide learners with positive evidence. At the same time learners must process each sentence for its meaning in order to complete the task.

Assessment Instruments and Scoring

Pre-tests were administered to the participants one week before the beginning of the instructional period. In order to address the questions raised in the present study, two tests were developed: an interpretation task and a production task. The post-tests were administered immediately after the end of the instructional treatment and again three weeks later to measure possible delayed effects.

Sample items from one version of the sentence-level interpretation task are provided in Figure 4.4. The interpretation task was an aural task which was developed to measure knowledge gained by learners at interpreting passive sentences in English. The task consisted of 20 audio-taped target sentences recorded by a native speaker of English speaking at a normal speed. Participants were required to listen to each sentence and to select one of two pictures that matched their interpretation. The two pictures differed in terms of who was performing the action. For the assessment task, learners also had the option of indicating that they were not sure who performed the action. In order to measure real-time comprehension, we did not repeat the items. Learners had only one opportunity to hear and interpret a sentence. Correct responses were given a score of 1 and each incorrect response a score of 0. The maximum score on this test was 10 points and the minimum 0. Distracters (non target items)were not scored.

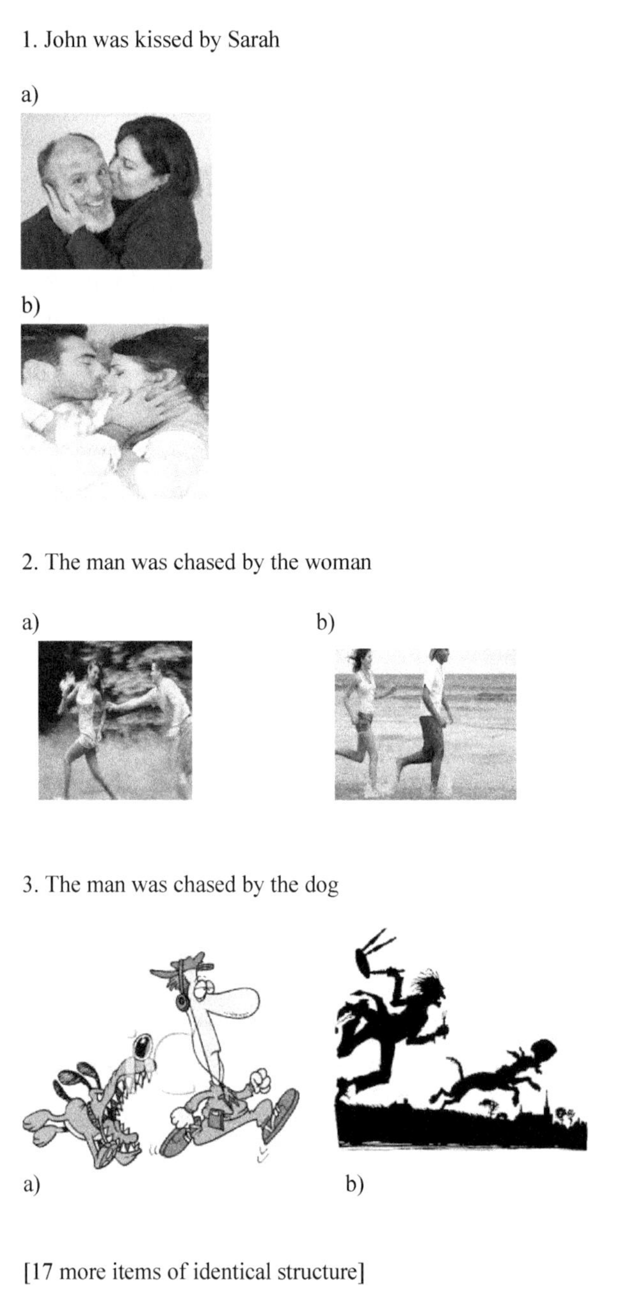

Figure 4.4 Interpretation task

Fill in the gaps writing the correct passive construction form. Use the verb and the tense provided in the brackets.	
1. The house ________________	by Janet. (to build – Simple Past)
2. Michael's table ___________	by Amy. (to make – Simple Past)
3. The word ________________	by the teacher. (to explain – Simple Present)
4. The letter ________________	the day before yesterday. (to send – Simple Past)
5. John's car ________________	by Paul. (to steal – Simple Past)
6. The cow _________________	by the horse. (to kick – Simple Past).
7. Ken's new restaurant _______	yesterday. (to open – Simple Past)
8. Jake ____________________	by Sara. (to kiss – Simple Past)
9. Jane ____________________	by Samuel to a party. (to invite – Simple Present)
10. Jane ___________________	the book by Jo last Sunday. (to give – Simple Past)

Figure 4.5 Production task

Sample items from the sentence-level written production task are provided in Figure 4.5. It was developed to measure learners' ability to produce correct English passive verb forms. The production test consisted of ten incomplete sentences in English. They were given the agent (already marked appropriately in the passives) and object and had to provide the correct verb form. All ten sentences were critical items (i.e., passives). Learners scored 1 point for each correct sentence produced and 0 points for incorrect ones. The maximum possible score was 10 points and the minimum 0.

Results

One-way analyses of variance (ANOVAs) were conducted on the raw scores for all pre-tests to determine whether there were any statistical differences among the two age groups prior to the beginning of the experiment. Repeated measures ANOVAs were used to determine whether there were any relevant differences between the two treatment groups after instruction and between the scores on the two post-tests.

Interpretation Data

Table 4.1 provides the means and standard deviations (SD) for the three administrations of the interpretation test. A one-way ANOVA conducted on the interpretation pre-test revealed no significant difference among the groups' means (F (1, 28) = 1.959, p = .359). Both age groups began instruction with equivalent knowledge of the target structure.

		Pre-test		Immediate post-test		Delayed post-test	
Variable	*n*	*Mean*	*SD*	*Mean*	*SD*	*Mean*	*SD*
PI (c)	17	1.352	1.057	7.294	1.649	6.117	1.218
PI (a)	12	1.283	1.922	6.831	1.994	6.083	1.250

Table 4.1 Means and standard deviations for interpretation task: pre-test, immediate post-test, and delayed post-test

The means in Table 4.1 suggest that both age groups made equal improvements from pre-test to post-tests. The processing instruction children-group and the processing instruction adults-group improved over 60% from pre-test to post-test scores. Their gains decreased between 8 and 11% between the first post-test and the delayed post-test.

A repeated measured ANOVA was conducted on the raw scores of the interpretation task (pre-test and post-test). Age Group (children and adult) was the between-subjects factor, whereas Time (pre-test, post-test) was the within-subjects factor. The results from the statistical analysis revealed a significant main effect for Time (F (1, 28) = 353.101, p = .000); no significant main effect for Age Group (F (1, 28) = 114.614, p = .139); and no significant interaction between Age Group and Time (F (2, 28) = 101.376, p = .121). These results indicate that both age groups benefited equally from instruction. To address the question of delayed effects, a second ANOVA was conducted on the two interpretation post-tests. The results from the statistical analysis revealed a significant main effect for Time (F (1, 28) = 278.451, p = .005); no significant main effect for Age Group (F (1, 28) = 103.654, p = .158); and no significant interaction between Age Group and Time (F (2, 28) = 61.476, p = .141).

Learners from the two processing groups maintained their ability to process and parse English passive forms at interpretation sentence-level between the post-test and the delayed post-test. These results indicate that both age groups retained the benefits of instruction.

Production Data

Table 4.2 provides the means and standard deviations for the three administrations of the production test. The raw scores for learners' performance on the sentence-level written production pre-test were submitted to a one-way ANOVA. The results of this analysis showed that there was no significant difference between the two groups before instruction (F (1, 28) = .357, p = .468). Both children and adults began instruction with equivalent knowledge of the target structure.

		Pre-test		**Immediate post-test**		**Delayed post-test**	
Variable	*n*	*Mean*	*SD*	*Mean*	*SD*	*Mean*	*SD*
PI (c)	17	1.176	1.014	6.294	1.358	5.058	.966
PI (a)	12	1.306	.657	6.165	1.055	5.121	.678

Table 4.2 Means and standard deviations for production task: pre-test, immediate post-test, and delayed post-test

The means displayed in Table 4.2 show that the gains made by the two age groups were very similar. The instructional training received by these two groups resulted in an improvement of about 50% from pre-test to post-test scores. Although the groups' scores decreased about 10% from post-test to delayed post-test, the positive effects of the instructional treatment are evident. The raw scores from the pre-test and the post-test in the production task were submitted to an ANOVA with repeated measures. The statistical analysis show a significant main effect for Time (F (1, 28) = 145.151, p = .000); no significant main effect for Age Group (F (1, 28) = 50.277, p = .101); and no significant interaction between Treatment and Time (F (1, 28) = 46.066, p = .179). These results indicate that both age groups benefited equally from instruction. To investigate the question of delayed effects, another ANOVA was conducted on the raw scores of the two production post-tests. The results from the statistical analysis revealed a significant main effect for Time (F (1, 28) = 208.224, p = .002); no significant main effect for Age Group (F (1, 28) = 113.235, p = .279); and no significant interaction between Age Group and Time (F (2, 28) = 74.139, p = .171).

These results indicate that both age groups retained the benefits of instruction.

Discussion and Conclusion

The three main objectives of the present study were:

(1) to examine the effectiveness of processing instruction on the acquisition of the English passive constructions by training L2 learners to circumvent the First Noun Principle;
(2) to provide further evidence of the positive effects of processing instruction by directly comparing the performance of school-aged and adult learners whose native language (Turkish) has not yet been examined in the processing instruction database;
(3) to determine possible delayed effects for processing instruction.

The results of the classroom experimental study presented in this chapter provide positive answers to the three research questions and support the hypotheses of this study.

1) Research question one (supported)
The first question formulated in the present study was 'Would the two processing groups (children and adults) make equal gains in the correct interpretation of passive sentences in English?'

The analysis of the data collected through the interpretation task clearly showed that the children and adults improved equally from pre-test to post-test in their ability to interpret English passive forms at sentence-level.

2) Research question two (supported)
The second question formulated in the present study was: 'Would the two processing groups (adults and children) make equal gains in the correct production of passive sentences in English?'

The statistical analysis indicated that both children and adults made equal gains from pre-test to post-test. Learners in these groups improved in their ability to produce English passive forms at sentence-level.

3) Research question three (supported)
The third question in this study attempted to address possible delayed effects for instruction. 'Would the possible positive effects for instruction be retained over time by the two age groups (children and adults)?' In order to address this question, a delayed

> post-test was used to collect data three weeks after the immediate post-test. Data were collected through sentence-level interpretation and production tasks. Despite a small decrease in performance, both age groups maintained their improvement three weeks after the end of the instructional period. Overall, the main findings confirm the third hypothesis and provide new information to the processing instruction research database.

Based on some of the limitations in the processing instruction research agenda, the aim of the present study was threefold:

- to explore the effects of processing instruction on L2 learners' ability to interpret and produce sentences containing a new linguistic item of English: namely English passive forms;
- to compare directly the effects of processing instruction on school-aged and adult learners who were native speakers of Turkish;
- to explore possible durable effects for processing instruction and structured input practice.

The results indicate that both age groups equally improved in all tasks (interpretation and written production). Processing instruction is successful in altering L2 learners' reliance on the first noun to identify the agent in passive sentences. The results also support previous findings investigating the effects of processing instruction on the First Noun Principle (VanPatten and Wong, 2004). The present study also suggests that the earlier findings can be generalized for a different structure and a different language.

The research presented in this chapter on English passive forms was carried out on school-aged children and adults. The main outcome of the present study provides direct rather than indirect support to the Age Hypothesis. Work presented in this chapter also strengthens the Native Language Hypothesis. Previous findings on the effects of processing instruction was carried out on native speakers of Italian (Lee and Benati, 2007), Chinese and Greek (Benati, 2005) and Korean native speakers (Benati, Lee and Houghton, 2008). The research presented here on English was carried out on Turkish native speakers.

Finally, the results presented in this chapter confirmed that processing instruction has a durable effect.

Despite the positive outcomes in this study, there are a number of limitations to be mentioned. Only a relatively small number of subjects participated (29 participants) in the final experiment. Further research should address this problem and replicate the experiment with a larger sample. Future research should also take into consideration the effects of other possible variables, which were not measured in this study, such as time on task and the amount of exposure to the grammatical feature.

Notes

1. Celik-Yazici (2007) reported comparing the effects of processing instruction to traditional instruction with native speakers of Turkish. His processing instruction treatment was, however, questionable. The sample affective structured input activity provided in his paper is in fact a production task. The referential activities uses seemed more a multiple choice preference task rather than a structured input activity.

References

Benati, A. (2005). The effects of processing instruction, traditional instruction and meaning-output instruction on the acquisition of the English past simple tense. *Language Teaching Research*, 9(1), 67–93.

Benati, A., and Lee, J. F. (2008). *Grammar Acquisition and Processing Instruction: Secondary and Cumulative Effects*. Bristol: Multilingual Matters.

Benati, A., and Lee, J. F. (2010). *Processing Instruction and Discourse*. London: Continuum.

Benati A., Lee, J. F., and Houghton, S. D. (2008). Chapter 4: From processing instruction on the acquisition of English past tense to secondary transfer-of-training effects on English third person singular present tense. In Benati, A. and Lee, J. F., *Grammar Acquisition and Processing Instruction: Secondary and Cumulative Effects* (pp. 88–120). Bristol: Multilingual Matters.

Bever, T. G. (1970). The cognitive basis for linguistic structures. In Hayes, R. (ed.), *Cognition and Language Development* (pp. 279–362). New York: Wiley and Sons.

Celik-Yazici, I. (2007). A study of the effects of processing instruction on the development of English WH-questions by Turkish EFL learners. *Interlinguistica*, 17, 250–60.

Ervin-Tripp, S. (1974). Is second language learning like the first? *TESOL Quarterly*, 8, 111–127.

Farley A. (2005). *Structured Input: Grammar Instruction for the Acquisition-Oriented Classroom*. New York: McGraw-Hill.

Lee, J. F. (1987). Comprehending the Spanish subjunctive: an information processing perspective. *Modern Language Journal*, 71, 50–57.

Lee, J. F. (2004). On the generalizability, limits, and potential future directions of processing instruction research. In VanPatten, B. (ed.). *Processing Instruction: Theory, Research, and Commentary* (pp. 311–23). Mahwah, NJ: Erlbaum.

Lee, J. F., and Benati, A. G. (2007). *Delivering Processing Instruction in Classrooms and Virtual Contexts: Research and Practice*. London: Equinox.

Lee, J. F., and Benati, A. G. (2009). *Research and Perspectives on Processing Instruction*. Berlin: Mouton de Gruyter.

Lee, J., and VanPatten, B. 2003 [1995]. *Making Communicative Language Teaching Happen*. 2nd edn. New York: McGraw-Hill.

LoCoco, V. (1987). Learner comprehension of oral and written importance of word order. In VanPatten, B., Dvorak, T. and Lee, J. F. (eds), *Foreign Language Learning: A Research Perspective* (pp. 119–29). Rowley, MA: Newbury House.

Nam, E. (1975). Child and adult perceptual strategies in second language acquisition. Paper presented at the annual TESOL Convention, Los Angeles.

Plèh, C. (1989). The development of sentence interpretation in Hungarian. In MacWhinney, B. and Bates, E. (eds), *The Cross-Linguistic Study of Sentence Processing* (pp. 158–84). Cambridge: Cambridge University Press.

VanPatten, B. (1984). Learners' comprehension of clitic pronouns: more evidence for a word order strategy. *Hispanic Linguistics*, 1, 57–67.

VanPatten, B. (1996). *Input Processing and Grammar Instruction: Theory and Research*. Norwood, NJ: Ablex Pub.

VanPatten, B., and Cadierno, T. (1993). Explicit instruction and input processing. *Studies in Second Language Acquisition*, 15, 225–43.

VanPatten, B., and Oikennon, S. (1996). Explanation vs. structured input in processing instruction. *Studies in Second Language Acquisition*, 18, 495–510.

VanPatten, B., and Wong, W. (2004). Processing instruction and the French causative: another replication. In VanPatten, B. (ed.), *Processing Instruction: Theory, Research, and Commentary* (pp. 97–118). Mahwah, NJ: Erlbaum.

Appendix A

Activity 1

'You will hear 10 sentences and you need to determine whether the sentences are active or passive sentences.'

	Active	Passive
1)	☐	☐
2)	☐	☐
3)	☐	☐
4)	☐	☐
5)	☐	☐
6)	☐	☐
7)	☐	☐
8)	☐	☐
9)	☐	☐
10)	☐	☐

Activity 1: Sentences heard by the learners

1) The artist was painted by his son – Passive
2) Jane kissed Mark – Active
3) Tina's present was opened by Kerry – Passive
4) Paul was helped by John – Passive
5) John listened to music – Active
6) The pen was lost by John – Passive
7) Alex watched football with Paul – Active
8) Mark was kissed by Jane – Passive
9) John lost the pen – Active
10) Paul helped John to repair the car – Active

Activity 2

Circle the option, which you think is passive.

1.
   a) Mr Jones watched the film.
   b) The film was watched by Mr Jones.
2.
   a) Jake was beaten at volleyball by John.
   b) Jake and John played volleyball.
3.
   a) The song was sung by Paul.
   b) Paul sung a song.
4.
   a) Mark was taught English by Emma.
   b) Emma taught English to Mark.
5.
   a) Eliot read a book to Sam.
   b) Sam was read a book by Eliot.
6.
   a) Lara's photo was taken by Charlie.
   b) Charlie took photos of Lara.
7.
   a) Michael's housework was done by Steven.
   b) Steven did Michael's housework.
8.
   a) The policemen helped the children.
   b) The children were helped by the policemen.
9.
   a) Jamie wrote a text message to Sarah.
   b) Sarah received a text message from Jamie.
10.
   a) John kissed Sarah.
   b) Sarah was kissed by John.

Activity 3

You will hear three sentences. Circle the picture that you think represents the sentence.

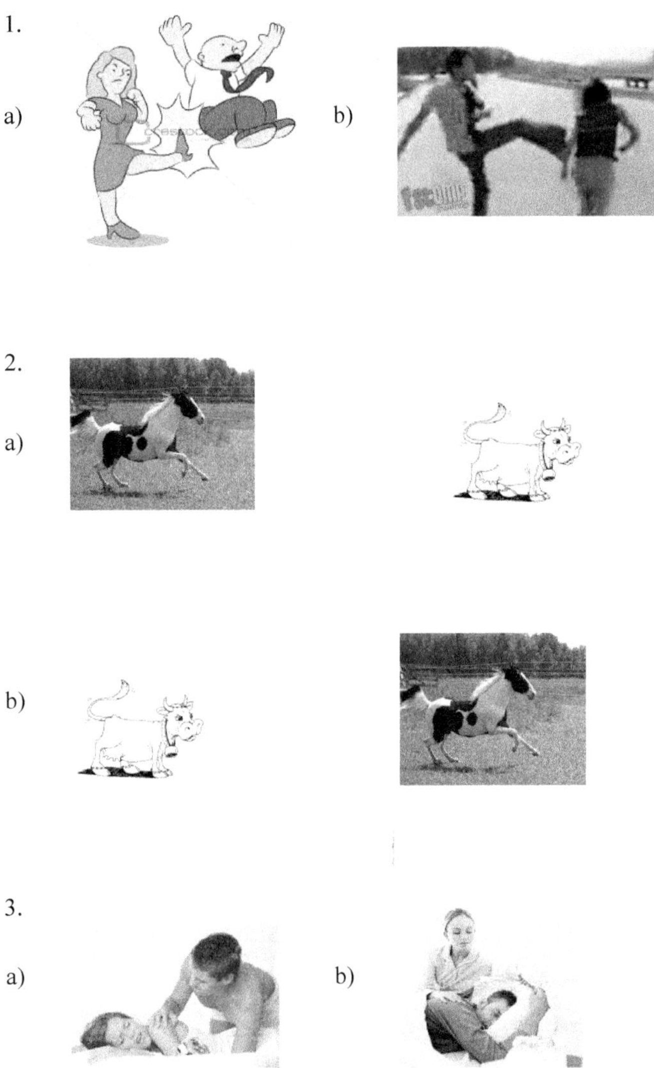

The activity continues in similar fashion.

Activity 3: Sentences heard by the learners

1. The man was kicked by the woman.
2. The cow was chased by the horse.
3. The woman was woken up by the man.

5 The Age Factor on the Primary, Secondary and Cumulative Transfer-of-Training Effects of Processing Instruction on the Acquisition of French as a Second Language

Cecile Laval, University of Greenwich (UK)*

Introduction

Research on processing instruction (PI) has assessed its direct or primary effects investigating whether PI would alter inappropriate processing strategies and/or instill appropriate ones. The positive results of the direct and primary effects of PI on second language acquisition have been validated by numerous studies (see review of these studies in Lee and Benati, 2009) and have demonstrated that PI is a powerful tool for resolving second language learners' processing problems.

Within the processing instruction research framework, a specific line of research has also established the transfer-of-training effects of processing

* **Cécile Laval** received a BA in Teaching French as a Foreign Language from the University of Grenoble, France, and an MA in Management of Language Learning from the University of Greenwich, UK. She is currently the Programme Leader of the BA (Hons) in International Studies and the French co-ordinator in the School of Humanities and Social Sciences at the University of Greenwich. She is actively involved as a researcher in the areas of applied linguistics and second language acquisition. Her research focuses on how L2 learners process incoming linguistic information at input level and more precisely in the area of processing instruction. She has published in the area of second language acquisition and language instruction in journal articles and book chapters.

instruction. Transfer-of-training can be either secondary or cumulative as defined in Benati and Lee (2008). The term 'secondary effects' is used when the processing principle is shared by the two linguistic features investigated. For example, in the case of the linguistic features investigated in the present study, both French imperfect and French subjunctive expose L2 learners to a morphological processing problem defined by VanPatten (2004) as the Lexical Preference Principle and the Sentence Location Principle. The term 'cumulative effects' is used when the processing principles are completely different for the two linguistic features investigated. Once again, if we look at the linguistic features investigated in the present study, the French imperfect and the French causative with *faire* involve two different processing problems: the Lexical Preference Principle and the First Noun Principle (VanPatten, 2004).

Based on research findings on the transfer-of training effects of processing instruction (see for a full review Lee and Benati, 2009) the Secondary Transfer-of-Training Hypothesis has been formulated by Benati and Lee (2008):

> *The Secondary Transfer-of Training Hypothesis*: Learners who receive training on one type of processing strategy for one specific form will appropriately transfer the use of that strategy to other forms without further instruction in PI (Benati and Lee 2008: 168).

Empirical evidence also showed that PI had a cumulative effect and based on this evidence Benati and Lee (2008) formulated the Cumulative Transfer-of-Training Hypothesis:

> *The Cumulative Transfer-of-Training Hypothesis*: Learners who receive training on one type of processing strategy will begin to work differently with primary linguistic data (Benati and Lee, 2008: 168).

In most cases, experimental studies investigating the effectiveness of processing instruction have used adult learners with only a few studies using younger learners (Benati, 2005; Benati, Lee and Houghton, 2008; Marsden, 2006; VanPatten and Oikennon, 1996). Based on these empirical results Benati and Lee (2008) formulated the Age Hypothesis:

> *The Age Hypothesis*. PI will be just as effective as an intervention with younger learners as it is with older learners (Benati and Lee, 2008: 168).

In this chapter we will provide further evidence in support of the *Secondary Transfer-of-Training Hypothesis*, the *Cumulative Transfer-of-Training Hypothesis* and the *Age Hypothesis* by measuring the effects of processing instruction on the acquisition of past imperfective aspect, subjunctive mood and causative constructions in French with school-aged children (9–10 years old).

Previous Research on Processing Instruction

Studies in Support of the Secondary Transfer-of-Training Hypothesis

Four studies have been carried out to provide support to the Secondary Transfer-of-Training Hypothesis. Benati and Lee (2008) carried out a study to investigate the secondary transfer-of-training effects of processing instruction on the acquisition of noun-adjective agreement in Italian. The main purpose of this study was to measure primary and secondary effects of processing instruction and to establish whether the processing instruction group could transfer the training received on noun-adjective agreement to the acquisition of Italian future tense morphology affected by the same processing principles, namely the Preference for Non-Redundancy Principle and the Lexical Preference (VanPatten, 2004). Twenty-five English native speakers participated in this study. They were undergraduate adult-learners of Italian. A pre-test/post-test design was adopted in this experiment. Participants were randomly assigned to three groups: processing instruction, traditional output-based instruction, and a control group that did not receive instruction on the two linguistic features. Two sets of materials were developed: one for the processing instruction group and one for the traditional instruction group. Two assessment tasks were used (interpretation and production sentence-level tasks). The results of the interpretation task measuring the primary effects revealed that the processing instruction group performed better than the other two groups. The results of the production task measuring the primary effects showed that the processing instruction group and the traditional instruction group performed equally well and better than the control group. The results of the interpretation task measuring the secondary effects revealed that the processing instruction group outperformed the other two groups. The findings from the production task showed that the processing instruction group and the traditional instruction group made similar gains. The overall outcome of this study was that, in terms of measuring primary effects, processing instruction is superior to traditional instruction in interpretation tasks and equally efficient in production tasks. In terms of measuring secondary transfer-of-training effects processing instruction is superior to traditional instruction in the interpretation task.

Benati, Lee and Houghton (2008) conducted an investigation on the acquisition of English as a foreign language. The aim of this study was to investigate the secondary transfer-of-training effects of processing instruction on the acquisition of the past tense in English and to establish whether the processing instruction group could transfer the training received on the past tense *–ed* in English to the acquisition of the third person singular present tense. Twenty-five Korean native speakers studying beginner-level English in a middle school in Korea participated in this study. Participants were randomly assigned to two groups: processing instruction and traditional output-based instruction. A pre- and post-tests procedure and two assessment tasks (interpretation and production sentence-level) were used. The results of the interpretation task and the production task measuring the secondary effects revealed that the processing instruction group outperformed the traditional group. These findings confirmed that L2 learners in the processing instruction group were able to transfer the instructional training on the English past tense to another word final temporal morpheme affected by the same processing principles.

Benati (2009) investigated the secondary transfer-of-training effects of processing instruction on the acquisition of the use of affirmative vs. negative present tense in Japanese and to establish whether the learners receiving processing instruction on the present tense could transfer that training and process Japanese past tense morphology. Twenty-four Italian native speakers studying beginner-level Japanese in a private school in Italy participated in this study. Participants were randomly assigned to three groups: processing instruction group; traditional instruction group; and control group. A pre- and post-tests procedure and two assessment tasks (interpretation and production sentence-level) were used. Once again, the results of the interpretation task measuring the secondary effects revealed that the processing instruction group outperformed the traditional group and the control group. The processing instruction group and traditional instruction group improved on the production task and both groups outperformed the control group. These findings confirmed that L2 learners in the processing instruction group were able to transfer the instructional training on the Japanese present tense and process the Japanese past tense affected by the same processing principles, namely the Lexical Preference Principle and the Sentence Location Principle (VanPatten, 2004).

Benati, Lee and Laval (2008) carried out a study to investigate the secondary transfer-of-training effects of processing instruction on the acquisition of the French imperfect tense. The main purpose of this study was to measure primary and secondary effects of processing instruction and establish whether the processing instruction group could transfer the training received on the French imperfect tense to the acquisition of the French subjunctive used for expression of doubt affected by the same processing principles, namely the Lexical Preference Principle and the Sentence Location Principle (VanPatten, 2004). Thirty-three English native speakers studying intermediate-level French as part of their undergraduate degree participated in this study. Participants were randomly assigned to three groups: processing instruction group; traditional instruction group; and control group. A pre- and post-tests procedure and two assessment tasks (interpretation and production sentence-level) were used. The results of the interpretation task and the production task measuring the secondary effects revealed that the processing instruction group outperformed the traditional group and the control group. These findings confirmed that L2 learners in the processing instruction group were able to transfer the instructional training received on the French imperfect to another linguistic form in French (subjunctive of doubt) affected by the same processing principles.

Study in Support of the Cumulative Transfer-of-Training Hypothesis

Benati, Lee and Laval (2008), in the study reviewed above, also sought to measure the cumulative transfer-of-training effects of processing instruction by measuring whether the processing instruction group could transfer the instructional training received on the French imperfect tense to the acquisition of French causative constructions with *faire*. From French imperfect to French causatives with *faire* is a move from morphology to syntax and the French imperfect and the French causatives with *faire* are affected by two very different processing problems: the Lexical Preference Principle and the First Noun Principle (VanPatten, 2004). The results on the cumulative transfer-of-training effects indicated that the processing instruction group outperformed the traditional group and the control group on both the interpretation and production tasks. These findings showed that L2 learners in the processing instruction group were able to transfer the instructional training received on the French imperfect to another linguistic form in French (causative constructions with *faire*) affected by different processing principles.

Studies in Support of the Age Hypothesis

VanPatten and Oikennon (1996) investigated the effects of explicit information and structured input practice on the acquisition of Spanish direct object pronouns. The main objective of this classroom-based study was to establish which factor within the processing instruction approach is the most effective. Fifty-nine English native speakers studying Spanish in their second year in secondary school (15–16 years old) participated in this study. A pre-test/post-test design was adopted in this experiment. Participants were randomly assigned to three groups: the full processing instruction group; the explicit information only group; and the structured input practice only group. Two assessment tasks were used (interpretation and production sentence-level tasks). The results of the interpretation task measuring the primary effects revealed that the processing instruction group performed better than the other two groups. The materials, assessment tasks and scoring procedures that VanPatten and Cadierno (1993) produced and used for their investigation were also utilized in the case of this experimental study. The results of the interpretation and production tasks revealed that the processing instruction group and the structured input only group improved significantly and equally and that they outperformed the explicit information only group. These findings revealed that structured input practice was responsible for high-school-aged L2 learners' gains in interpretation and production on sentence-level tasks.

Benati (2005) demonstrated the positive effects of processing instruction on the English past tense marker *–ed* with 12–13-year-old Greek and Chinese children studying English in their home countries. Marsden (2006) demonstrated positive effects of processing instruction on French present indicative tense with 13–14 year olds using a wide variety of tests (speaking, reading, writing and listening). Benati, Lee and Houghton (2008), as reviewed previously, in their investigation on the secondary transfer-of-training effects of processing instruction in the acquisition of the past tense in English demonstrated that middle-school-aged L2 learners of English in the processing instruction group experienced positive primary effects of instruction and were able to transfer the instructional training received on the English past tense to the acquisition of the third person singular present tense, another word final temporal morpheme affected by the same processing principles.

Research Questions

Empirical evidence has demonstrated secondary transfer-of-training effects and cumulative transfer-of-training effects of processing instruction supporting the view that the effects of processing instruction are not restricted to primary effects nor to simply adult learners. The purpose of the partial replication of Benati, Lee and Laval's study (2008) reported in this chapter is threefold. First, the aim of this study is to reinforce the findings and deepen the understanding of the concept of transfer-of-training effects of processing instruction and in particular to further demonstrate the secondary transfer-of-training effects of processing instruction. Secondly, the purpose of this study is to provide new evidence for the positive cumulative transfer-of-training effects of processing instruction. Thirdly, to provide further evidence of the positive effects of processing instruction and transfer-of-training effects of processing instruction on school-aged learners. The specific research questions formulated in this study are as follows:

> Q1: Are there primary effects of processing instruction on L2 school-aged learners from receiving instruction on French past tense imperfective aspect as measured by an interpretation and a production task?
>
> Q2: Are there secondary effects of processing instruction on L2 school-aged learners from receiving instruction on French past tense imperfective aspect to French subjunctive mood morphology as measured by an interpretation and a production task?
>
> Q3: Are there cumulative effects of processing instruction on L2 school-aged learners from receiving instruction on French past tense imperfective aspect to French causative constructions with *faire* as measured by an interpretation and a production task?
>
> Q4: How do the possible transfer-of-training effects of processing instruction on the acquisition of French *imparfait* on L2 adult learners and L2 school-aged learners compare when measured by an interpretation and a production task?

Based on previous empirical findings presented in the background section the following hypotheses related to the four research questions were formulated:

> H1. The group receiving processing instruction treatment should increase its performance when interpreting and producing sentences containing the French imperfect (primary linguistic target). The results from the interpretation and production tasks should provide further evidence in support of the primary effects of processing instruction on L2 school-aged learners.
>
> H2. The group receiving processing instruction treatment should increase its performance when interpreting and producing sentences containing

French subjunctive mood morphology (secondary linguistic target). The results from the interpretation and production tasks should provide evidence in support of the secondary effects of processing instruction on L2 school-aged learners.

H3. The group receiving the processing instruction treatment should increase its performance when interpreting and producing sentences containing French causative constructions with *faire* (cumulative linguistic target). The results from the interpretation and production tasks should provide further evidence in support of the cumulative effects of processing instruction on L2 school-aged learners.

H4. L2 adult learners and L2 school-aged learners receiving processing instruction should equally benefit from the positive transfer-of-training effects of processing instruction.

Method

Participants

The present study was carried out at Junior King's School, a private school in Canterbury (England). Participants were drawn from a group of year 7 pupils studying French. All were in the second semester of their school year. The participants were all 9–10 years old and were all English native speakers. Their learning of French was limited to classroom instruction, and they had no previous knowledge of the target forms. Three main considerations were taken into account when deciding to select year 7 pupils: level of proficiency; vocabulary familiarity; and no previous exposure to any of the linguistic targets, namely, French past tense imperfective aspect, French subjunctive mood morphology and French causative constructions with *faire*. The original data pool consisting of 20 subjects was reduced to 14. As in the case of Benati, Lee and Laval (2008) all participants completed the pre-tests, and subjects who scored more than 50% in the pre-tests (interpretation and production) were not included in the final pool. A randomization procedure (see Figure 5.1) was adopted to randomly assign the participants in the final pool (n = 14) to the following two groups: processing instruction group (n = 9); control group (n = 5). Three immediate post-tests on the three grammatical features were administered to the two groups. Only participants who had participated in each stage of the experiment (pre-tests, instructional treatment and post-tests) were included in the final pool.

Procedures

The six pre-tests (two per linguistic item) were administered two weeks before the instructional treatments took place (see Figure 5.1 for an overview of the experimental procedures). The processing instruction group was taught for a total of two hours over a one-day period by the researcher. Considering the young age of the participants and the structure of the school teaching blocks, minor alterations to the delivery of the processing instruction treatment had to be made and breaks of five minutes were given to participants for every 20 minutes of instruction. As in Benati, Lee and Laval (2008) the processing instruction group was given explicit information about the forms and function of the imperfective past tense as well as information about processing strategies and was finally given structured input activities (referential and affective activities) as practice. A sample referential activity is given in Figure 5.2.

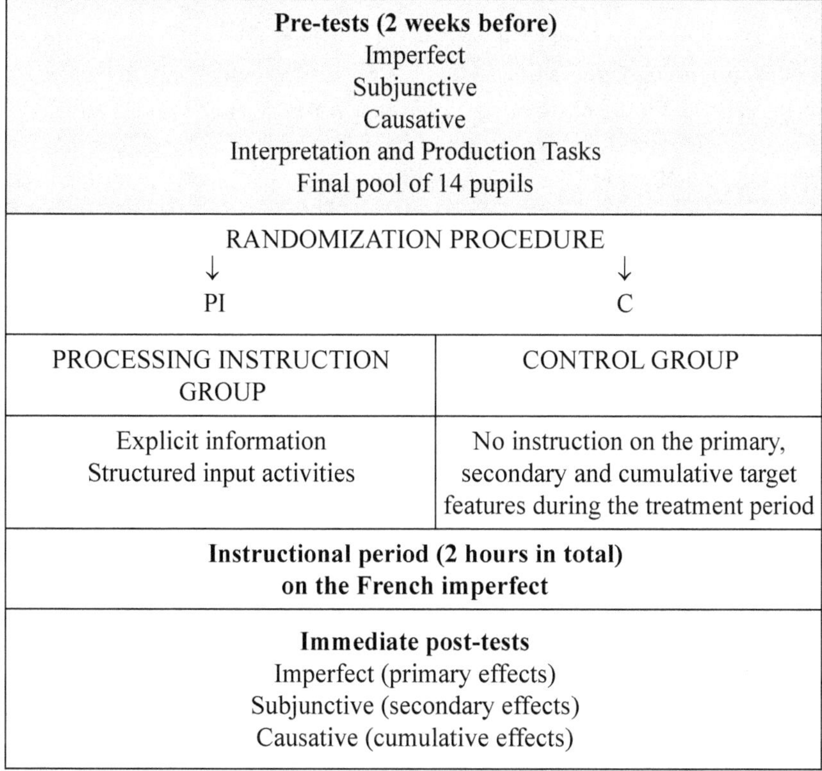

Figure 5.1 Overview of the experiment

The processing instruction group received explicit information and structured input practice to help participants alter their reliance on the Lexical Preference Principle and the Sentence Location Principle so that they could process the French imperfective past tense accurately and efficiently. All temporal adverbs and lexical cues to past time and imperfective aspect were removed. L2 learners in the processing instruction group were engaged in processing input sentences to make better form-meaning connections. At no point during the instructional period were participants in the processing instruction group asked to produce the correct verb inflection in the French imperfect. The control group was given no instruction on the primary, secondary and cumulative target features during the treatment period, but were exposed to a comparable amount of the target language for the same amount of time.

The Target Linguistic Feature

The aim of this study was to measure possible secondary and cumulative transfer-of-training effects of processing instruction on younger L2 learners, so three linguistic features affected by similar and different processing principles had to be chosen. As described in Benati, Lee and Laval (2008) the three linguistic features (the French imperfect, the French subjunctive and the French causative with *faire*) were selected in relation to their processing principles (see VanPatten, 2004). Both French imperfect and French subjunctive expose L2 learners to a morphological processing problem defined by VanPatten (2004) as the Lexical Preference Principle and the Sentence Location Principle whereas the French imperfect and the French causative with *faire* involve two different processing problems, the Lexical Preference Principle and the First Noun Principle (VanPatten, 2004).

Materials

The set of materials for the processing instruction treatment used in Benati, Lee and Laval (2008) was used for the present study (see more examples of referential structured input activities in the Appendix). Only minor lexical changes were made to adapt both vocabulary and context to 9 to 10 year olds. For example one of the referential activities entitled 'First day at university: what a day!' in Benati, Lee and Laval (2008) was changed to 'First day at school: what a day!', and the statements in the affective activity entitled 'In their teens...' used in Benati, Lee and Laval (2008) were slightly altered to ensure the meaning of the sentences was appropriate for 9 to 10 year olds (see Figure 5.2). The materials contained explicit information and structured input activities including an equal number of referential and affective activities (10 activities).

Referential Activity: Zinédine Zidane: avant et après…		
• **Step 1** Listen to the following statements made by a journalist about the life of Zinédine Zidane and decide whether each statement is referring to his past life as a professional football player or his life now as a retired football player.		
Professional football player	Retired football player	[Sentence heard] *Zinédine Zidane…*
❑	❑	*1… jouait au football dans le monde entier.*
❑	❑	*2…gagnait beaucoup de coupes.*
❑	❑	*3… passe du temps avec sa famille.*
❑	❑	*4… participait à beaucoup de dîners officiels.*
❑	❑	*5… s'entrainait avec Ronaldo.*
❑	❑	*6… s'occupe de ses enfants.*
❑	❑	*7… est directeur de l'association française de football.*
❑	❑	*8… téléphone à ses amis pour discuter.*
❑	❑	*9… marquait beaucoup de buts.*
❑	❑	*10… était le meilleur joueur de football au monde.*

- **Step 2**
  Now decide if Zinédine Zidane was busier when he was a professional football player or now that he is retired.

Figure 5.2 Sample referential activity

In affective activities there are no right or wrong answers. In the affective activity in Figure 5.3 (adapted from Farley, 2005), all items use the past tense imperfective aspect and participants must process each sentence for its meaning in order to complete the task.

Affective Activity 8 (adapted from Farley, 2005): In their teens…			
• **Step 1** Imagine what your parent's life was like as a teenager many years ago. What about another relative and your teacher? Can you imagine who worked hard? Who argued with his/her teacher a lot? Read over each statement and decide whether each individual (parent, relative or instructor) did these things or not.			
Il/Elle…			
… *se disputait avec son professeur.*	Parent	Relative	Teacher
… *ne passait pas ses examens.*	❑	❑	❑
… *écoutait de la musique.*	❑	❑	❑
… *avait de très bonnes notes.*	❑	❑	❑
… *étudiait beaucoup.*	❑	❑	❑
… *faisait des bêtises.*	❑	❑	❑
… *visitait beaucoup de pays.*	❑	❑	❑
… *organisait des soirées avec ses amis.*	❑	❑	❑
• **Step 2** Find out if your instructor did any of the above. Are you surprised?			

Figure 5.3 Sample affective activity

Assessment Instruments and Scoring

Pre- and post-tests were used for measuring the primary effects of instruction on the primary target (French past tense imperfective aspect); the secondary effects on the second target (French subjunctive mood morphology), and the cumulative effects on the third target (French causative constructions with *faire*). Both groups received the same version of the pre-tests and post-tests. They consisted of a sentence-level interpretation task, in which participants were only allowed to listen to the sentences once as no repetition was provided, and a sentence-level production task, shown in Figure 5.4. The sentence-level interpretation and production tasks were identical to the ones used in Benati, Lee and Laval (2008) except for the pre-test (production task) on the *imparfait* in which the protagonist was changed from *Madonna* to *Justin Bieber* since the latter is more familiar to 9 to 10 year olds. Apart from this slight amendment the tasks remained the same as in Benati, Lee and Laval (2008). Participants had to fill the blanks in a short passage by producing the correct form of the verb. A two, one, zero point system (for a possible maximum score of twenty points) was used to score the production task. Participants received two points if the sentence completion contained a verb in the correct past tense form. However, a score of one point was allocated if the verb was in the past tense but with the wrong person or if the learner had switched verb category endings. Any other response received a score of zero points.

Fill the gaps writing the verbs in brackets in the correct form. Use the verb provided in the brackets.

Hier j'_________ (être) au supermarché avec mon ami Charles. A côté de moi, à ma droite, un jeune garçon grand et blond ________(porter) des lunettes de soleil noires. Bizarre dans un supermarché, non ?

Je _________(montrer) discrètement ce garçon à Charles. Il _________ (marcher) dans notre direction, quelques secondes plus tard, il __________ (enlever) ses lunettes de soleil et il (sourire) ____________. Je __________ (rester) paralysée, je ne _________ (pouvoir) pas parler et je ___________ (penser) « oh mon Dieu, je rêve ! ». Charles me dit alors: « ce garçon blond aux lunettes de soleil : c'est Justin Bieber ! » et deux minutes plus tard Charles __________ (avoir) son autographe.

Figure 5.4. Sample production task

Pre-tests were administered to the students two weeks before the beginning of the instructional period and the post-tests were administered immediately after the end of the instructional treatment.

Results

Primary, secondary and cumulative effects were measured at the end of the instructional treatment. To address the research questions guiding this study, one-way ANOVA analyses were conducted on the raw scores for all pre-tests to measure whether there were any statistical differences among the three groups prior to the beginning of the experiment. The raw scores of the sentence-level interpretation and production pre-tests and post-tests were also submitted to a two-way ANOVA with repeated measures to assert whether there were any relevant differences between the two treatments and between pre-tests and post-tests. Treatment (processing instruction versus control group) was the between-subjects variable, whereas Time (pre-test vs. post-test) was the within-subjects repeated measures variable.

Primary Effects of Processing Instruction on French Imperfect

Interpretation Data

Means and standard deviations for the interpretation task are presented in Table 5.1. A one-way ANOVA on the pre-test scores for the interpretation and the production tasks was conducted to determine whether there were any statistically significant differences between the three groups before the beginning of the experimental period. The results of the one-way ANOVA conducted on the interpretation pre-test for the French imperfect revealed no significant differences among the groups' means before the treatment period (F (1, 13) = 3.198, p = .099). The mean scores on French imperfect tense forms measuring primary effect in Table 5.1 suggest that the processing instruction group

		Pre-test		Post-test	
Variable	*N*	*Mean*	*SD*	*Mean*	*SD*
PI	9	1.888	1.054	8.333	1.000
C	5	3.000	1.224	2.200	.8366

Table 5.1 Means and standard deviations (French *imparfait*) for interpretation task pre-test and post-test

made an improvement from pre-test to post-test, whereas the control group's performance decreased from pre-test to post-test.

These results demonstrate that the processing instruction group gained about 64% from pre-test to post-test scores in their ability to interpret the French imperfect. The control group decreased by 8% from pre-test to post-test scores. Adult learners in Benati, Lee and Laval (2008) gained about 58% from pre-test to post-test scores.

The two-way ANOVA showed a significant effect for Time (F (1, 13) = 37.214, p = .000) and Treatment (F (1, 13) = 53.002, p = .000) as well as a significant interaction between Time and Treatment (F (1, 13) = 61.301, p = .000). The main findings from the interpretation data showed that only the processing instruction group gained in their ability to interpret the French imperfect.

Production Data

Means and standard deviations for the production task are given in Table 5.2. The one-way ANOVA conducted on the written production task pre-test scores for the primary linguistic target showed no significant difference between groups prior to instruction (F (1, 13) = .000, p = .000). This was not surprising, given that all learners scored zero on the production pre-test. The means scores on the primary linguistic target in Table 5.2 show improvement for the processing instruction group.

		Pre-test		**Post-test**	
Variable	*N*	*Mean*	*SD*	*Mean*	*SD*
PI	9	.000	.000	15.888	5.230
C	5	.000	.000	.000	.000

Table 5.2 Means and standard deviation (French *imparfait*) for production task pre-test and post-test

The processing instruction group gained about 159% from pre-test to post-test scores. The control group made no improvements. Once again, the results are consistent with Benati, Lee and Laval (2008). In their study adult learners in the processing instruction group gained about 140% from pre-test to post-test scores.

The two-way ANOVA showed a significant effect for Time (F (1, 13) = 44.487, p = .000) and Treatment (F (1, 13) = 44.487, p = .000) as well as a significant interaction between Time and Treatment (F (1, 13) = 44.487, p = .000).

The mean scores of the post-tests for both the interpretation and the production tasks measuring primary effects showed that likewise in Benati, Lee and Laval (2008) the processing instruction group made some significant gains (64% improvement in the interpretation task and 159% in the production task). The control group did not.

Secondary Effects of Processing Instruction on French Subjunctive

Interpretation Data

Means and standard deviations for the interpretation task are given in Table 5.3. The one-way ANOVA on the pre-test interpretation task scores for French subjunctive showed no significant differences among the groups' means (F (1, 13) = .008, p = .930) before the treatment period. The mean scores on French subjunctive forms measuring secondary effect in Table 5.3 suggest that the processing instruction group made a significant improvement from pre-test to post-test, whereas the control group made no significant improvement.

		Pre-test		Post-test	
Variable	*N*	*Mean*	*SD*	*Mean*	*SD*
PI	9	.222	.440	5.666	1.000
C	5	.200	.447	.2000	.447

Table 5.3 Means and standard deviation (French subjunctive) for interpretation task pre-test and post-test

The two-way ANOVA showed a significant effect for Time (F (1, 13) = 139.054, p = .000) and Treatment (F (1, 13) = 82.482, p = .000) as well as a significant interaction between Time and Treatment (F (1, 13) = 139.054, p = .000).

These results demonstrate that the processing instruction group gained about 55% from pre-test to post-test scores. The control group made no improvements from pre-test to post-test scores. The results are significantly higher than those of adult learners in Benati, Lee and Laval (2008) who gained about 20% from pre-test to post-test scores.

Production Data

Means and standard deviations for the production task are given in Table 5.4. The one-way ANOVA conducted on the written production task pre-test scores for the secondary linguistic target showed no significant difference between groups prior to instruction; again this was not surprising, given that all learners scored zero on the production pre-test. The means scores on the secondary linguistic target in Table 5.4 indicate that both the processing instruction group and the control group made no improvements from pre-test to post-test.

		Pre-test		Post-test	
Variable	*N*	*Mean*	*SD*	*Mean*	*SD*
PI	9	.000	.000	.000	.000
C	5	.000	.000	.000	.000

Table 5.4 Means and standard deviation (French subjunctive) for production task pre-test and post-test

These results of the statistical analysis for the production task are not surprising since participants scored 0 for both pre-test and post-test. The aspect of task complexity might explain the fact that participants made no improvement from pre-test to post-test and would also be consistent with the findings of Benati, Lee and Laval (2008), since in their study adult learners in the processing instruction group only made a modest, yet significant, 10% improvement from pre-test to post-test on producing the subjunctive.

The mean scores of the post-tests for the interpretation task measuring primary effects are once again consistent with findings in Benati, Lee and Laval (2008) and with the findings in the other three studies reviewed in the introduction investigating the secondary transfer-of-training effects of processing instruction. Although the processing instruction group did not improve from pre-test to post-test in the written production task the positive effects of the instructional treatment is still measurable for the interpretation task. The processing instruction group made some significant gains in interpretation (64%) and the results demonstrate once again the secondary transfer-of-training effects for processing instruction and for the first time with school-aged learners.

Cumulative Effects of Processing Instruction on French Causative Construction with *Faire*

Interpretation Data

Means and standard deviations for the interpretation task are given in Table 5.5. The one-way ANOVA on the pre-test interpretation task scores for French causative construction with *faire* showed no significant differences among the groups' means (F (1, 13) = .245, p = .630) before the treatment period. The mean scores on French causative forms measuring cumulative effect in Table 5.5 suggest that the processing instruction group made a significant improvement from pre-test to post-test, whereas the control group made no significant improvement.

		Pre-test		Post-test	
Variable	*N*	*Mean*	*SD*	*Mean*	*SD*
PI	9	.333	.500	5.333	1.732
C	5	.200	.447	.000	.000

Table 5.5 Means and standard deviation (French causative) for interpretation task pre-test and post-test

The two-way ANOVA showed a significant effect for Time (F (1, 13) = 28.853, p = .000) and Treatment (F (1, 13) = 50.556, p = .000) as well as a significant interaction between Time and Treatment (F (1, 13) = 43.457, p = .000).

The processing instruction group gained about 50% from pre-test to post-test scores. The control group made no improvements from pre-test to post-test scores. The results are consistent with those in Benati, Lee and Laval (2008) where adult learners in the processing instruction group gained about 34% from pre-test to post-test scores.

Production Data

Means and standard deviations for the production task are given in Table 5.6. The one-way ANOVA conducted on the written production task pre-test scores for the cumulative linguistic target showed no significant difference between groups prior to instruction; again this was not surprising since all learners scored zero on the production pre-test. The means scores on the secondary linguistic target in Table 5.6 indicate an improvement for the processing instruction group and no improvements for the control group from pre-test to post-test scores.

		Pre-test		Post-test	
Variable	*N*	*Mean*	*SD*	*Mean*	*SD*
PI	9	.000	.000	3.333	3.278
C	5	.000	.000	.000	.000

Table 5.6 Means and standard deviation (French causative) for production task pre-test and post-test

The processing instruction group gained about 30% from pre-test to post-test scores. The control group made no improvements from pre-test to post-test scores.

The two-way ANOVA showed a significant effect for Time (F (1, 13) = 4.983, p = .045) and Treatment (F (1, 13) = 4.983, p = .045) as well as a significant interaction between Time and Treatment (F (1, 13) = 4.983, p = .045).

The results are consistent with those in Benati, Lee and Laval (2008) where adult learners in the processing instruction group gained a modest yet significant 10% from pre-test to post-test scores. These results demonstrate once again the cumulative transfer-of-training effects for processing instruction. For the first time these results are demonstrated with school-aged learners.

Discussion and Conclusion

The four main objectives of the present study were:

1. To offer further evidence of the positive effects of processing instruction on the acquisition of French past tense imperfective aspect and in particular on L2 school-aged learners.
2. To examine the possible secondary effects of processing instruction on L2 school-aged learners from receiving instruction on French past tense imperfective aspect to French subjunctive mood morphology.
3. To determine possible cumulative effects of processing instruction on L2 school-aged learners from receiving instruction on French past tense imperfective aspect to French causative constructions with *faire*.
4. To compare the possible transfer-of-training effects of processing instruction on the acquisition of French *imparfait* on L2 adult learners and L2 school-aged learners.

The results of the classroom experimental study presented in this chapter provide positive answers to the four questions and support the hypotheses of this study.

1) Research question one (supported)
   The analysis of the data collected through the interpretation and production tasks clearly showed that the processing instruction

		Benati, Lee and Laval, 2008	Laval, 2013	Benati, Lee and Laval, 2008	Laval, 2013	Benati, Lee and Laval, 2008	Laval, 2013
Linguistic feature/ Language	Treatment and Results	Means Scores Pre-test	Means Scores Pre-test	Means Scores Post-test	Means Scores Post-test	Improvement	Improvement
		ADULTS	CHILDREN	ADULTS	CHILDREN	ADULTS	CHILDREN
French imperfect	*Primary effects*	*Int.* PI = 2.3 C= 2.6 *Prod.* PI = 0.1 C = 1.0	*Int.* PI = 1.9 C= 3.0 *Prod.* PI = 0 C = 0	*Int.* PI = 8.1 C = 2.8 *Prod.* PI = 14.1 C =1.6	*Int.* PI = 8.3 C=2.2 *Prod.* PI = 15.9 C = 0	*Int.* PI = 58% C = 2% *Prod.* PI = 140% C = 16%	*Int.* PI = 64% C = - 8% *Prod.* PI = 159% C = 0%
French subjunctive	*Secondary effects*	*Int.* PI = 1.7 C = 1.6 *Prod.* PI = 0 C = 0	*Int.* PI = 0.2 C= 0.2 *Prod.* PI = 0 C = 0	*Int.* PI = 3.6 C = 1.1 *Prod.* PI = 1.0 C = 0	*Int.* PI = 5.7 C= 0.2 *Prod.* PI = 0 C = 0	*Int.* PI = 19% C = 5% *Prod.* PI = 10% C = 0%	*Int.* PI = 55% C= 0% *Prod.* PI = 0% C = 0%
French *faire* causative	*Cumulative effects*	*Int.* PI = 1.2 C= 1.1 *Prod.* PI = 0 C = 0	*Int.* PI = 0.3 C= 0.2 *Prod.* PI = 0 C =0	*Int.* PI = 4.6 C= 0.8 *Prod.* PI = 1.0 C = 0	*Int.* PI = 5.3 C= 0 *Prod.* PI =3.3 C =0	*Int.* PI = 34% C= -3% *Prod.* PI = 10% C = 0%	*Int.* PI = 50% C= - 2% *Prod.* PI = 33% C = 0 %

Table 5.7 Pre-test and post-test results of studies investigating primary, secondary and cumulative effects for processing instruction on the acquisition of French as a second language – adults and children

group performed better than the control group. Learners in the processing instruction group improved in their ability to interpret and produce sentences containing the French imperfect form. The results demonstrate the primary effects of processing instruction on L2 school-aged learners.

2) Research question two (partially supported)
Again, the statistical analysis indicated that the processing instruction group performed better than the control group in the interpretation task. Both the processing instruction group and the control group did not improve from pre-test to post-test in the written production task; however, the positive effects of the instructional treatment is still measurable for the interpretation task. The processing instruction group made some significant gains in interpreting the French subjunctive and the results provide further evidence in support of the secondary transfer-of-training effects for processing instruction. These findings demonstrate for the first time secondary transfer-of-training effects for processing instruction on school-aged learners.
3) Research question three (supported)
The analysis of the data collected through the interpretation and production tasks clearly demonstrated that the processing instruction group performed better than the control group in both interpretation and production tasks. The processing instruction group made some significant gains in the interpretation and production of the French causative with *faire*. These results provide further evidence in support of the secondary transfer-of-training effects for processing instruction and demonstrate for the first time such effects on school-aged learners.
4) Research question four (supported)
The results of our investigation confirm Benati and Lee's (2008) Age Hypothesis. We have summarized in Table 5.7 the percentage change in scores from pre-test to post-test on both the interpretation and production tasks for the primary, secondary and cumulative effects of processing instruction for both school-aged learners and adult learners in Benati, Lee and Laval (2008). The results showed in Table 5.7 provide evidence that processing instruction is as effective an intervention with younger learners as it is with older learners.

The results obtained in measuring the primary effects show processing instruction is as effective in helping adult L2 learners and younger L2 learners at interpreting and producing sentences containing French imperfect form as detailed in Table 5.7. The results also support previous findings (Cadierno, 1995; Benati, 2001; Farley, 2001a; Farley, 2001b; Benati, 2005; Gely, 2005; Marsden, 2006; Lee and Benati, 2007; Benati and Lee, 2008; Benati, Lee and Houghton, 2008; Benati, Lee and Laval, 2008) showing that processing instruction is successful at altering the Lexical Preference Principle and Sentence Location Principle.

The findings of the present study obtained in measuring the secondary effects show participants in the processing instruction group were able to transfer the processing instruction training received on the French imperfect to another linguistic form in French (subjunctive) affected by similar processing problems. As detailed in Table 5.7 the results presented in this chapter confirmed the secondary transfer-of-training effects of processing instruction and also suggests that the earlier findings for the interpretation task can be generalized for school-aged learners.

The results obtained in measuring the cumulative effects also show participants in the processing instruction group were able to transfer the processing instruction training received on the French imperfect to another linguistic form in French (causative with *faire*) affected by different processing problems. The findings presented in this chapter confirmed the cumulative transfer-of-training effects of processing instruction and also suggests that the earlier findings (Benati, Lee and Laval, 2008) can be generalized for school-aged learners (see Table 5.7).

Finally, the results of the present study confirm processing instruction is as effective as an intervention with younger learners as it is with older learners and support previous findings (VanPatten and Oikennon, 1996; Benati, Lee and Houghton, 2008). These results lend support to the Age Hypothesis.

The most important findings of the present study, arguably, is that processing instruction offers both adult learners and school-aged learners primary, secondary and cumulative transfer-of-training effects.

While we underscore the positive outcomes in this study, as with all empirical research, we acknowledge certain limitations. Only a small number of school-aged learners (14) participated in the final experiment. Further research could replicate our study with a larger sample size.

References

Benati, A. (2001). A comparative study of the effects of processing instruction and output-based instruction on the acquisition of the Italian future tense. *Language Teaching Research*, 5, 95–127.

Benati, A. (2005). The effects of PI, TO and MOI in the acquisition of English simple past tense. *Language Awareness*, 13, 67–80.

Benati, A. (ed.) (2009). *Issue in Second Language Proficiency*. London: Continuum.

Benati, A., and Lee, J. F. (2008). *Grammar Acquisition and Processing Instruction: Secondary and Cumulative Effects*. Clevedon: Multilingual Matters.

Benati, A., Lee, J. F., and Houghton, S. D. (2008). Chapter 4: From processing instruction on the acquisition of English past tense to secondary transfer-of-training effects on English third person singular present tense. In Benati, A. and Lee, J. F., *Grammar Acquisition and Processing Instruction: Secondary and Cumulative Effects* (pp. 88–120). Bristol: Multilingual Matters.

Benati, A., Lee, J. F., and Laval, C. (2008). Chapter 5: From processing instruction on the acquisition of French imparfait to secondary transfer-of-training effects on French subjunctive and to cumulative transfer-of-training effects with French causative constructions. In Benati, A. and Lee, J. F., *Grammar Acquisition and Processing Instruction: Secondary and Cumulative Effects* (pp. 121–57). Bristol: Multilingual Matters.

Cadierno, T. (1995). Formal instruction from processing perspective: an investigation into the Spanish past tense. *Modern Language Journal*, 79, 179–93.

Farley, A. P. (2001a). The effect of processing instruction and meaning-based output instruction. *Spanish Applied Linguistics*, 5, 57–94.

Farley, A. P. (2001b). Authentic processing instruction and the Spanish subjunctive. *Hispania*, 84, 289–99.

Farley A. (2005). *Structured Input: Grammar Instruction for the Acquisition-Oriented Classroom*. New York: McGraw-Hill. ADDed

Gely, A. (2005) Output-based instruction versus processing instruction on the acquisition of the French imperfect tense. MA thesis, University of Greenwich, London.

Lee, J. F., and Benati, A. (2007). *Second Language Processing: An Analysis of Theory, Problems and Solutions.* London: Continuum.

Lee, J. F., and Benati, A. (2009). *Research and Perspectives on Processing Instruction.* New York: Mouton de Gruyter.

Marsden, E. (2006). Exploring input processing in the classroom: an experimental comparison of processing instruction and enriched input. *Language Learning*, 12, 268–97.

VanPatten, B. (2004). Input processing in second language acquisition. In VanPatten, B. (ed.), *Processing Instruction: Theory, Research and Commentary* (pp. 5–31). Mahwah, NJ: Erlbaum.

VanPatten, B., and Cadierno, T. (1993). Explicit instruction and input processing. *Studies in Second Language Acquisition*, 15, 225–43.

VanPatten, B., and Oikennon, S. (1996). The causative variables in processing instruction: explanations versus structured input activities. *Studies in Second Language Acquisition*, 18, 225–43.

Appendix

Referential Activity:	**Things people were doing last summer or now**	
• Step 1 Listen to the following statements and decide whether each statement refers to an activity that was taking place last summer or takes place now.		
LAST SUMMER	NOW	[Sentence heard] *On...*
❑	❑	*1... avait chaud.*
❑	❑	*2... regarde beaucoup la télévision.*
❑	❑	*3... allait à la plage.*
❑	❑	*4... dansait.*
❑	❑	*5... travaille beaucoup.*
❑	❑	*6... voyage en train.*
❑	❑	*7... visitait Paris.*
❑	❑	*8... lisait des livres.*
❑	❑	*9... est fatigué.*
❑	❑	*10... étudie beaucoup.*

Referential Activity: **Stress!**		
• **Step 1** **You will hear a series of sentences about what Cécile was doing last week. Decide if what you hear is something that relieved her stress or contributed to her being stressed.**		
RELIEVED STRESS	CONTRIBUTED TO STRESS	[Sentence heard] *Je...*
❑	❑	*1. ... faisais du yoga.*
❑	❑	*2. .... parlais de mes vacances à mes amies.*
❑	❑	*3. ... avais besoin de plus de temps pour faire mes devoirs.*
❑	❑	*4. ... venais à l'école en vélo.*
❑	❑	*5. ... avais besoins d'argent pour acheter une glace.*
❑	❑	*6. ... étudiais beaucoup.*
❑	❑	*7. ... me relaxais à la piscine.*
❑	❑	*8. ... nettoyais ma chambre.*
❑	❑	*9. ... travaillais beaucoup*
❑	❑	*10. .... faisais du sport avec mon ami Charles*
• **Step 2** **Who was more stressed last week, you or Cécile?**		

Referential Activity: **What's Appropriate?**		
• **Step 1** **Read each sentence then decide whether or not it is typical of your teacher's behaviour.**		
Mon professeur…	**C'est typique**	**Ce n'est pas typique**
… dormait toute la journée.	❑	❑
… travaillait chez MacDonald's.	❑	❑
… faisait la vaisselle tous les soirs.	❑	❑
… notait les examens.	❑	❑
… venait à l'école en voiture.	❑	❑
… préparait sa classe.	❑	❑
… portait un jean et des baskets.	❑	❑
… se couchait à 5 heures du matin.	❑	❑
… écoutait de la musique forte.	❑	❑
… lisait le journal tous les jours.	❑	❑
• **Step 2** **Which statement do you think is the least typical for your teacher to have done? And why?**		

6 Processing Instruction and the Age Factor: Can Adults and School-age Native Speakers of German Process English Simple Past Tense Correctly?

Tanja Angelovska, University of Munich (Germany)* and
Alessandro G. Benati, University of Greenwich (UK)**

Introduction

This study addresses the question of whether age plays a significant role in the effectiveness of a type of grammar instruction called 'processing instruction' (VanPatten, 1996, 2004, 2007). VanPatten's model of input processing (1996) is the theoretical base that directly informs the practices of processing

* **Tanja Angelovska** holds a PhD in English Linguistics and Language Teaching from University of Munich (LMU), Germany. She has taught courses in second language acquisition (SLA), applied linguistics, psycholinguistics, and multilingualism. Her research focuses on language processing in second and additional language acquisition. Since 2012, she has also been involved in a Leverhulme Trust post-doctoral research project on individual differences in SLA at the University of Greenwich.

** **Alessandro Benati** is Director of Research and Enterprise in the School of Humanities and Social Sciences at the University of Greenwich. He is an academic scholar in the area of second language acquisition. His research focuses on how language learners process incoming linguistic information at input level. He has worked extensively with James Lee on various projects. He has published books and journal papers in the areas of second language teaching and language acquisition. He is editor of an international book series in Instructed Second Language Research (Continuum Publishing).

instruction. Input processing refers to 'the initial process by which learners connect grammatical forms with their meanings as well as how they interpret the roles of nouns in relationship to verbs' (VanPatten, 2004: 5). The main purpose of processing instruction is 'to help learners circumvent ineffective processing strategies or to instill appropriate processing strategies, so that they derive better intake from the input' (Lee and Benati, 2007: 16).

Processing instruction is an input-based approach to grammar instruction. The effects of processing instruction have been compared to other approaches to grammar (for a full review of these studies see Lee and Benati, 2009). The effects of processing instruction have been measured through sentence and discourse level tasks (see Benati and Lee, 2010).

The overall findings from studies conducted to measure the effects of PI have clearly indicated that PI helps L2 learners to process certain grammatical forms or structures that may be affected by various processing problems (e.g. syntactic, perceptual, and semantic processing problems). The majority of studies investigating the effectiveness of processing instruction have utilized adult learners, with a few exceptions where the population used was school-age learners (see for example Benati, 2005; Marsden, 2006; and Benati, Lee and Houghton, 2008). In Benati (2005) and Benati, Lee and Houghton (2008) the participants were children studying English in secondary schools. In both studies the target grammar feature under investigation was the English past simple tense.

Based on these empirical findings, Benati and Lee (2008) formulated *the Age Hypothesis*. According to this hypothesis, processing instruction is an effective intervention with younger learners as well as with older learners (Benati and Lee, 2008: 168).

Primary Target Item: The Past Simple Tense of Regular Verbs

The English past simple tense was chosen for a number of reasons. First, it is affected by the Lexical Preference Principle. According to this principle, 'learners will tend to rely on lexical items as supposed to grammatical form to get meaning when both encode the same semantic information' (VanPatten, 2007: 118). There is consistent and strong evidence suggesting that L2 learners process a lexical item before a grammatical form when both encode the same meaning. According to VanPatten, this is a processing strategy used by early stage learners who are more likely to process temporal adverbials over morphological markers when interpreting tenses. Secondly, German speakers are not always successful in making the distinction between the present perfect (German, *das Perfekt*) and the past simple (German, *Präteritum*). Indeed, many dialects (such as the Southern Bavarian) do not even use a simple past, which is thus mostly reserved for written narrations. German speakers sometimes mix the two tenses indiscriminately. In colloquial conversation, they tend to use exclusively the present perfect to express actions in the past. For example, the English sentence '*Mary cleaned the kitchen yesterday*' can be expressed in German in two ways: '*Mary hat die Küche gestern geputzt*', or '*Mary putzte die Küche gestern*'. Hence, a German learner of English will experience difficulties in mapping the past simple marker (*–ed*) in English to the past time framework, because '[L2 learners] may borrow the concept of past tense in their L1 as the starting point' (Benati, 2005: 76) or 'L2 learners may be processing according to a strategy that has been developed during L1 acquisition' (Doughty, 2004: 190, 193). The third reason that we selected the English past tense *–ed* marker for investigation is that it has previously been examined within the PI research framework (Benati, 2005; Benati, Lee and Houghton, 2008). Therefore, expanding the research line on this particular linguistic feature will contribute to the generalizibility of the effects of PI on the past simple across target and native languages.

Previous Research in Processing Instruction

Benati (2005) conducted a study investigating the effects of processing instruction, traditional instruction and meaningful output-based instruction on the acquisition of English past simple tense. This form is affected by the so-called Lexical Preference Principle. The participants involved in Benati's study were 47 Chinese and 30 Greek school-age learners (12–13 years old) of English residing in their respective countries. The participants in both schools were divided into three groups: processing instruction, traditional instruction and meaning output-based instruction. One interpretation and one production measure were administered using a pre- and post-test design. The results from this parallel study were similar and revealed that processing instruction had positive effects on the processing and acquisition of the target feature. Benati, Lee and Houghton (2008) examined whether learners who received processing instruction on the English simple past tense (primary effects) can transfer this instructional training to the acquisition of the third person singular present tense (secondary effects). Twenty-six subjects participated in this classroom experiment. They were all Korean native speakers and they were studying beginner-level English in a secondary school in Korea (13 years old). These school-aged learners were randomly assigned to two groups: the processing instruction group and the traditional instruction group. A pre- and post-tests procedure was used in this study with two different assessment tasks (interpretation and production sentence-level). The overall outcomes of this study indicated that processing instruction not only provides learners with the primary benefit of learning to process and produce the morphological form on which they receive instruction, but also a secondary benefit in that they transferred that training to processing and producing another morphological form on which they had received no instruction.

In both experimental studies, processing instruction was effective in making the redundant and non-salient grammatical meaning-form relationships more salient in the learner's input. In both studies, participants were not native speakers of English but were 'adolescent native speakers of Korean' (Benati, Lee and Houghton, 2008: 91), and 'Chinese and Greek students studying English in a secondary school in China' (Benati, 2005: 74).

The present study will investigate whether two different age groups would benefit equally from PI in altering their reliance on lexical temporal indicators and redirect their attention to verb forms. This study includes native speakers of German, a language not previously investigated within the PI research paradigm.[1]

Research Questions

In the attempt to provide further empirical evidence to the *Age Hypothesis* and the *Native Language Hypothesis* (Benati and Lee, 2008) the present study aims at more systematically measuring the effects of PI on the acquisition of English simple past tense among school-age and adult native speakers of German. For the present study, we advance the following two hypotheses:

> The Age Hypothesis: PI will be just as effective as in intervention with younger learners as it is with older learners (Benati and Lee, 2008: 168).
>
> The Native Language Hypothesis: PI will be effective for instilling target language specific processing strategies, no matter the native language of the learners (Benati and Lee, 2008: 169).

PI was used in this study to alter learners' processing strategies as captured in one of the processing principles formulated by VanPatten (1996): namely the Lexical Preference Principle. The aim of the study is threefold:

- to test the effects of the PI treatment on groups of two different age ranges;
- to test the effects of the PI treatment on a different foreign language: namely German;
- to measure any durable effects for the PI treatment.

The research that guided this study is framed by the following questions:

(Q1): Will PI equally affect children and adult native speakers of German in their ability to process the past simple regular tense *–ed* as measured by two interpretation sentence-level tasks?
(Q2): Will the positive effects of instruction be retained over time by both age groups?

Method

Participants

Two parallel classroom experiments were conducted in two institutions in Germany. The participants belonged to two different age groups: adults and children. The adults-group was composed of students learning English as a foreign language (mean age 26 years old) and the children-group was composed of German fifth-grade pupils (mean age 10.5 years old). Both types of participants were recruited in Germany at their institutions: Maria Ward Gymnasium Nymphenburg (German high school) and the Language Centre of University of Munich (LMU), Germany. All participants completed a consent form agreeing to take part in the experiment. They were all German native speakers and were living in Germany. They were all studying English and they did not have any previous knowledge of the target feature. All participants were pre-tested on the ability to interpret the target feature and an exclusion criterion of 60% was used to select the final pool. Twenty-three adults and 75 children were included in the final pool following a randomization procedure. Adult students were tested with the *Oxford Quick Placement Test* and they were all at A1/A2 language proficiency level. The children had learned English for two years and their level of English was also at A1/A2 language proficiency level. Their language proficiency level was set in accordance with the CEFR (Common European Framework of Reference for Languages) and with the years of instruction, and assessed through oral exams (*mündliche Prüfungen*) for their specific school type (regulated in §54, 1, 1 of the School Rule for Grammar Schools in Bavaria – *Schulordnung für die Gymnasien in Bayern*). Both age groups were split into two additional groups using a random procedure at the beginning of the two parallel experiments. The following four groups were formed and included in the two parallel experiments:

- Group 1: children who were treated with existing referential structured input activities ('matching-based', i.e. matching the temporal adverb with the verb inflection in the input sentence), $n = 34$;
- Group 2: adults who underwent the same treatment as group 1 children, $n = 11$;
- Group 3: children who were treated with modified referential structured input activities (new sentence-level interpretation task), i.e. learners were required to derive the sentence meaning based only on the verb inflection without any given temporal adverb to match it to the input sentence, but rather a logical reasoning based on the sentence time frame, $n = 41$;
- Group 4: adults who underwent the same treatment as group 3 children, $n = 12$.

Participants' learning was limited to classroom instruction and only the ones who had been exposed to all phases of the instructional treatment were included in the final data pool.

Procedures

In both studies, the four groups were taught for a total of two hours over a two-day period. In both experiments one of the researchers was also the instructor. The researcher acted only as facilitator during the experiments and she presented the target feature by explaining how it works in the target language and she followed the instructional materials to the letter. The experiments were designed and carried out to make the results as objective as possible within the constraints imposed by a number of variables (e.g. foreign language curriculum).

Two parallel experiments were conducted using processing instruction as the independent factor (see Figure 6.1). During the instructional treatment limited feedback was provided to the participants. Learners in the four groups were told whether they were right or wrong but no explanation was given.

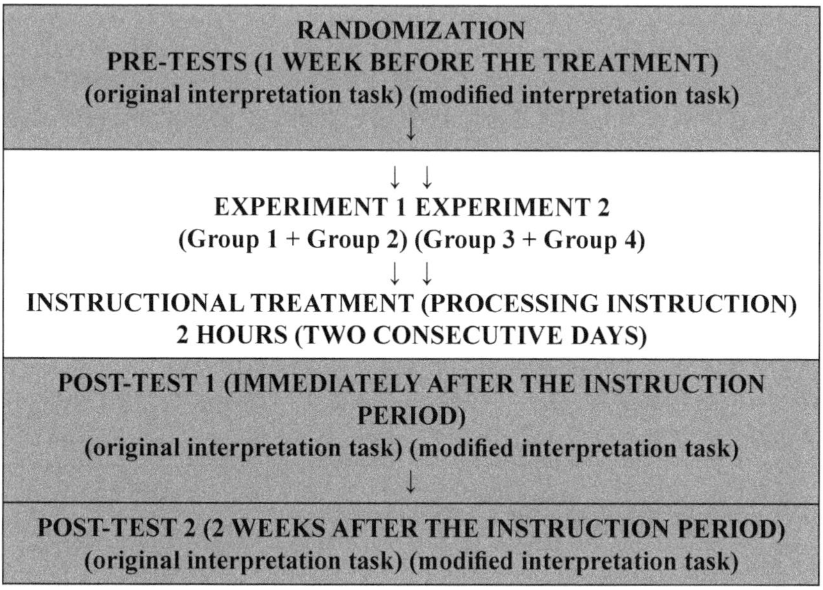

RANDOMIZATION PRE-TESTS (1 WEEK BEFORE THE TREATMENT) (original interpretation task) (modified interpretation task) ↓
↓ ↓ EXPERIMENT 1 EXPERIMENT 2 (Group 1 + Group 2) (Group 3 + Group 4) ↓ ↓ INSTRUCTIONAL TREATMENT (PROCESSING INSTRUCTION) 2 HOURS (TWO CONSECUTIVE DAYS)
POST-TEST 1 (IMMEDIATELY AFTER THE INSTRUCTION PERIOD) (original interpretation task) (modified interpretation task) ↓
POST-TEST 2 (2 WEEKS AFTER THE INSTRUCTION PERIOD) (original interpretation task) (modified interpretation task)

Figure 6.1 Overview of the experiment

Materials

The material was developed following processing instruction guidelines (Lee and VanPatten, 1995; VanPatten and Sanz, 1995). The processing instruction treatment had the following two characteristics:

1. Presentation of the target feature pointing out to learners possible processing problems.
2. Use of referential and affective structured input activities in which learners have to respond to the content of sentences.

In the processing instruction treatment, lexical markers (temporal adverbs) were removed from the structured input activities, so that learners' attention was directed towards the verb endings (*–ed*) as the indicator of tense. As processing instruction aims at making learners interpret the linguistic feature more efficiently and appropriately, learners were never asked to produce a sentence with the past tense. They were engaged in processing input sentences in a controlled situation so that they could make better form-meaning connections. The input was structured so that the grammatical item carried the important meaning and learners had to rely on the target item to complete the task. The structured input activities in this instructional treatment were all communicative and meaningful, constructed in an attempt to 'force' learners to attend to the form to complete the task (i.e. to get the meaning). As there were no lexical indicators, learners had to use verbal morphology as the indicator of tense.

The material included three referential and two affective structured input activities (see Appendices B and C) and highly frequent vocabulary items were chosen. Those vocabulary items which were new for the participants were explained to them and translated in their L1. The task instructions were presented to them in English and translated in German in order to avoid comprehension difficulties. In both experiments, all participants were exposed to the same amount of explicit information (see Appendix A) and structured input practice (two-hour instruction).

Assessment and Scoring Procedures

A pre-test and post-test design (immediate and delayed post-tests) was used (see Figure 6.1). Pre-tests were administered to the subjects two weeks before the beginning of the instructional period. The pre-test was also used to eliminate subjects from the original pool (anyone who scored more than 60% on the assessment measures was not included in the final pool). Tests were balanced in terms of difficulty and vocabulary. One interpretation task (see Figure 6.2) was adopted from previous research (Benati, 2005) and a second interpretation task (see Figure 6.3) was developed especially for this experiment. Both interpretation tasks consisted of 20 sentences each (10 distractor items in the present simple or the present perfect tense) of which 10 were in the English past simple tense (only regular forms). The participants had to listen to the sentences and indicate (interpret) whether the sentence they heard was related to a past or present action. Temporal adverbs were removed from all sentences. No repetition was provided, so that the test would measure real-time comprehension. Only the target items were scored. The maximal possible score was 10 for the first interpretation task (existing 'matching-based' interpretation task) and 10 for the second interpretation task (new sentence-level interpretation task) on all tests. The raw scores were calculated as follows: incorrect response – 0 point; correct response – 1 point. No partial credit was given. All input sentences were recorded by a native speaker of English and presented to the subjects on a CD-player.

Previous research on PI has investigated the relative effects of this input-based approach on the acquisition of different linguistic features by utilizing an interpretation task, which measured learners' ability to process sentences containing the target feature. In the present study an additional interpretation task was developed (see Figure 6.3).

Rationale for Including a Modified Interpretation Task

We followed two main arguments for the inclusion of a modified interpretation task. Clearly, the first reason was the structure of the learners' 'native language' – German. Clearly, the first reason for including a second interpretation task is, as previously said, that L1 German learners might have some difficulties in distinguishing pastness. They could very likely end up with false mapping of the meaning 'pastness' to a verb in present perfect simple when presented with a target sentence in English containing a verb

Sentence-level interpretation task:

Listen to the sentences and decide whether 'last year' or 'right now' is more appropriate for each. You will hear the sentences only once and you have five seconds to make the correct choice.

[Sample sentences heard by the students: John finished graduate school.]

	LAST YEAR	RIGHT NOW	CAN'T TELL
1)	X	________	________

Figure 6.2 Interpretation task adapted from Benati (2005)

New/modified sentence-level interpretation task:

Read the questions before you listen to each of the sentences and then choose the correct answer. Try to choose the most suitable answer (offered as an option) and choose the 'can't tell option' only if you do not know the answer at all. You will hear the sentences only once. You have five seconds to read the question for each sentence and five seconds to make the correct choice.

[Sample sentence heard by the students: John chopped his finger with a knife.]

1) Is John still in pain?

YES ( ) NO ( ) CAN'T TELL ( )

Figure 6.3 Second interpretation task

in present perfect, because this is done in their L1 German. Therefore, we aimed for a purposeful inclusion of distractor sentences which are known to pose difficulties in the interpretation of pastness by German learners of English. We confronted learners with input sentences which contained identical lexical items, but only different verb forms and we presented these input sentences one after another followed by the same type of questions.

The main purpose of the use of a modified interpretation task was the attempt to 'train' their ability to interpret input by exposing them to input sentences in different time frames, for example, a sentence with present perfect verb form (used to express finished past action in the L1, i.e. correct for expressing finished past action in their L1 but erroneous for the L2 use, where past simple tense is needed), and a sentence in the past simple, i.e. the tested verb form). Hence, we eliminated the effort required to process different lexical items in each sentence, which may have exhausted attentional capacity.

The on-task demands for the modified interpretation task are to match the grammatical form (*–ed*) with the meaning of the whole utterance (finished past action) without a given temporal adverbial as an option to choose from, but rather to attend to the meaning of the whole utterance by reasoning, i.e. to decide whether there is a possibility that the action which started in the past may have continued in the present (present perfect). If the input sentence is in past simple, the learner's correct choice would be to exclude the possibility that the action has continued in the present. On the other hand, if the input sentence was given as a distractor, i.e. containing a verb in 'present perfect', the learner should reason that the action which began in the past could/may have continued in the present, as well.

Results

Experiment 1

Interpretation task 1

Table 6.1 provides the mean scores and standard deviations for both age groups (adults and children) on the sentence-level interpretation task administered in this first experiment. The descriptive statistics show the gains made from pre-test to post-test scores by the two age groups and, at the same time, the descriptive statistics show an extremely small difference between the first post-test and the delayed post-test. A one-way ANOVA conducted on the pre-test scores showed no significant differences between the two

Groups	Pre-test		Post-test		Delayed Post-test	
	M	*SD*	*M*	*SD*	*M*	*SD*
PI(c) ($n = 34$)	3.11	1.88	5.73	2.2	5.35	1.61
PI(a) ($n = 11$)	3.90	1.81	5.63	2.57	4.81	2.99

Table 6.1 Descriptive statistics for first sentence-level interpretation task

groups before instruction (F (1, 44) = .010, $p = .904$). Both age groups began instruction with equivalent knowledge of the target structure. Any differences found after instruction will be attributed to the effects of instruction.

The raw scores of the sentence-level interpretation pre-test and post-tests were submitted to a two-way ANOVA with repeated measures. The ANOVA showed a significant main effect for Time (F (2, 44) = 15.034, p = .000); there was no significant effect for Age Group (F (2, 44) = 2.674, p = .109); and no significant interaction between Age Group and Time (F (2, 44) = 317.027, p = .922). These results demonstrate that both age groups gained in their ability to interpret English past tense forms as measured by a sentence-level interpretation task.

Experiment 2

Interpretation task 2

Table 6.2 provides the mean scores and standard deviations for both age groups (adults and children) on the sentence-level interpretation task administered in this second experiment. The descriptive statistics show the gains made from pre-test to post-test by the adults-group and, at the same time, that these gains are retained in the delayed post-tests. A one-way ANOVA conducted on the pre-test scores showed no significant differences between the two groups before instruction (F (1, 51) = .959, $p = .332$). Both age groups began instruction with equivalent knowledge of the target structure. Any differences found after instruction will be attributed to the effects of instruction.

Groups	Pre-test		Post-test		Delayed Post-test	
	M	*SD*	*M*	*SD*	*M*	*SD*
PI(c) ($n = 41$)	3.04	1.89	3.75	1.63	4.43	1.70
PI(a) ($n = 12$)	3.66	2.01	6.08	2.93	6.66	2.01

Table 6.2 Descriptive statistics for second sentence-level interpretation task

The raw scores of the sentence-level interpretation (from the second experiment) pre-test and post-tests were tabulated and a two-way ANOVA with repeated measures was performed. The results of the ANOVA revealed a significant main effect for Time (F (2, 51) = 28.538, p = .000); a significant effect for Age Group (F (2, 51) = 12.664, p = .001); and a significant interaction between Age Group and Time (F (2, 51) = 435.120, p = .000). The significant interaction indicates that there may be differential effects of instruction for the different age groups.

Post hoc means comparisons on the scores for the two age groups were carried out. It was confirmed that from the pre-test to post-test 1 (immediate) and from the pre-test to post-test 2 (delayed) the scores are significantly different. PI(a) > PI(c) (p = .000 and p = .000, respectively). The difference in scores from post-test 1 (immediate) and post-test 2 (delayed) was significantly different. PI(a) > (PI(c) (p = .004).

Discussion and Conclusion

The results from this study has provided further evidence that the processing instruction approach is an effective instructional treatment in helping L2 learners to make accurate form-meaning connections. The interpretation tasks included in this study required both adults and children to interpret the target form in the input. They were asked to process the form (morpheme –*ed*) to its meaning (expressing an action in the past, which was completed).

The results from the first sentence-level interpretation task showed that processing instruction has positive and equal effects on both age groups (children and adults). The positive effects of instruction were maintained over the delayed post-test for both age groups who make similar gains on the immediate post-test.

The results from the second sentence-level interpretation task indicated that the adults made greater gains than the children. However, both groups retained the positive effects of the instruction over time. The difference in gains between the two age groups on the second sentence-level interpretation tasks can be explained in terms of cognitive processing load. In the sentence-level interpretation task from the second experiment, L2 learners were exposed to verb forms with 'conflicting' meanings and therefore to a more demanding task. As argued by Schmidt (1990: 143), 'task demands are a powerful determinant of what is noticed' (or extended, 'what is noticed, processed and acquired'). Similarly, as VanPatten affirms, 'the issue of capacity (that is, limited resources) is not the same for everyone' (VanPatten, 2004: 22). Task demand and individual processing capacity can provide an explanation for the results on the second experiment.

Overall, the results from the present study provide further evidence of the *Age Hypothesis* (Benati and Lee, 2008) as processing instruction is equally effective with primary-school-age learners as well as older learners. It also offers further support for the *Native Language Hypothesis* in terms of offering additional evidence for the effects of processing instruction on different age groups, i.e. children and adults with German as L1.

The present study is a valuable contribution to the processing instruction research agenda as it provides further evidence for the effects of processing instruction on the acquisition of a verbal morphology feature (past tense) of the English grammatical system, which is affected by the Lexical Preference Principle.

Despite the positive outcomes, there are a number of limitations. One of them is the limited cell size for our study (23 adult learners and 75 children). It would need to be replicated before we could comment with more confidence on the generalizability of its findings. However, the similarities between the results of this study and previous empirical research on the impact of processing instruction do lend validity to the findings presented in this chapter. Furthermore, the long-term effects of the variables under investigation should be re-examined as the long-lasting effects of instruction in this study were measured only over a period of two weeks. Finally, it could be argued that the fact that the instructor of the four groups was also the researcher meant that she could have been biased towards one group or the other although we do not believe so. On the other hand, the fact that the experimenter and the instructor were the same person eliminated the incomparability of having various instructors with different teaching abilities, styles, preferences, and habits. Further research is needed in order to compare the effects of processing instruction on the acquisition of different linguistic features in English. Moreover, future PI studies should focus on comparing the PI effects on a number of linguistic features between children and adults who share the same native language. In addition, future studies should aim to go beyond the so far employed pool of native speakers of German, Greek, Chinese and Korean, but should rather conduct experiments with native speakers of other less explored languages.

Authors' Note

This study was supported by a Leverhulme Trust post-doctoral fellowship grant. We would like to thank to the participants from the grammar school 'Maria Ward Gymnasium' Nymphenburg and from the language centre of the Ludwig Maximilians University of Munich in Germany. We appreciate the willingness of their teachers to support this research. We also express special gratitude to Angela Hahn and Bettina Raaf for helping us in the collection of the data presented in this study.

Notes

1. Benati, Lee and McNulty (2010) profiled the native language backgrounds of a group of learners who were not native speakers of English. Among the seven was one native speaker of German. The present study included only native speakers of German.

References

Benati, A. (2005). The effects of processing instruction, traditional instruction and meaning-output instruction on the acquisition of the English past simple tense. *Language Teaching Research*, 9(1), 67–93.

Benati, A., and Lee, J. F. (2008). *Grammar Acquisition and Processing Instruction: Secondary and Cumulative Effects*. Bristol: Multilingual Matters.

Benati, A., and Lee, J. F. (2010). *Processing Instruction and Discourse*. London: Continuum.

Benati, A., Lee, J. F., and Houghton, S. D. (2008). Chapter 4: From processing instruction on the acquisition of English past tense to secondary transfer-of-training effects on English third person singular present tense. In Benati, A. and Lee, J. F., *Grammar Acquisition and Processing Instruction: Secondary and Cumulative Effects* (pp. 88–120). Bristol: Multilingual Matters.

Benati, A. G., Lee, J. F., and McNulty, E. M. (2010). Exploring the effects of processing instruction on a discourse level guided composition with the Spanish subjunctive after the adverb *cuando*. In Benati, A.G. and Lee, J. F., *Processing Instruction and Discourse* (pp. 97–147). London: Continuum.

Doughty, C. (2004). Effects of instruction on learning a second language: a critique of instructed SLA research. In VanPatten, B., Williams, J. and Rott, S. (eds), *Form-Meaning Connections in Second Language Acquisition* (pp. 189–212). Mahwah, NJ: Lawrence Erlbaum.

Lee, J. F., and Benati, A.G. (2007). *Delivering Processing Instruction in Classrooms and Virtual Contexts: Research and Practice*. London: Equinox.

Lee, J. F., and Benati, A. G. (2009). *Research and Perspectives on Processing Instruction*. Berlin: Mouton de Gruyter.

Lee, J., and VanPatten, B. (1995). *Making Communicative Language Teaching Happen*. New York: McGraw-Hill.

Marsden, E. (2006) Exploring input processing in the classroom: an experimental comparison of processing instruction and enriched input. *Language Learning*, 56(3), 507–566.

Schmidt, R. (1990). The role of consciousness in second language learning. *Applied Linguistics*, 11, 127–58.

VanPatten, B. (1996). *Input Processing and Grammar Instruction in Second Language Acquisition*. Norwood, NJ: Ablex Pub.

VanPatten, B. (2004). *Processing Instruction: Theory, Research, and Commentary*. Mahwah, NJ: Erlbaum.

VanPatten, B. (2007). Input processing in adult second language acquisition. In VanPatten, B. and Williams, J. (eds), *Theories in Second Language Acquisition: An Introduction* (pp. 115–35). Mahwah, NJ: Lawrence Erlbaum Associates.

VanPatten, B., and Sanz, C. (1995). From input to output: processing instruction and communicative tasks. In Eckman, F. R., Highland, D., Lee, P. W., Mileham, J. and Weber, R. R. (eds), *Second Language Acquisition Theory and Pedagogy* (pp. 169–85). Mahwah, NJ: Erlbaum.

Appendix A: Instructional Component of PI

The past simple tense

- The past simple tense is one of the tenses most used to talk about events in the past. It does refer to finished actions and events. Very often the English past simple tense ends in –ed. This is the regular past tense.

  Examples:

  I invited John for lunch

  I played tennis with Paula

- When you talk about a finished time in the past, the English past simple tense is often accompanied by a temporal adverb.

  Example:

  Yesterday, I smoked 20 cigarettes

Attention

- DO NOT RELY ON THE TEMPORAL ADVERB (e.g. Yesterday) TO UNDERSTAND WHEN THE ACTION TAKES PLACE AS SOMETIME YOU CAN HEAR A SENTENCE WITHOUT THE TEMPORAL ADVERB.
- You must pay attention to the form of the verb (e.g. *–ed*) to understand when the action takes place.
- In the case of describing past events pay attention to the ending of the verb: *-ed*.
- However, you may see an auxiliary "have/has" in front of a verb form ending with *–ed*. In that case the action expressed is not past and has not finished.

Appendix B: Referential Activities

Referential Activity 1: Things People Did Now and Last Summer

Listen to the following statements and decide whether each statement refers to an activity that takes place now or took place last summer in London.

	LAST SUMMER	NOW
1)	❑	❑
2)	❑	❑
3)	❑	❑
	(...)	

Referential Activity 2: David Beckham: Now and After

Step 1
Listen to the following statements made by a journalist about the life of the footballer David Beckham and decide whether each statement is referring to his past life as a Manchester United player in England or his life now as a Real Madrid player in Spain.

	MANCHESTER UNITED PLAYER (PAST)	REAL MADRID PLAYER (NOW)
1)	❑	❑
2)	❑	❑
3)	❑	❑
4)	❑	❑
	(...)	

Step 2
Now read the sentences you have just listened to and decide (in pairs) if David Beckham was more famous when he was a Manchester United player or a Real Madrid player.

Referential Activity 3: Has the Action Finished or Not?

Read the questions underneath before you listen to the sentences. Then listen and decide.

Step 1:
S/he did it and could do it, but can s/he still do it?

1) Is her coat new?
YES ( ) NO ( ) CAN'T TELL ( )
Sentence heard: 'I have received a new coat'.
2) Do you think he is still in pain?
YES ( ) NO ( ) CAN'T TELL ( )
Sentence heard: 'John chopped his finger with a knife'.
3) Decide whether Mozart can still compose operas.
YES ( ) NO ( ) CAN'T TELL ( )
Sentence heard: 'Mozart composed many operas'.
4) Decide whether Bill can still create business plans.
YES ( ) NO ( ) CAN'T TELL ( )
Sentence heard: 'Bob has created a new business plan'.

Step 2:
Listen to the sentences you will hear and decide whether the action has finished or not.

1) Decide whether the week when s/he learnt three songs has finished or not:
FINISHED ( ) NOT FINISHED ( ) CAN'T TELL ( )
Sentence heard: 'I learned three songs'.
2) The cooking of the dinner is:
FINISHED ( ) NOT FINISHED ( ) CAN'T TELL ( )
Sentence heard: 'I cooked a dinner for Peter'.
3) The action is:
FINISHED ( ) NOT FINISHED ( ) CAN'T TELL ( )
Sentence heard: 'I visited Mexico'.
4) The action is:
FINISHED ( ) NOT FINISHED ( ) CAN'T TELL ( )
Sentence heard: 'I have received a phone call'.

Step 3:

Looking for verb endings

Now read the following sentences and decide whether the statements are true (T), false (F) or if you CAN'T TELL (C).

1) *Mary has received a new bike.*
   ⇨ Her bike (the only one she has) is new. T/F/C
2) *John chopped his finger with a knife.*
   ⇨ He is in pain now. T/F/C
3) *Mozart composed one opera.*
   ⇨ He cannot compose any other operas. T/F/C
4) *Marc has composed one opera.*
   ⇨ Marc cannot compose any operas. T/F/C
5) *I visited Mexico.*
   ⇨ Now I am not in Mexico T/F/C
6) *I have received a phone call.*
   ⇨ I am still on the phone. T/F/C

Step 4

Discuss your decision with the partner sitting next to you. Ask the teacher to give you the correct answers. What can you conclude?

My conclusion:

____

____

Appendix C: Affective Activities

Affective Activity 1

Step 1:
Read the following activities and indicate whether you did similar or different things at the last New Year celebrations:

		Yes	No
1)	I visited my relatives	❑	❑
2)	I received gifts	❑	❑
3)	I mailed New Year cards to friends	❑	❑
4)	I celebrated in the street with friends	❑	❑
5)	I enjoyed myself	❑	❑
6)	I decorated my home	❑	❑
7)	I danced at a club	❑	❑
8)	I decided on a New Year resolution	❑	❑

Step 2
Compare your results with your partner to find out how many similar things you did.

Affective Activity 2: My First Day in London

Step 1

Listen to the following story that a student told about his first day in London and decide whether the statements are true (T) or false (F).

	THE STUDENT.....	TRUE OR FALSE
1)	...wanted to see Buckingham Palace.	T/F
2)	...showed pictures of Hyde Park to his parents.	T/F
3)	...stayed in bed most of the morning.	T/F
4)	...liked Covent Garden.	T/F
5)	...phoned his parents.	T/F
6)	...liked English trains.	T/F
7)	...visited Madame Tussaud's.	T/F
8)	...travelled on the bus.	T/F
9)	...really liked the clowns in Oxford Circus.	T/F
10)	...arrived home early.	T/F

Step 2:

Now read the text you have just listened to and check your answers. Would you like to change any of your answers?
(Instructor's script)

I really wanted to see Madame Tussaud's, so early in the morning I took a quick shower and washed myself, and travelled by train to Baker Street station. I had my picture taken with David Beckham, well the wax model that is. I also visited Trafalgar Square and saw Nelson's Column. There were so many pigeons there I think they owned the place! In the afternoon, I waited for ages for a train to take me to Covent Garden. I really hated London trains; they are awful. Covent Garden was fantastic, I watched the different street performers, and I really enjoyed listening to the musicians. I finished my exploration and sunbathed for a bit in Hyde Park – London's most famous and largest open space. I arrived home quite late and called my parents back in China and talked about my day. All in all, I had a wonderful time today.

Step 3:

Ask your teacher to give you the answers.

Step 4:

Read the text again. Do you know any of the famous places mentioned above? Would you like to go to any of them?

7 Exploring Possible Effects of Gender and Enhanced vs. Unenhanced Processing Instruction on the Acquisition of Case Marking in L2 German

Zoe Agiasophiti, Research Visiting Fellow, University of Greenwich, UK*

Introduction

Input enhancement (IE) and processing instruction (PI) manipulate input in different ways in order to draw learners' attention to the target linguistic form. For IE the objective is to make input salient to make it more likely to become processed (Sharwood Smith, 1991; 1993). For PI the aim is to force learners to process the target form in order to decode the meaning of the sentence (VanPatten, 1996; 2004).

In the literature there are various types of IE such as input flood; corrective feedback; recasts; elicitation; metalinguistic clues; clarification requests; repetition of learner's error; textual/typographical IE (TTIE) and PI (see Wong, 2003, 2005; Lee and Benati, 2007). TTIE involves written input that is enhanced by visually altering its appearance in the text (see also Rutherford and Sharwood Smith, 1987; Wong, 2005: 49). The target item can be

* **Zoe Agiasophiti** obtained her MA in German as a Foreign Language from Heidelberg University, Germany. She later attended the University of Sunderland, where she graduated with a Master's Degree in Business Administration (MBA). She obtained her PhD from Newcastle University and she is currently a Research Visiting Fellow at the University of Greenwich with an interest in the areas of applied linguistics and second language acquisition.

manipulated in various ways: it can be bolded, italicized, capitalized, underlined, highlighted or enhanced with colours.

On the contrary, PI has a more rigid type of instruction. PI consists of four main components (full PI paradigm), namely explicit grammar instruction, referential activities and affective activities (referred to as 'structured input activities') and a set of guidelines, e.g. they assist instructors in developing the materials (VanPatten, 1996, 2004; VanPatten and Cadierno, 1993; VanPatten and Fernandez, 2004; Wong, 2004). Studies have also utilized PI excluding the explicit grammar component (SI only paradigm) in the treatment package (for instance Culman *et al.*, 2009; Farley, 2004; Sanz, 2004b; Sanz and Morgan-Short, 2004; VanPatten and Borst, 2012; VanPatten and Oikennon, 1996). Results in both types of PI studies have shown positive effects of PI instruction.

Findings of IE studies are inconclusive, as some have reported positive effects (Doughty, 1991; Jourdenais *et al.*, 1995; Leeman *et al.*, 1995, among many) and others no effects (Alanen, 1995; Leow, 1997, 2001; Overstreet, 1998, among many) in language learning.

Meta-analyses of IE and PI studies suggest that the more explicit, more obtrusive and more elaborate a type of instruction is, the more effective it seems to be compared to implicit, less obtrusive and/or less elaborate types of instruction. According to these classifications, PI is considered a more obtrusive-explicit type of intervention than IE (Doughty, 2003; Lee and Huang, 2008; Norris and Ortega, 2000).

In the literature it has been suggested that individual differences play a significant role in second language acquisition. Dörnyei (2005: 2) argues that individual differences are 'the most consistent predictor of (second language) success'. There are many factors that are classified under the category of individual differences, such as learning styles; learning strategies; learning aptitude; affective variables; gender; age; culture; and other demographic variables. The focus of this study is on gender, investigating whether it can be an affecting factor in second language acquisition (SLA) using PI solely and/or in combination with IE, as teaching interventions. In the field of IE and PI the role and interaction of individual differences with the specific instructional approaches have not been explored.

Previous Research on Processing Instruction and Input Enhancement

IE and PI are two different but interrelated approaches that draw, to some extent, on common psycholinguistic theories. Both approaches are based on the notion that attention has a facilitative role in the acquisition of a target form and therefore plays a crucial role in the way both IE and PI operate. In the literature attention remains a vexed issue. There are various characteristics attributed to attention; however the main issue remains whether attention and awareness are two overlapping but not isomorphic concepts that promote second language learning through noticing understood as conscious processing (see Schmidt, 1990, 1993, 1995, 2001; see also FonF/IE[1] studies, for instance Alanen, 1995; Jourdenais *et al.*, 1995; Leow, 1997). Others argue against this notion and dissociate attention from awareness. In this case attention is seen as a process involving three stages, namely alertness, orientation and detection. During the process of detection we can become conscious of processing without dismissing the fact that even within detection, processing occurs without conscious awareness (Tomlin and Villa, 1994; see also Sharwood Smith, 1991, 1993; VanPatten, 1996; Truscott, 1998). Despite the fact that for both approaches the key element is attention, both have failed to provide a detailed explanation of how exactly attention affects the language learning mechanisms; what are the processes involved during learning and acquisition; or how attention could be operationalized in a teaching intervention, such as IE and PI, in order for learning/acquisition to take place (Carroll, 2004; Collentine, 2004; DeKeyser *et al.*, 2002; Harrington, 2004; Salaberry, 1998; Sharwood Smith and Trenkic, 2001).

This study combines the two instructional methods, namely PI and IE, using TTIE with colour enhancement and explores whether and to what extent they can have a positive impact on second language acquisition. Lee and Benati (2007) explored the effects of textually enhanced versus unenhanced SI activities in the acquisition of future tense morphology, partially replicating Benati (2001; 2004). Twenty first-semester undergraduate students were randomly assigned to two groups, an enhanced SI (n = 10) and an unenhanced SI group (n = 10). The type of enhancement used in the referential activities was oral enhancement of the target form by pronouncing the targeted verb ending more loudly (Lee and Benati, 2007: 102). For the affective activities, textual enhancement was applied with the target form verb ending being bolded and underlined (Lee and Benati, 2007: 103). Results from the interpretation task showed that both groups made significant gains post-instruction; however, no significant differences were reported between groups. The same results were revealed for the written production task. Lee and Benati (2007: 109) concluded that SI enhanced or unenhanced is the main factor contributing towards accurate comprehension and production of the target form (similar to Sanz, 2004a; Sanz and Morgan-Short, 2004; VanPatten and Oikennon, 1996).

Findings of the Lee and Benati (2007) study are important since they compare PI to another input-based approach, namely IE, applying aural and textual enhancement. The study provides evidence that SI can be an effective teaching intervention when combined or not with IE. However, the sample size of the study and the lack of the delayed post-test cannot provide reliable and generalizable conclusions regarding the effectiveness of the proposed teaching intervention. The fact that the enhancement variable was not isolated, i.e. both types of enhancement were applied, namely aural and textual enhancement, does not allow conclusions regarding which of the two types of enhancement is most effective.

Furthermore, the study investigates whether an individual difference, such as gender, can be an affecting factor when applying one or the two types of teaching intervention. In the field of IE and PI, gender has not been considered as a variable affecting L2 learning. Research findings in other areas of L2 acquisition are inconclusive. Studies investigating the acquisition of phonology have found gender a significant factor with females making greater gains than males in accuracy of phonological production (Díaz-Campos, 2004; Farhady, 1982; Nyikos, 1990); others have found advantages for males (Boyle, 1987); and others have found no differences between genders (Bacon, 1992). Studies investigating gender and SLA focusing on the differences in learning strategies have revealed that females utilize more language-learning strategies than males (Gass and Varonis, 1986; Ehrman and Oxford, 1989; Larsen-Freeman and Long, 1991; Oxford, 1993; Politzer, 1983). Findings also suggest that females may be more motivated and may have a more positive attitude towards an L2 (Gardner and Lambert, 1972; Ellis, 1994; Spolsky, 1989). Despite the fact that females appear to outperform males in learning strategies and motivation, performance differences are not clearly shown with regards to gender, as an individual difference affecting acquisition (see also Sanz, 2004a).

A theoretical framework is therefore necessary in order to provide a detailed explanation of how the two instructional methods can operate in isolation and/or combination and to better understand the processes involved and the possible factors, such as individual differences, that may affect language learning development, when applying one or the combined instructional methods in language learning and acquisition. Both IE and PI (through input processing) have to date – to some extent – attempted to provide such information with existing theories and models without however adopting and/or integrating one. Lack of full compatibility, weaknesses in fully explaining all the processes involved when applying IE and PI, are some of the reasons that have created this gap (see VanPatten, 1996, 2004, 2007, 2009). A recently developed language processing framework, Modular Online Growth and Use of Language (MOGUL), proposed by Sharwood Smith and Truscott (2005 and in press; see also Truscott and Sharwood Smith, 2004a, 2004b) may be a suitable candidate in filling in the existing gap. MOGUL adopts an interdisciplinary and modular approach to language development, in terms of integrating UG representations (developed by Fodor, 1981, 1983, and Jackendoff, 1987, 1997, 2002, 2007) with a theory of real-time processing connectionist approaches, such as the 'Competition Model' (Bates and MacWhinney, 1987), and Baars's (1988) ideas of the 'Global Workspace Theory' in relating the role of consciousness to language learning and acquisition. With 'Acquisition by Processing Theory' (APT), MOGUL provides an adaptation of the previously mentioned theories and models in order to explain language learning.

Following Jackendoff (1987, 1997, 2002, 2007), there is a parallel domain language specific module, which consists of the phonological (PS) and morphosyntactical (SS) systems and a conceptual system (CS). Structures can work both in isolation or can communicate information with each other through the interfaces in a modular way, as Figure 7.1 depicts.

The language module, otherwise referred to as the core language system, is considered in MOGUL as a 'blind spot' as we cannot become consciously aware of the processing of phonological and morphosyntactical structures. On the contrary, the conceptual store can process both linguistic and non-linguistic information, which can be communicated through the interfaces with the language module. Additionally, information processing in the conceptual structure (CS) can reach high levels of consciousness, thus we can become consciously aware of CS. For Sharwood Smith and Truscott (in press) the CS is located outside the language module because of the innate universal properties the latter entails (Truscott and Sharwood Smith, 2004: 4; see also Jackendoff, 1990). However, all modules are also connected to the non-linguistic perception system through a 'composite blackboard' of extralinguistic modules, i.e. auditory, kinaesthetic, olfactory, gustatory and visual processors, for perceptual processing and representations of sensory input, called Perceptual Output Structures (POpS). POpS serve as the basis for higher-level processing and are therefore accessible to consciousness because of their rich interconnectivity. As Figure 7.2 also illustrates, MOGUL is bi-directional, i.e. it accounts for both comprehension and production (Sharwood Smith and Truscott, in press).

The processing activity results in what APT refers to as 'indexing' and 'co-indexing'. Indexing 'has the effect of matching up a representation in different modules', while co-indexing refers to the activity of a representational chain formulation. Co-indexing is not limited in indexing only a

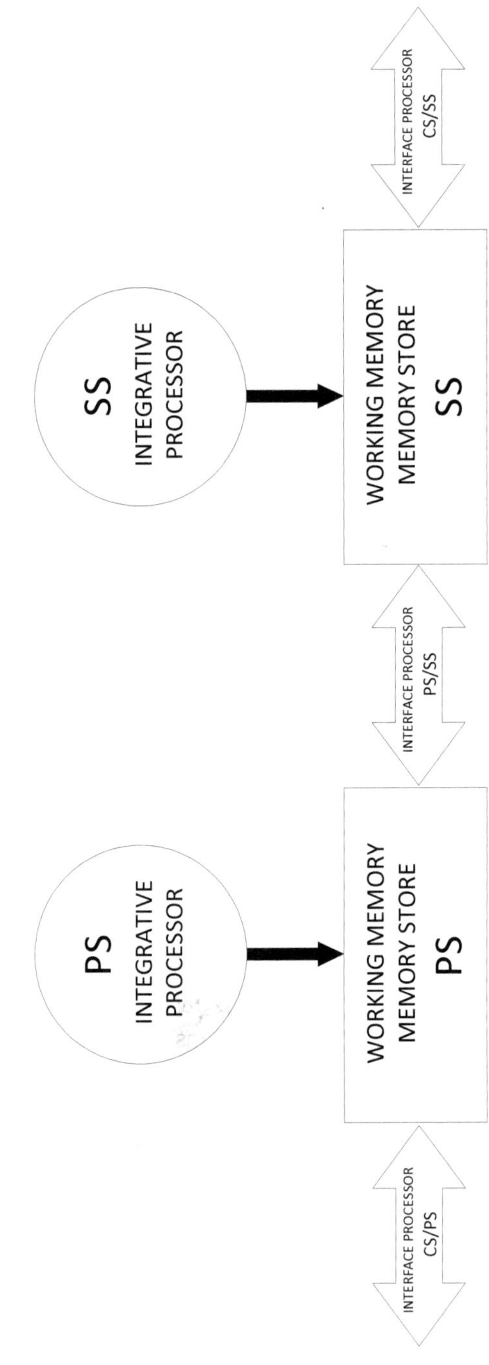

Figure 7.1 MOGUL memory stores, processors and interfaces (adapted from Sharwood Smith and Truscott, in press)

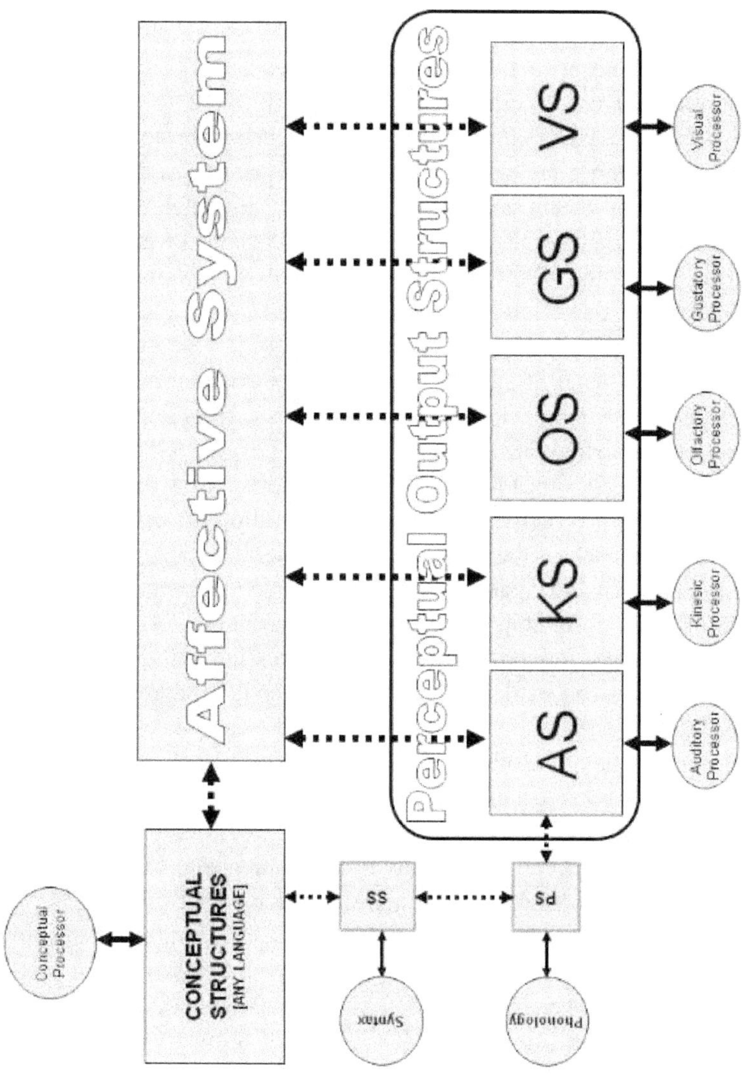

Figure 7.2 MOGUL architecture in a nutshell (Sharwood Smith and Truscott, in press)

phonological representation in the phonological structure, as it can also include a chain of structures, i.e. PS<=>SS<=>CS matched up with affective and/or POpS structures, while it can occur with or without any awareness at the level of understanding or even noticing. However, if co-indexing occurs with a very highly active perceptual representation it can become a conscious representation and therefore can have more chances (although there is no guarantee) of succeeding in becoming a form-meaning connection (Sharwood Smith and Truscott, in press, cited with permission).

Activation levels and competition play a significant role in MOGUL. Each structure has resting, current, high or low levels of activation. As soon as a representation enters one of the processors, structures that have high activation levels are the ones that have a greater chance to win the competition during processing. The 'resting level' is the starting point for each item and it determines if and how quickly an item will become available for processing, and/or incorporated into a representation. On the other hand, the current activation level of an item determines its availability for inclusion in the current processing activity. When an item's current level is activated then spreading activation also occurs (similar to Levelt, 1999; Levelt, Roelofs and Meyer, 1999), meaning that if the PS structure is activated then the SS and CS can also be activated. Spreading activation can also refer to the activation within each of the sub-modules, as interfaces trigger stimulation and try to match the information with any available representation from the LTM store of the sub-module that is activated (see Figure 7.3).

Given that POpS are connected to other processing units, processing in the POpS is influenced by the activity taking place in these units and therefore processing of a representation takes place in the same way, as would processing occur in one of the other structures. Sharwood Smith and Truscott (in press) argue that a representation's current level can be raised at a higher level of activation than other representations that are processed in the language module and/or the conceptual structure, if information enters through POpS. It is the exceptionally high level of activation that POpS can achieve that makes them unique in being able to trigger conscious awareness therefore providing an advantage for SLA (Sharwood Smith and Truscott, in press).

Learning occurs when an indexed item hits an empty node and thus creates a new item. Acquisition or, in MOGUL terms 'growth of language', is the 'lingering effect of processing' (Sharwood Smith and Truscott, in press: 59). Thus, acquisition in MOGUL is not failure driven, as argued by Carroll (2001) but is viewed as an automatic procedure, since the 'parser is constructed so as to automatically acquire (even if the effects are often fleeting)' (Sharwood Smith and Truscott, 2005: 233 and in press; see also Truscott and

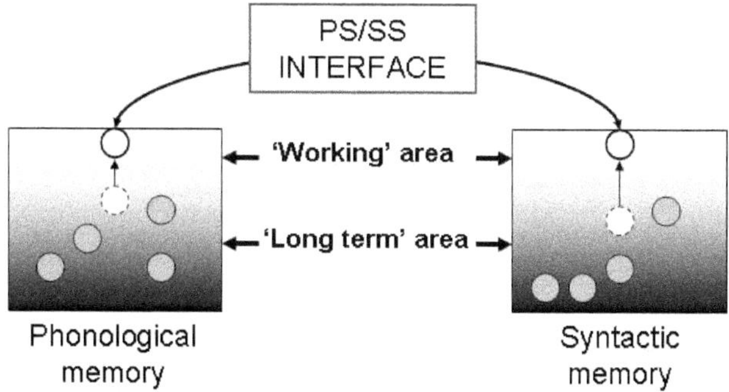

Figure 7.3 Memory stores and activation levels in MOGUL (Sharwood Smith and Truscott, in press, cited with permission)[2]

Sharwood Smith, 2004). MOGUL offers an interdisciplinary approach for a potentially coherent transition theory for SLA; however empirical evidence is necessary, as it remains at a theoretical stage.

Research Questions

The aim of this study is to provide further data on the ongoing PI research focusing on the acquisition of case marking in German L2. The main contribution of this study is therefore:

- to provide further insight regarding the possible positive effects of enhanced/unenhanced PI on the acquisition of L2 case marking in German in the short and long term.
- to investigate whether and to what extent enhanced/unenhanced PI alters learners processing strategies, namely the First Noun Principle (FNP).
- to examine whether an individual difference, such as gender, has an impact on the acquisition of case marking in German in the short and long term when applying enhanced/unenhanced PI as a teaching intervention.

The rationale behind this study stems from the fact that input manipulation results in drawing learners' attention to specific items of the input in order to help the process of input becoming intake and thus getting further processed through the language learning mechanisms (Schmidt, 1990, 1993, 1995, 2001; Sharwood Smith, 1991, 1993; Tomlin and Villa, 1994; VanPatten,

1996, 2004, 2007, 2009). The research questions of the present study have been formulated as follows:

1. Will there be any statistical significant differences in L2 learners' performance in the acquisition of case marking in German when using typographically coloured enhanced or unenhanced PI and/or no instruction in the short and long term in the interpretation task?
2. Is instruction using coloured typographical IE with PI of the target linguistic form more effective than unenhanced PI and/or no instruction in the short and long term in the fill-in-the-gap tasks?
3. Does an individual difference, i.e., gender, have an effect in acquiring case marking in German L2 when applying enhanced, unenhanced PI and/or no instruction in the short and long term?

Based on the results and meta-analyses of previous studies the following hypotheses have been formulated:

Hypothesis 1: Enhanced PI, being more elaborate, obtrusive and explicit than PI, will be a more effective teaching intervention in the short and long term in the interpretation task. No improvement is expected for the control group.

Hypothesis 2: Enhanced PI using colour will be more effective than unenhanced PI in the fill-in-the-gap task in the short and long term.

Hypothesis 3: It is expected that individual differences, i.e., gender, will not have an impact on learners' performance in the short and long term, regardless of type of instruction.

Method

Participants

Participants were secondary-school learners from five different secondary schools in the UK. Initially, 102 English learners of German in their second year, tested roughly after 100 hours of learning German, participated in the study. The final number of participants was 99, since some participants did not attend all four sessions. Participants ranged from Year 8–Year 10 and were aged between 12 and 14 years old. Participants also took an online placement test available from the Goethe Institute (http://www.goethe.de/cgi-bin/einstufungstest/einstufungstest.pl), in order to have an independent assessment of their proficiency in German. The placement test revealed that the majority of participants were at the A2 level; however, two learners were placed on level A1. The range of score placing participants either at level A1 and A2 confirmed that participants in each class were of mixed abilities, a fact that is in line with the different set of classes (higher vs. bottom sets) and the teachers' reports noting that participants in all six classes were of mixed abilities. There is also variability with regard to the teaching hours per week, the course books and teaching materials. Participants were randomly assigned into three different groups, namely Group 1 having typographically coloured IE with PI (+IE+PI) consisting of 34 participants (n = 34); Group 2 having unenhanced PI (–IE+PI) consisting of 33 participants (n = 33); and Group 3 the control group (–IE–PI) that received no instruction in the target form consisting of 32 participants (n = 32).In the first group (Group 1) the sample size consisted of 18 female and 16 male participants (n = 18F, n = 16M). The unenhanced PI group (Group 2) included 16 female and 17 male participants (n = 16F, n = 17M), while the control group (Group 3) included 17 female and 15 male participants (n = 17F, n = 15M).

Procedures

The time line for the present study is given in Figure 7.4. The pre-test and the placement test were administered online one week before training. In the second week of the study a one-and-a-half-hour treatment was followed by the immediate post-test. Twelve to fourteen weeks later the delayed post-test was administered, as Figure 7.4 illustrates.

Pre-test	Treatment 1 1 hour	Treatment 2 (half an hour) + Immediate post-test (IPT) half an hour	Delayed post-test (DPT)
Week 1	Week 2	Week 2	12–14 weeks after treatment and IPT

Figure 7.4 Overview of the timescale of the study

Materials

The target form is the German object–verb–subject (OVS) structure and the marking of accusative case on the definite article. German's canonical surface sentence structure is subject–verb–object (SVO) word order, as in (1).

(1) *Der Mann küsst die Frau.*
The (Nom) man–SUB kisses the woman–OBJ (The man kisses the woman)

However, in German, the subject, object and indirect objects can move freely within a sentence as long as the verb stays in second position (in the case of a main clause). A grammatical OVS sentence structure appears in (2).

(2) *Den Mann küsst die Frau.*
The (Acc) man–OBJ kisses the woman–SUB (The woman kisses the man)

The only cue that German speakers have when interpreting sentences like (2) is that subjects/objects can be identified by their definite article endings, if the object is masculine, because it has a different form from the nominative. As seen in Table 7.1, the endings of the definite articles in German can change on the basis of both gender and case.

An additional cue for German speakers when interpreting OVS sentences is available from stress intonation when sentences are produced orally. At a discourse level, stress intonation is added at the object of the structure, which is placed at the beginning of the sentence indicating the differences in pragmatics, as well as acting as an additional cue for context and topicalization. English learners do not have this sort of variable word order or case marking on determiners in their L1, nor do they have grammatical gender, as German nouns (feminine, masculine or neuter) have.

Case	Masculine	Feminine	Neuter	Plural
Subject (Nominative)	der	die	das	die
Object (Accusative)	den	die	das	die
Indirect Object (Dative)	dem	der	dem	den
Possessive (Genitive)	des	der	des	der

Table 7.1 German definite article system

All treatment and testing materials focused on written tasks. Due to the nature of the target form and the use of coloured typographical input enhancement all input sentences were given in the written form. Participants of the two groups (+IE+PI, –IE+PI) received the full PI paradigm. For the coloured typographically enhanced group (+IE+PI) cases were enhanced with different colours in bold, i.e. for the Masculine Nominative light blue; for the Masculine Accusative dark blue; for the Feminine Nominative and Accusative pink and for the Neuter Nominative and Accusative, green. The explicit information for the two groups covered two main points: (1) the German nominative and accusative case markings on articles; (2) SVO versus inverted OVS word order in German with examples. Figures 7.5 and 7.6 provide an illustration of the explicit instruction the two groups received.

During practice with SI activities learners could not access the grammatical explanation. Feedback, in terms of which answers were correct/incorrect and/or overall score, was also not provided.

SI activities followed and were split into referential and affective activities. Referential activities required the learners to attend to the meaning in order to decode the target form. Activities of this type were interpretation activities; the target form was provided in German and four possible responses were

The meaning is the same but the word order is not.

If you see or hear 'den' in front of the noun, this means that the noun is not performing the action.

Be careful to notice the article before the nouns. The noun that comes first in the sentence is not always the one that performs the action. You should pay attention to the case in order to establish who is doing what.

Figure 7.5 Extract from the unenhanced PI group's explicit instruction

The meaning is the same but the word order is not!
If you see or hear '**den**' in front of the noun, this means that the noun is **not performing the action**.
BE CAREFUL to notice the article before the nouns. The noun that comes first in the sentence is not always the one that performs the action. You should pay attention to the case in order to establish who is doing what.

Figure 7.6 Extract from the typographically coloured enhanced PI group's explicit instruction

Den Mann ärgert die Frau

Figure 7.7 Extract materials from a referential activity for the unenhanced PI group

available to the participant. Alternatively, a sentence in German was provided and participants were requested to decide which picture corresponded best to the sentence (and vice versa), as illustrated in Figure 7.7 (see also Appendix for further examples).

Choose which picture corresponds to the sentence. If you are not sure, choose (c) I am not sure.

Similarly, for the typographically enhanced with colour PI group the exact same activities were provided with the appropriate colour coding, as illustrated in Figure 7.8 (see also Appendix for further examples).

Choose which picture corresponds to the sentence. If you are not sure, choose (c) I am not sure.

Affective activities were also available during treatment in order to provide more examples of the target linguistic form. For the +IE+PI group the

***Den** Mann ärgert die Frau*

Figure 7.8 Extract materials from a referential activity for the coloured typographically enhanced PI group

target form was typographically enhanced with colour, according to the colour coding (see Appendix for more examples). Here any attention to form would have been incidental to the task, since in these types of activities there were no right or wrong questions, according to the PI guidelines (see VanPatten, 1996, 2004).

Participants in the control group did not receive explicit instruction or treatment tasks focusing on the target form. The instructional package contained reading comprehension, matching and ranking activities, focused either on verbs and/or vocabulary.

Assessment Instruments and Scoring

Testing materials were also computerized and available online. The testing materials included an interpretation task and a fill-in-the-gap task. One version of the same test was used for the three conditions (pre-, immediate and delayed post-test); participants did not receive any feedback, in terms of which responses were correct or incorrect, or a score for each task and/or total at the end of the test.

The interpretation task comprised of ten items, six target forms and four distracters. The format of the task was the same as in the treatment package of the enhanced/unenhanced PI groups. It contained a German sentence and two possible English interpretations, the first interpreting the sentence as an SVO and the second as an OVS structure; a third option claiming that the aforementioned options (a) and (b) are possible interpretations, as well as a fourth option 'I am not sure'. The third and fourth options were included to prevent participants providing responses based on guess work. Option c served as a distractor, while option d was used to avoid participants choosing one of the three available responses based on chance, as Figure 7.9 illustrates (see also Appendix for further examples).

Participants received two points for each correct answer and zero points for any of the three incorrect options. The maximum score that one could achieve in this task was twelve points.

In the fill-in-the-gap task, participants were presented with a picture and a German sentence containing a gap (always at the beginning of the sentence). They were asked to fill the gap with the target form. As previously mentioned the option 'I am not sure' served as a control in providing responses based on guess work, as Figure 7.10 illustrates (see also Appendix for further examples).

Altogether the task comprised of thirty terms, sixteen target items and fourteen distracters. Only target items were scored, receiving one point for

Choose which sentence corresponds better to the German sentence.

1. Den Opa fragt das Kind.

- a. The grandfather asks the child.
- b. The child asks the grandfather.
- c. Both a and b options correspond to the German sentence.
- d. I am not sure.

Figure 7.9 Interpretation task, extract from the testing materials

Figure 7.10 Fill-in-the-gap task – extract from the testing materials

each correct response. The maximum score one could achieve in this task was sixteen points.

Results

Interpretation Task

The mean scores for the interpretation task are presented in Table 7.2. A one-way ANOVA on the interpretation task showed no statistical significant differences between groups ($F(2, 96) = .407$, $p = .666$) on the pre-test.

		Pre-test		Immediate post-test		Delayed post-test	
Variable	*n*	*Mean*	*SD*	*Mean*	*SD*	*Mean*	*SD*
+IE+PI Feminine	16	.50	1.155	9.13	4.617	4.50	5.292
+IE+PI Masculine	18	.11	.471	9.22	3.300	5.78	5.219
–IE+PI Feminine	16	.25	.683	8.00	5.060	4.13	3.052
–IE+PI Masculine	17	.47	.874	7.53	5.076	5.29	5.193
–IE–PI Feminine	17	.47	1.125	.82	1.590	.35	1.057
–IE–PI Masculine	15	.53	1.187	.93	1.486	.67	1.633

Table 7.2 Means and standard deviations for interpretation task: pre-, immediate and delayed post-test

Levene's homogeneity of variance test ($p = .187$) confirmed that the three groups were equal prior to instruction. The mean scores suggest that treatment groups improved from the pre- to the immediate and delayed post-test conditions. Feminine and masculine participants of the experimental groups seem to have improved equally in the two testing conditions. The control group made no apparent improvement. Gains to the delayed post-test condition appear to be maintained for both treatment groups regardless of gender; however, scores declined.

The means were submitted to a repeated measures ANOVA with Treatment and Gender as the between-groups variables and Time as the repeated measure. The results of the repeated measures ANOVA with a Greenhouse-Geisser correction determined a significant main effect for the Time (F (1.882, 178.819) = 81.209, $p = .001$); a significant interaction between Time and Treatment (F (3.765, 178.819) = 18.022, $p = .001$); and no significant interaction between Time and Gender (F (1.882, 178.819) = .865, $p = .417$). Post-hoc Scheffe and Bonferonni tests comparing paired groups performance in the interpretation task revealed that the two experimental groups were not statistically significantly different ($p > .05$), while there were significant differences between the two experimental groups and the control group ($p < .001$). Further, two-way ANOVA tests were conducted that examined the possible effect of gender in type of instruction and interpretation task scores. Treatment and Gender were the between-groups variables and Time was the dependent variable. No significant interaction was revealed between Gender, Group and Treatment in the pre-test condition F (2, 93) = .939, $p = .395$; in the immediate post-test F (2, 93) = .061, $p = .941$; and in the delayed post-test condition F (2, 93) = .139, $p = .870$. Pairwise comparisons of groups' performance in the interpretation task revealed that the two experimental groups were not statistically significantly different ($p > .05$) in all three testing conditions (pre-, immediate and delayed post-tests); while there were significant differences between the two experimental groups and the control group ($p < .001$), in all three testing conditions. No significant differences were reported from pairwise gender comparisons in all three testing conditions in the three groups ($p < .05$).

Fill-in-the-Gap Task

The mean scores for the fill-in-the-gap task are presented in Table 7.3. In the pre-test condition of the fill-in-the-gap task no points were scored in all three groups. The mean score performance in the immediate and delayed post-test conditions shows that the two experimental groups made significant gains after instruction, while the control group did not improve at all. Standard deviation in both treatment groups in the immediate and delayed post-tests indicates that there is great variability within groups, as Table 7.3 illustrates.

The means were submitted to a repeated measures ANOVA with Treatment and Gender as the between-groups variables and Time as the repeated measure. The results of the repeated measures ANOVA determined a significant main effect for Time (F (2, 190) = 55.946, $p = .001$); a significant interaction between Time and Treatment (F (2, 190) = 17.697, $p = .001$); and no significant interaction between Time and Gender (F (2, 190) = 1.051, $p = .352$). Post-hoc Scheffe and Bonferonni tests comparing paired groups performance in the fill-in-the-gap task revealed that the two experimental groups were statistically significantly different ($p. < .05$), while there were

		Pre-test		**Immediate post-test**		**Delayed post-test**	
Variable	*n*	*Mean*	*SD*	*Mean*	*SD*	*Mean*	*SD*
+IE+PI Feminine	16	.00	.000	8.37	5.175	3.31	5.095
+IE+PI Masculine	18	.00	.000	7.50	4.342	3.67	5.145
–IE+PI Feminine	16	.00	.000	4.69	4.715	1.06	3.750
–IE+PI Masculine	17	.00	.000	3.94	4.956	2.41	4.473
–IE–PI Feminine	17	.00	.000	.00	.000	.00	.000
–IE–PI Masculine	15	.00	.000	.00	.000	.00	.000

Table 7.3 Means and standard deviations for the fill in the gap task: pre-, immediate and delayed post-test

significant differences between the two experimental groups and the control group ($p < .001$).

Further, two-way ANOVA tests were conducted that examined the possible effect of gender in type of instruction and interpretation task scores. Treatment and Gender were the between-groups variables and Time was the dependent variable. Results were reported only for the immediate and delayed post-test conditions, as participants received no points in the pre-test condition for the fill-in-the-gap task. No significant interaction was revealed between Gender, Group and Treatment in the immediate post-test F (2, 93) = .116, p = .890; and in the delayed post-test condition F (2, 93) = .271, p = .763. Pairwise comparisons of groups' performance in the fill-in-the-gap task revealed that the two experimental groups were statistically significantly different ($p. < .05$) in the immediate post-test condition. No significant differences between the two experimental groups were revealed in the delayed post-test condition ($p. > .05$). Pairwise group comparisons between the two experimental groups and the control group showed significant differences in the immediate and delayed post-test conditions ($p < .001$).

Discussion and Conclusion

The analysis of results showed that overall the two treatment groups, namely the Coloured Typographical Input Enhancement with Processing Instruction group (enhanced PI) and the Processing Instruction Group (unenhanced PI), significantly improved post-instruction, while the control group made no improvement. Effects are maintained for both experimental groups; however at a lower scale, in the long term.

Findings show that overall the two experimental groups made significant improvement post-instruction. Both improved equally in the interpretation task. Based on the mean score performance, findings show that the two groups significantly improved in the fill-in-the-gap task. However, the enhanced PI group outperformed the unenhanced PI group in the immediate post-test. No significant differences between the two experimental groups were reported in the delayed post-test. Despite a small decrease in score performance, gains were maintained 12–14 weeks post-instruction equally in both treatment groups, thus suggesting that effects of treatment, whether enhanced or unenhanced PI, are long term. Further analysis showed that individual difference, such as gender, is not a significant factor affecting performance regardless of enhanced or unenhanced PI. However, standard deviation in mean score performance in all three groups indicates that there is great variability within groups. Further research is necessary to establish whether this is the outcome of individual differences, as factors such as age; mixed abilities of original groups; exposure to the target language with different teaching styles and materials; and the use of online teaching and testing tasks may have affected results of the present study.

The main outcome of the present study is that PI, whether enhanced or unenhanced, is successful in forcing learners to process the form in order to decode the meaning of the sentence. Through its theoretical framework, namely input processing (IP), findings support that PI is successful in altering learners' processing strategies – the First Noun Principle (FNP), namely, learners relying on the first noun of the sentence in order to decode the meaning. In this study learners were forced to process the accusative case marking in German instead of relying on the FNP in order to establish who performs the action in the given sentence (German SVO vs. OVS sentences). It seems that the use of full PI type of instruction with the inclusion of explicit rule explanation has succeeded in helping learners make initial form-meaning connections. Referential activities seem to have assisted learners in establishing correct form-meaning connections, whereas affective activities reinforced correct processing (see Lee and VanPatten, 1995, 2003; VanPatten, 1996, 2002, 2004, 2007, 2009). In line with previous PI studies, results show that both experimental groups were able to produce the target form in the fill-in-the-gap task, despite the fact that participants were only engaged in input-based activities, as production of the target form was not part of the enhanced and unenhanced PI treatment package (Culman *et al.*, 2009; Fernández, 2008; VanPatten and Cadierno, 1993; VanPatten and Wong, 2004).

In addition, findings indicate that typographical IE using colour in combination with PI has also been successful in drawing learners' attention to the target linguistic form and has made the target form more salient to participants of the enhanced PI group. In turn, the external typographical input manipulation has had a positive effect in making input salient internally and in getting further processed by the language learning mechanisms (Sharwood Smith, 1991, 1993). However, further research is necessary in order to investigate the effects of typographically enhanced PI using colour.

Meta-analyses of PI and IE studies have distinguished studies between explicit and implicit types of L2 instruction (Doughty, 2003; Lee and Huang, 2008; Norris and Ortega, 2000). Based on these analyses and mean score performance of groups, it could be argued that the enhanced PI group performed better than the unenhanced PI group due to instruction type being more explicit, more obtrusive and more elaborate in making input more salient and forcing learners to make correct form-meaning connections by paying attention to the target form. However, limitations for such claims apply, as the role of coloured typographical input enhancement in combination with PI requires further investigation. The significance of the attention drawing factor that both IE and PI place seems to validate the claim that attention has a facilitative role in language learning and acquisition, according to the findings of the current study. However, neither PI nor IE provide adequate information regarding the effect and/or the operationalization of attention in the learning and acquisition process. Moreover, there is no sufficient explanation about the role of attention and how it could be utilized in a teaching intervention, as proposed by IE and/or PI in order to become more effective (Carroll, 2004; Collentine, 2004; DeKeyser *et al.*, 2002; Sharwood Smith and Trenkic, 2001). Thus, there are no adequate theoretical explanations, and it remains rather vague for both approaches, why in the present study the enhanced PI group performed better than the unenhanced PI group based on mean score performance. A plausible explanation could be that typographically coloured IE in combination with PI may have induced further attention to the target form. However, further research and theoretical support is necessary in order to validate claims and draw generalizable conclusions.

According to MOGUL, information entering through our sensory system, e.g. through POpS, can serve as the basis for higher-level processing due to the rich interconnectivity of POpS, which give rise to conscious experience (Sharwood Smith and Truscott, in press). In this study, all three groups received written input only and therefore information entering the perceptual system was available through the visual system, part of POpS. The two experimental groups did not vary quantitatively in the amount of input received. However, they did vary qualitatively, in terms of the way the input was manipulated in order to draw learners' attention and stimulate processing of the target form in the language learning system.

Regarding the enhanced PI group performing better than the unenhanced PI group, the two groups only differed in the amount of POpS available for processing. Both groups received (a) the same amount of explicit instruction; (b) the same SI activities at a sentence level; and (c) the same set of pictures. Thus, at this level groups were exactly the same in terms of exposure to input. Both groups received information through the visual structure via written input, i.e. sentences and pictures. Information entering through the visual processor was stimulating and at the same time was trying to match information from the language module, concentrating on the syntactical memory processor (as there was no oral input available) in order to formulate a conceptual structure. In IP and PI terms, this process would be translated into processing the form in order to decode the meaning of the sentence/picture. Successful processing in terms of participants' correct responses can be interpreted as the making of correct form-meaning connections for IP and PI. For MOGUL, successful processing is the build-up of a chain of structures consisting of VS–PS–SS–CS.[3] At this point processing is common for both the enhanced and unenhanced PI groups, focusing mainly on the 'blind spot', i.e. the syntactical structure, in order to stimulate and match activation at the conceptual structure to decode meaning. Processing at this stage is considered to take place without conscious awareness (Carroll, 1999, 2001, 2007; Jackendoff, 1987, 1997, 2002, 2007; Truscott and Sharwood Smith, 2004a, 2004b and Sharwood Smith and Truscott, in press). It could be hypothesized that through the coloured IE, the enhanced PI group received a greater stimulation of POpS and therefore an increase in the activation levels of conscious awareness of the processing of the structure. The written input entered the sensory system through the visual structure, while stimulation and activation generated in the language module and the conceptual structure began the process of 'indexing' (i.e. match perceptual structures and/or create new nodes), in the same way as in the unenhanced PI group. In contrast to the unenhanced PI group, coloured enhancement of the target form could have generated a parallel activation of another set of POpS processing, which focused on decoding colour from form, as well as matching form to one of the few possibly activated structures in the corresponding language module, conceptual and/or visual structures. In other words, for the second set of POpS, information that entered through the visual structure was stimulating activation in the syntactical memory store in order to match the colour to a syntactical structure (i.e. assign the nominative for light blue, the accusative case for the masculine nouns for dark blue, while pink was used for feminine and green for neuter nouns) as well as activation to the conceptual structure in order to assign meaning. The type of processing described for the enhanced PI group generates greater POpS interconnectivity than the one provided for the unenhanced PI group.

The obtained hierarchy (enhanced PI > unenhanced PI > control group) provided from mean score performance can be explained with MOGUL through successful indexing, matching (co-indexing) and high activation levels of the target structure. The differences in performance between groups indicate that the enhanced PI instructional technique has been more successful first of all in creating an index for the target structure in the lexicon. In turn, the enhanced PI teaching intervention has been effective in stimulating processing of the structure, raising its current activation levels, as well as increasing the structure's resting activation levels more frequently. It could also be argued that the enhanced PI with the integration of PI and coloured IE has achieved greater POpS interconnectivity because of the second set of POpS and has brought the target structure to higher levels of conscious awareness during online processing. In this way matching of perceptual structures with syntactical and conceptual memory structures (co-indexing) achieved through stimulation has been more effective due to frequency of activation, resulting in the making of correct form-meaning connections. Based on these findings, it could be therefore argued that coloured typographical input enhancement in combination with PI is a successful teaching intervention that could be applied in pedagogical interventions in order for learners to benefit more than the sole application of coloured typographical IE and/or PI. Gender did not have an impact on learners' performance. Standard deviation, though, showed great variability within groups, suggesting that individual differences had an effect on participants' performance, regardless of experimental group. It remains unclear to what extent there was an effect and/or which individual difference may have been a crucial factor. Based on MOGUL, this variation could be attributed to the differences in participants' own activation levels and the ability to form an index and a co-index of the particular structure, thus creating a node that will lead to 'acquisition' (or in MOGUL terms, 'growth of language').

The results of this study show that processing instruction (PI) is successful in altering the reliance of L2 learners on the First Noun Principle (FNP) and they lend support to previous studies' findings. Typographical/textual input enhancement (TTIE) with colour seems to have an effect on drawing learners' attention to the target form and in inducing saliency of the target form, resulting in the form getting further processed in the language learning mechanisms. Results show that PI can be a successful teaching intervention whether enhanced and/or unenhanced, since both groups improved post-instruction. Gains were maintained in the immediate and delayed conditions, suggesting that treatment effects are short and long term. However, based on the mean score performance it seems that coloured typographical enhanced PI can be more beneficial than unenhanced PI. Thus, it could be applied as a pedagogical intervention; however further research is necessary in order to provide generalizable conclusions. Attention seems to have a facilitative role in learning and acquiring a target form. Given the importance that attention has in the IE and PI field, further research and theoretical support is necessary in order to provide a detailed explanation about its role and operation within the two fields. Modular Online Growth and Use of Language (MOGUL) could provide the theoretical underpinnings for both approaches in providing a detailed explanation of how the two teaching interventions operate in isolation and/or in combination, as well as explain findings of studies linking theory with empirical evidence. However, limitations apply, as MOGUL is a new account of language processing, and further empirical evidence is necessary.

Notes

1. In the literature there is an overlap between the use of terms Focus on Form (FonF) and Input Enhancement (IE). In the present study the later definition is adopted.
2. Note that the circles in the model depict the different structures that can be activated once processing of a new representation begins. Depending on the activation levels that one existing structure holds the structure rises until it wins the competition and reaches the current level of activation. This is the reason why the circles are not placed all in the same level, as well as by comparison the number of circles between the phonological and syntactical memory store as depicted in the figure do not contain the same number of circles; suggesting that each structure may activate different number of structures and in different elevation stage. A fact that further shows how each structure operates not only autonomously but also in a modular way through the interfaces (similar to Cowan, 1993, 2001; Ruchkin et al., 2003; Miyake and Shah, 1999; Sharwood Smith and Truscott, 2005 and in prep; Truscott and Sharwood Smith, 2004a, 2004b).
3. Visual Structure (VS) – Phonological Structure (PS) – Syntactical Structure (SS) – Conceptual Structure (CS).

References

Alanen, R. (1995). Input enhancement and rule presentation in second language acquisition. In Schmidt, R. (ed.), *Attention and Awareness in Foreign Language Teaching* (pp. 259–301). Honolulu: University of Hawai'i Press.

Baars, B. (1988). *A Cognitive Theory of Consciousness*. New York: Cambridge University Press.

Bacon, S. M. (1992). The relationship between gender, comprehension, processing strategies and cognitive and affective response in foreign language listening. *Modern Language Journal*, 76, 160–78.

Bates, E., and MacWhinney, B. (1987). Competition, variation and language learning. In MacWhinney, B. (ed.), *Mechanisms of Language Acquisition*. Hillsdale, NJ: Lawrence Erlbaum.

Benati, A. (2001). A comparative study of the effects of processing instruction and output-based instruction on the acquisition of the Italian future tense. *Language Teaching Research*, 5, 95–127.

Benati, A. (2004). The effects of structured input activities and explicit information

on the acquisition of the Italian future tense. In VanPatten, B. (eds.), *Processing Instruction: Theory, Research, and Commentary* (pp. 207–226). Mahwah, NJ: Lawrence Erlbaum.
Boyle, J. P. (1987). Sex differences in listening vocabulary. *Language Learning*, 37, 273–84.
Carroll, S. E. (1999). Putting 'input' in its proper place. *Second Language Research*, 15, 337–88.
Carroll, S. E. (2001). *Input and Evidence*. Amsterdam: John Benjamins.
Carroll, S. E. (2004). Some comments on input processing and processing instruction. In VanPatten, B. (eds), *Processing Instruction: Theory, Research, and Commentary* (pp. 293–309). Mahwah, NJ: Lawrence Erlbaum.
Carroll, S. E. (2007). Autonomous induction theory. In VanPatten, B. and Williams, J. (eds), *Theories in Second Language Acquisition* (pp. 155–73). Mahwah, NJ: Lawrence Erlbaum Associates.
Collentine, J. (2004). Commentary: where PI research has been and where it should be going. In VanPatten, B. (ed.), *Processing Instruction: Theory, Research, and Commentary* (pp. 144–69). Mahwah, NJ: Lawrence Erlbaum.
Cowan, N. (1993). Activation, attention, and short-term memory. *Memory and Cognition*, 21, 162–67. (Reprinted in *Readings in Cognitive Psychology*, eds R. J. Sternberg and R. K. Wagner [Fort Worth, TX: Harcourt Brace, 1999]).
Cowan, N. (2001). The magical number 4 in short-term memory: a reconsideration of mental storage capacity. *Behavioral and Brain Sciences*, 24, 87–185.
Culman, H., Henry, N., and VanPatten, B. (2009). The role of explicit information in instructed SLA: an on-line study with processing instruction and German accusative case inflections. *Die Unterrichtspraxis Teaching German*, 42, 19–31.
DeKeyser, R., Salaberry, R., Robinson, P., and Harrington, M. (2002). What gets processed in processing instruction? A commentary on Bill VanPatten's processing instruction: an update. *Language Learning*, 52, 805–823.
Díaz-Campos, M. (2004). Context of learning in the acquisition of Spanish second language phonology. *Studies in Second Language Acquisition*, 26, 249–74.
Dörnyei, Z. (2005). *The Psychology of the Language Learner: Individual Differences in Second Language Acquisition*. Mahwah, NJ: Erlbaum.
Doughty, C. J. (1991). Second language instruction does make a difference. *Studies in Second Language Acquisition*, 13, 431–69.
Doughty, C. J. (2003). Instructed SLA: constraints, compensation, and enhancement. In Doughty, C. J. and Long, M. (eds) (2003), *The Handbook of Second Language Acquisition* (pp. 256–310). Malden, MA: Blackwell.
Ehrman, M. L., and Oxford, R. L. (1989). Effects of sex differences, career choice, and psychological type on adult language learning strategies. *Modern Language Journal*, 73, 1–13.
Ellis, R. (1994). *The Study of Second Language Acquisition*. Oxford: Oxford University Press.
Farhady, H. (1982). Measures of language proficiency from the learner's perspective. *TESOL Quarterly*, 16(1), 43–59.
Farley, A. P. (2004). Processing instruction and the Spanish subjunctive: is explicit information needed? In VanPatten, B. (eds), *Processing Instruction: Theory, Research, and Commentary* (pp. 227–39). Mahwah, NJ: Lawrence Erlbaum.

Fernández, C. (2008). Re-examining the role of explicit information in processing instruction. *Studies in Second Language Acquisition*, 30, 277–305.

Fodor, J. (1981). The mind-body problem. *Scientific American*, 244, 114–25.

Fodor, J. (1983). *The Modularity of Mind*. Cambridge, MA: MIT Press.

Gardner, R. C., and Lambert, W. (1972). *Attitudes and Motivation in Second Language Learning*. Rowley, MA: Newbury House.

Gass, S., and Varonis, E. (1986). Sex differences in non-native speaker – non-native speaker interactions. In Day, R. (ed.), *Talking to Learn* (pp. 327–52). Rowley, MA: Newbury House.

Harrington, M. (2004). Commentary: input processing as theory of processing input. In VanPatten, B. (eds), *Processing Instruction: Theory, Research, and Commentary* (pp. 79–93). Mahwah, NJ: Lawrence Erlbaum.

Jackendoff, R. (1987). *Consciousness and the Computational Mind*. Cambridge, MA: MIT Press.

Jackendoff, R. (1990). *Semantic Structures*. Cambridge, MA: MIT Press.

Jackendoff, R. (1997). *The Architecture of the Language Faculty*. Cambridge, MA: MIT Press.

Jackendoff, R. (2002). *Foundations of Language: Brain, Meaning, Grammar, Evolution*. Oxford: Oxford University Press.

Jackendoff, R. (2007). A parallel architecture perspective on language processing. *Brain Research*, 1146, 2–22.

Jourdenais, R., Ota, M., Stauffer, S., Boyson, B., and Doughty, C. (1995). Does textual enhancement promote noticing? In Schmidt, R. (eds), *Attention and Awareness in Foreign Language Teaching* (pp. 183–216). Honolulu: University of Hawai'i Press.

Larsen-Freeman, D., and Long, M. (1991). *An Introduction to Second Language Acquisition Research*. London: Longman.

Lee, J., and Benati, A. (2007). *Second Language Processing: An Analysis of Theory, Problems and Possible Solutions*. London: Continuum.

Lee, S. K., and Huang, H. T. (2008). Visual input enhancement and grammar learning: a meta-analytic review. *Studies in Second Language Acquisition*, 30, 307–331.

Lee, J. F., and VanPatten, B. (2003) [1995]. *Making Communicative Language Teaching Happen*, 2nd edn. New York: McGraw-Hill.

Leeman, J., Arteagoitia, I., Fridman, B., and Doughty, C. (1995). Integrating attention to form and meaning: focus on form in content- based Spanish instruction. In Schmidt, R. (eds), *Attention and Awareness in Foreign Language Teaching* (pp. 217–58). Honolulu: University of Hawai'i Press.

Leow, R. (1997). The effects of input enhancement and text length on adult L2 readers' comprehension and intake in second language acquisition. *Applied Language Learning*, 8, 151–82.

Leow, R. (2001). Do learners notice enhanced forms while interacting with the L2?: an online and offline study of the role of written input enhancement in L2 reading. *Hispania*, 84, 496–509.

Levelt, W. (1999). Producing spoken language: a blueprint of the speaker. In Brown, C. and Hagoort, P. (eds), *The Neurocognition of Language* (pp. 83–154). Oxford: Oxford University Press.

Levelt, W. J. M., Roelofs, A. P. A., and Meyer, A. S. (1999). A theory of lexical access in speech production. *Behavioral and Brain Sciences*, 22, 1–37.

Miyake, A., and Shah, P. (1999). *Models of Working Memory*. New York: Cambridge University Press.

Norris, J., and Ortega, L. (2000). Effectiveness of L2 instruction. *Language Learning*, 50, 417–528.

Nyikos, M. (1990). Sex-related differences in adult language learning: socialization and memory factors. *Modern Language Journal*, 74, 273–87.

Overstreet, M. (1998). Text enhancement and content familiarity: the focus of learner attention. *Spanish Applied Linguistics*, 2, 229–58.

Oxford, R. L. (1993). *La différence continue...* Gender differences in second/foreign language learning styles and strategies. In Sutherland, J. (ed.), *Exploring Gender* (pp. 140–47). Englewood Cliffs, NJ: Prentice-Hall.

Politzer, R. L. (1983). An exploratory study of self reported language learning behaviors and their relation to achievement. *Studies in Second Language Acquisition*, 6, 55–68.

Ruchkin, D. S., Grafman, J., Cameron, K., and Berndt, R. S. (2003). Working memory retention systems: a state of activated long-term memory. *Behavioral and Brain Sciences*, 26, 709–728.

Rutherford, W., and Sharwood Smith, M. (1987). *Grammar and Second Language Teaching: A Book of Readings*. Rowley, MA: Newbury House.

Salaberry, R. (1998). On input processing, true language competence and pedagogical bandwagons: a reply to Sanz and VanPatten. *Canadian Modern Language Review*, 54, 274–84.

Sanz, C. (2004a). *Mind and Context in Adult Second Language Acquisition*. Washington, DC: Georgetown University Press.

Sanz, C. (2004b). Computer delivered implicit versus explicit feedback in processing instruction. In VanPatten, B. (eds), *Processing Instruction: Theory, Research, and Commentary* (pp. 241–55). Mahwah, NJ: Lawrence Erlbaum.

Sanz, C., and Morgan-Short, K. (2004). Positive evidence versus explicit rule presentation and explicit negative feedback: a computer-assisted study. *Language Learning*, 54, 5–79.

Schmidt, R. (1990). The role of consciousness in second language learning. *Applied Linguistics*, 11, 129–58.

Schmidt, R. (1993). Awareness and second language acquisition. *Annual Review of Applied Linguistics*, 13, 206–226.

Schmidt, R. (eds) (1995). *Attention and Awareness in Foreign Language Teaching*. Honolulu: University of Hawai'i Press.

Schmidt, R. (2001). Attention. In Robinson, P. (ed.), *Cognition and Second Language Instruction* (pp. 3–32). Cambridge: Cambridge University Press.

Sharwood Smith, M. (1991). Speaking to many minds: on the relevance of different types of language information for the L2 learner. *Second Language Research*, 7, 118–32.

Sharwood Smith, M. (1993). Input enhancement in instructed SLA: theoretical bases. *Studies in Second Language Acquisition*, 15, 165–79.

Sharwood Smith, M., and Trenkic, D. (2001). Re-evaluating theoretical and methodological aspects of focus on form research. Paper presented at EUROSLA 11, Paderborn, 26-29 September 2001.

Sharwood Smith, M., and Truscott, J. (2005). Stages or continua in second language acquisition: a mogul solution. *Applied Linguistics*, 22, 219–40.

Sharwood Smith, M., and Truscott, J. (in press). Modular growth and use of language: a processing perspective. Unpublished draft manuscript (cited with permission).

Spolsky, B. (1989). *Conditions for Second Language Learning*. Oxford: Oxford University Press.

Tomlin, R., and Villa, V. (1994). Attention in cognitive science and second language acquisition. *Studies in Second Language Acquisition*, 16, 183–204.

Truscott, J. (1998). Noticing in second language acquisition: a critical review. *Second Language Acquisition Research*, 14, 103–135.

Truscott, J., and Sharwood Smith, M. (2004a). How APT is your theory: present status and future prospects. *Bilingualism: Language and Cognition*, 7, 43–47.

Truscott, J., and Sharwood Smith, M. (2004b). Acquisition by processing: a modular perspective on language development. *Bilingualism: Language and Cognition*, 7, 1–20.

VanPatten, B. (1996). *Input Processing and Grammar Instruction*. Norwood, NJ: Ablex.

VanPatten, B. (2002). Processing instruction: an update. *Language Learning*, 52, 755–803.

VanPatten, B. (eds) (2004). *Processing Instruction: Theory, Research and Commentary*. Mahwah, NJ: Lawrence Erlbaum.

VanPatten, B. (2007). Input processing in adult second language acquisition. In VanPatten, B. and Williams, J. (eds), *Theories in Second Language Acquisition* (pp. 115–35). Mahwah, NJ: Lawrence Erlbaum.

VanPatten, B. (2009). Processing matters in input enhancement. In Piske, T. and Young-Scholten, M. (eds), *Input Matters in SLA* (pp. 47–61). Clevedon: Multilingual Matters.

VanPatten, B., and Borst, S. (2012). The roles of explicit information and grammatical sensitivity in processing instruction: nominative-accusative case marking and word order in German L2. *Foreign Language Annals*, 45, 92–109.

VanPatten, B., and Cadierno, T. (1993). Explicit instruction and input processing. *Studies in Second Language Acquisition*, 15, 225–44.

VanPatten, B., and Fernandez, C. (2004). The long-term effects of processing instruction. In VanPatten, B. (eds), *Processing Instruction: Theory, Research and Commentary* (pp. 273–89). Mahwah, NJ: Lawrence Erlbaum.

VanPatten, B., and Oikennon, S. (1996). Explanation vs. structured input in processing instruction. *Studies in Second Language Acquisition*, 18, 495–510.

VanPatten, B., and Wong, W. (2004). Processing instruction and the French causative: another replication. In VanPatten, B. (eds), *Processing Instruction: Theory, Research, and Commentary* (pp. 97–118). Mahwah, NJ: Lawrence Erlbaum.

Wong, W. (2003). Textual enhancement and simplified input: Effects on L2 comprehension and acquisition of non-meaningful grammatical form. *Applied Language Learning*, 13 (2):17-45.

Wong, W. (2004). The nature of processing instruction. In VanPatten, B. (eds), *Processing Instruction: Theory, Research and Commentary* (pp. 3–63). Mahwah, NJ: Lawrence Erlbaum.

Wong, W. (2005). *Input Enhancement: From Theory and Research to Classroom*. New York: McGraw-Hill.

Appendix

A. Treatment materials – Referential and Affective Activities

Unenhanced PI group

Choose (a) if the picture corresponds to the sentence, (b) if it does not, and (c) if you are not sure:

Den Freund vermisst das Mädchen.

a. yes
b. no
c. I am not sure

Enhanced PI group

Choose (a) if the picture corresponds to the sentence, (b) if it does not, and (c) if you are not sure:

Den Freund vermisst **das** Mädchen.

a. yes
b. no
c. I am not sure

Unenhanced PI group

Put the following sentences into a chronological order so that a story can be told.

a. Den Vater pflegt die Mutter. ____
b. Den Dieb sieht der Vater im Zimmer. ____
c. Der Vater ruft sofort die Polizei an. ____
d. Der Vater schlägt der Dieb und geht weg. ____
e. Den Vater weckt die Mutter. ____

Enhanced PI group

Put the following sentences into a chronological order so that a story can be told.

a. **Den** Vater pflegt die Mutter. ____
b. **Den** Dieb sieht der Vater im Zimmer. ____
c. Der Vater ruft sofort die Polizei an. ____
d. Der Vater schlägt der Dieb und geht weg. ____
e. **Den** Vater weckt die Mutter. ____

B. Testing materials

Examples of the interpretation task:

Choose which sentence corresponds better to the German sentence:

1. Den Bruder sucht die Schwester.
   a. The brother is looking for the sister.
   b. The sister is looking for the brother.
   c. Both (a) and (b) options correspond to the German sentence.
   d. I am not sure.
2. Den Vater weckt der Bruder.
   a. The father wakes up the brother.
   b. The brother wakes up the father.
   c. Both (a) and (b) options correspond to the German sentence.
   d. I am not sure.

Examples of the fill-in-the-gap task:

1. Fill in the gap according to the situation in the picture:

_____ Mann begrüßt die Frau.

a. I am not sure.
b. Answer:

2. Fill in the gap according to the situation in the picture:

______ Delfin reitet der Mann.

a. I am not sure.
b. Answer:

8 The Effects of Processing Instruction and Traditional Instruction on Two Different School-age Learners: The Case of English Present Simple Tense Third Person Singular

Marina Mavrantoni, New York College, Athens (Greece)*
and Alessandro G. Benati, University of Greenwich (UK)**

Introduction

The aim of the present study is to investigate the extent to which two different approaches to grammar instruction affect young learners of different ages in the acquisition of a specific grammatical feature, namely the third singular person of the English present simple tense. The participants were school-age learners studying English in two private schools in Greece. They

* **Marina Mavrantoni** studied English Language and Literature at the National Kapodistrian University of Athens and completed an MA in Management of Language Learning, at New York College, Athens. Her research focuses on the effects of processing instruction on the acquisition of the English present tense. She has been teaching English as a foreign language in Greece for the last ten years.

** **Alessandro Benati** is Director of Research and Enterprise in the School of Humanities and Social Sciences at the University of Greenwich. He is an academic scholar in the area of second language acquisition. His research focuses on how language learners process incoming linguistic information at input level. He has worked extensively with James Lee on various projects. He has published books and journal papers in the areas of second language teaching and language acquisition. He is editor of an international book series in Instructed Second Language Research (Continuum Publishing).

were native speakers of Greek and were 8–10 years old in the first school and 15–17 years old in the second school. The effects of processing instruction were compared to traditional instruction among two different school ages (pre-puberty and post-puberty). Processing instruction (PI) is an effective approach to grammar instruction that works with those processes the learners use to get linguistic data from the input. Traditional instruction (TI), on the other hand, provides explanation through rules and paradigms of the target structure and engages students in mechanical output-based practice.

The grammatical feature chosen for this study is the English third person singular present simple tense (*–s*). There are two main reasons as to why this form was chosen. First, it is a feature that has been investigated within the processing instruction research framework as a transfer-of-training effect (Benati, Lee and Houghton, 2008) but not as a direct or primary effect of instruction. Secondly, it is affected by a combination of processing principles: the Preference for Nonredundancy Principle and the Lexical Preference Principle (VanPatten, 2004, 2007). The meaning encoded in the inflection *–s* (action happening regularly) can be encoded through time expressions, too (every day, once a month, often). The study presented in this chapter aims at examining whether PI can manipulate these processing principles and whether it helps students equally from distinct age groups to interpret and produce sentences containing tense third person singular forms of the English present simple tense.

Previous Research on Processing Instruction

There is a large database of studies comparing the relative effects of processing instruction and traditional grammar instruction. VanPatten and Cadierno (1993) compared PI and TI in the acquisition of object pronouns and word order in Spanish. This feature is affected by the First Noun Principle which indicates that learners process the first element they encounter in a sentence as the agent of that sentence (VanPatten, 2004). Eighty students who were enrolled in their second year of Spanish at the University of Illinois participated in the study. They were divided into three groups (PI group, TI group and a control group). The results confirmed that the PI group performed better than the TI group in an interpretation task which measured learners' capacity to correctly interpret sentences containing the target feature. Both PI and TI groups performed equally well on the production task.

Cadierno (1995) investigated the effects of TI and PI on the acquisition of a different linguistic feature, the Spanish *preterit* tense (past simple). The target feature is affected by the Lexical Preference Principle which states that learners tend to rely on lexical items instead of the morphological markers to get meaning when both encode the same semantic information (VanPatten, 2004). The three treatment groups (TI, PI and a control group) consisted of students enrolled in their second year of Spanish at university. The results showed that the PI group outperformed the TI group on the interpretation task and the two groups made equal gains in the production task.

Cheng (1995) also researched the effects of PI and TI on the acquisition of the Spanish copular verbs *ser* and *estar* using a PI group, a TI group and a control group. The target feature investigated in this study is affected by the Preference for Nonredundancy Principle which states that L2 learners are more likely to process non-redundant meaningful grammatical forms before they process redundant meaningful forms (VanPatten, 2004). Subjects were drawn from the same student population as in the two previous studies. The results confirmed the effectiveness of PI. The PI group outperformed the TI and control group on the comprehension task. On the sentence completion task and the composition task both treatment groups improved equally.

Benati (2001) compared the effects of PI and TI on the acquisition of the Italian future tense among university learners. Like the Spanish past tense, this feature is affected by the Lexical Preference Principle. For this experiment three groups were formed (PI, TI and a control group). Once again the results indicated that participants who had received PI performed better on the interpretation task than the TI group. Both PI and TI groups made equal gains on the production task.

VanPatten and Wong (2004) researched the effectiveness of PI and TI on the acquisition of the French causative *faire*. The processing principle affecting the target structure is the First Noun Principle. Three groups of undergraduate students learning French in two different universities were the sample population for this experiment. The results showed that the PI group performed significantly better than the TI group on the interpretation task and the two groups performed equally well on the written production test.

Benati (2005) also compared PI and TI on the acquisition of the English past simple tense, which is affected by the Lexical Preference Principle. This time a third group receiving a different and more meaningful output-based (MOI) approach to grammar instruction was used. The experiment was carried out in two different secondary schools in China and Greece with native speakers of Chinese and Greek, respectively. The results revealed that on the interpretation task both Chinese and Greek PI groups made significant progress compared to TI groups and the MOI groups which made no significant improvements. All treatment groups made equal gains on the written production task. This study is also notable as it is the second PI study to examine secondary school-aged learners, the first being VanPatten and Oikennon (1996).

Research Questions

The studies reviewed in the previous section demonstrate that PI is a better instructional treatment in affecting learners' ability to interpret and process language input. PI enhances learners' competence to make better form-meaning connections by providing structured input activities which force them to pay attention to forms in the input in order to process meaning. PI is also effective in enhancing learners' ability to produce the target structure. The vast majority of the classroom experiments comparing PI and TI involved adult second language learners studying at university level, with English as their mother tongue. The aim of the present study is to compare PI and TI using two participant groups from different school-age populations (pre-puberty and post-puberty) and with a language background that has been examined only once in PI research, i.e., Greek native-speaking school-age students learning English. The target structure is the English third person singular present simple tense. This linguistic feature has not been investigated before as a primary linguistic target within the processing instruction research framework. Two parallel studies were conducted among two distinct age groups and a set of three research questions were formulated.

1. What are the relative effects of PI and TI on the acquisition of the English third singular person present simple tense as measured by a sentence-level interpretation task?
2. What are the relative effects of PI and TI on the acquisition of the English third singular person present simple tense as measured by a production task?
3. Does the learners' age affect the performance of the two PI groups on a sentence-level interpretation task and a production task?

Method

Participants

The participants were school-age learners enrolled in two different private institutions in Greece. All were native speakers of Greek. In the first school, the original pool of 27 students aged 8–10 was reduced to 20. Learners were randomly distributed to the PI group (n = 10) and the TI group (n = 10). In the second school, a total of 19 students aged 15–17 was reduced to 14 following the implementation of a number of selection procedures. Learners in this second experiment were randomly assigned to the PI group (n = 7) and TI group (n = 7). Only learners who had received no previous instruction on the target feature were included in the final pool. To be included in the final data collection, participants had to score 50% or lower on the pre-test battery.

Procedures

The pre-test battery was administered to all participants a week before commencing both classroom experiments. The way teaching is scheduled in both schools allowed for the treatments to be carried out over two consecutive days for a total of three hours' instruction for each group in both experiments. One of the researchers served as the instructor of the two groups and participants were informed about the nature of the experiment. However, learners were reassured that their scores on the tests would not be taken into account as part of their final trimester marks. Post-tests were administered immediately after instruction.

Materials

Both groups in the two parallel studies received the same amount of explicit information and number of activities (10 for each treatment for a total of 100 target features) for three hours' instruction. Vocabulary and verbs used were the same in both instructional treatments. The only difference between the two groups was the instructional practice: input processing-based vs. output-based practice. Two instructional packets were developed for this experiment. Sample activities are provided in Appendix A and Appendix B. The PI packet consisted of a one-page handout containing explicit information on the target feature translated into Greek for the students and a set of structured input activities. The part of the handouts with the explicit information was also presented verbally by the instructor who informed learners about the processing problem affecting the acquisition of the target feature. Learners in the PI groups were told not to rely on pronouns or any lexical items to interpret who performed the action but rather to focus on the verb ending. The rest of the packet contained a balanced number of affective and referential structured input activities during which the students were asked to process and interpret the targeted form in order to complete the task. Learners in the PI groups were never asked to produce the target linguistic feature. Structured input activities were developed following the guidelines proposed by Lee and VanPatten (1995; 2003). For this study we developed a series of affective structured input activities. The purpose of affective activities is to provide learners with an input flood of the target structure which serves as positive evidence. Affective activities require learners to express their opinion or personal experiences by processing the target grammatical item which appeared in either aural or written form. A sample of a written affective activity is provided in Figure 8.1. Structured input activities were meaningful and communicative, and were developed so that learners had the opportunity to process the target form correctly and efficiently.

The TI packet, which is provided in Appendix B, also consisted of two parts: the explicit information handout which incorporated explicit information on the English present simple tense; and a set of production activities. The handout which included the explicit information was translated into Greek and was quite different to the one the PI group received because the target form was presented in a paradigmatic way to the TI groups. After learners were explained the rules, they were engaged in mechanical output-practice. Two examples of traditional practice are provided in Figure 8.2 which demonstrate that the TI groups had to produce all forms of the present simple tense.

What's right?

Step 1
Read each sentence and then decide whether or not it is right about your class teacher. Indicate your answer with an 'X'.

My Teacher…

	Right	Wrong
….. arrives to school early.	____	_____
….. wears colourful clothes.	____	_____
….. drinks coffee before each lesson.	____	_____

Step 2
Do you think your teacher is much different than other teachers in your school? Why?

Figure 8.1 Affective activity

1. Circle the correct word.

Every day my family and I (1) **wake/wakes** up at 7.30 am. We (2) **eat/eats** breakfast at 8 o'clock. Mum (3) **prepare/prepares** eggs... (The activity continues in a similar fashion)

2. Fill in the blanks with the present simple form of the verbs in brackets.
   1. I never................(drink) coffee.
   2. We often.............(eat) in the office.
   3. He .... (meet) his friend every day.

Figure 8.2 Traditional practice

Assessment Instruments and Scoring

A pre/post-test procedure using a split block design was utilized in order to assess the possible effects of the two treatments. Two versions of the test were developed and are provided in Appendix C. Both versions were balanced in terms of vocabulary and difficulty and included a sentence-level comprehension task and a written production task. The interpretation task consisted of 20 items, 10 targets (third person singular) and 10 distracters (third person plural). The participants were asked to listen to the items read by the instructor and indicate whether the action is performed by one agent or by multiple agents. In case students were not sure about their answer, they could choose the option *Not sure*. A sample from the interpretation task is provided in Figure 8.3.

Raw scores were calculated for the interpretation task. Each correct response on the target items was given a score of 1 point. No points were given for correct answers on the distracter items and for incorrect responses. The highest possible score was 10 points and the lowest was 0 points.

Listen to the following sentences and decide whether or not each sentence is referring to Patrick or his school friends.

Patrick	**school friends**	**not sure**	(Sentences heard by the students)
_______	_______	_______	plays basketball every day.
_______	_______	_______	reads a lot of comics.
_______	_______	_______	hates popcorn.

Figure 8.3 Sample from interpretation task

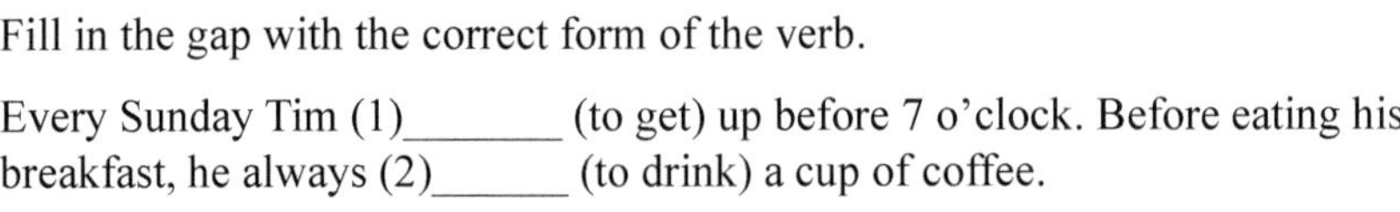
Fill in the gap with the correct form of the verb.

Every Sunday Tim (1)_______ (to get) up before 7 o'clock. Before eating his breakfast, he always (2)______ (to drink) a cup of coffee.

Figure 8.4 Sample from production task

The written production task was developed to measure the students' ability to produce the target form. Students were provided with a small passage which required them to fill in the blanks with the correct form of the verbs provided in brackets. The paragraph was referring to a person's daily routine and there were 10 gaps all of which required the production of the verb in the third person singular of the present simple tense. A sample of the production task is provided in Figure 8.4. The scoring procedure that was used in this task was 1 point if the students correctly produced the target form and 0 points for any incorrect responses. Again, students could achieve a maximum score of 10 points.

The pre-test design was administered one week prior to the experiment and the post-test ten minutes after the end of the instructional period. The raw scores for each test were submitted to separate analyses of variance (ANOVA) for which the between-groups variable was Instruction (PI, TI) and the within-group repeated measure was Time. The dependent variables were the scores on the interpretation and production tasks.

Results

First Experiment (School-age Learners 8–10)

Mean scores for the two groups are provided in Table 8.1. The one-way ANOVA carried out on the pre-test scores showed no significant differences among the instructional groups before the treatment period (F (1, 19) = 0.720, p = .496). Therefore any possible gains in the post-test scores will be attributed to the instructional interventions and not any previous knowledge of the subjects. The means show that the PI subjects improved from pre-test to post-test (55%). The TI group's performance not only did not improve but actually decreased. A repeated measures ANOVA was used on the raw scores of the interpretation data. The statistical analysis showed that there is a significant main effect for Instruction, F (1, 19) = 45.051, p = .000; a significant main effect for Time (F (1, 19) = 11.021, p = .000); and a significant interaction between Instruction and Time (F (2, 19) = 34.016, p = .000).

		Pre-test		Post-test	
Variable	*n*	*Mean*	*SD*	*Mean*	*SD*
PI	10	3.10	1.37	8.60	2.17
TI	10	3.20	1.68	1.60	1.71

Table 8.1 Means and standard deviations for interpretation task (pre-test and post-test) for learners aged 8–10

		Pre-test		Post-test	
Variable	*n*	*Mean*	*SD*	*Mean*	*SD*
PI	10	1.50	1.50	6.50	1.84
TI	10	1.80	0.78	5.50	1.58

Table 8.2 Means and standard deviations for production task (pre-test and post-test) for learners aged 8–10

These results demonstrate that the processing instruction group, aged 8–10, gained in its ability to interpret English third person singular present simple tense at the sentence-level but that the traditional instruction group did not.

Mean scores and standard deviations for both treatment groups are displayed in Table 8.2. The one-way ANOVA conducted on the pre-test scores for the production task revealed no statistically significant difference between the groups before the beginning of the instructional period (F (1, 19) = 1.226, p = .310). The means show that both treatment groups improved from pre-test to post-test. The PI group made an improvement of 50%, whereas the TI group made an improvement of 37%. A repeated measures ANOVA was used on the raw scores of the written production task. The statistical analysis showed that there is no significant main effect for Instruction (F (1, 19) = 15.891, p = .439; a significant main effect for Time (F (1, 19) = 65.179, p = .000); and no significant interaction between Instruction and and Time (F (1, 19) = 11.034, p = .195). These results demonstrate that the processing instruction group and the traditional instruction group made statistically equal gains in their ability to produce sentences containing English third person singular present simple tense forms.

Second Experiment (School-age Learners 15–17)

Table 8.3 provides the descriptive statistics on the performance for both the processing instruction groups and the traditional instruction group (learners

		Pre-test		Post-test	
Variable	*n*	*Mean*	*SD*	*Mean*	*SD*
PI	7	3.20	1.13	8.30	1.37
TI	7	3.34	1.32	2.46	1.12

Table 8.3 Means and standard deviations for interpretation task (pre-test and post-test) for learners aged 15–17

aged 15–17) on the sentence-level interpretation task. The one-way ANOVA conducted on the pre-test scores showed no significant differences between the two groups before instruction (F (1, 13) = 2.032, p = .678). Any differences found after instruction will be attributed to the effects of instruction. The processing instruction group improved from pre-test to post-test (59%), whereas the traditional instruction group made no gains.

The raw scores of the sentence-level interpretation pre-test and post-tests were submitted to a repeated measures ANOVA. The ANOVA showed a significant main effect for Instruction (F (1, 13) = 13.021, p = .000); a significant effect for Time (F (1, 13) = 22.134, p = .000); and a significant interaction between Instruction and Time (F (1, 13) = 34.036, p = .000). These results demonstrate that the processing instruction group gained in their ability to interpret English third person singular present simple tense but that the traditional instruction groups did not.

The descriptive statistics for the production task are displayed in Table 8.4. The one-way ANOVA conducted on the pre-test for the production task revealed no statistically significant difference between the groups before the beginning of the instructional period (F (1, 13) = 2.214, p = .456). The mean scores show that both treatment groups improved from pre-test to post-test. The PI group made an improvement of 50% whereas the TI group made an improvement of 52% from pre-test to post-test. A repeated measures ANOVA was used on the raw scores of the written production task.

		Pre-test		Post-test	
Variable	*n*	*Mean*	*SD*	*Mean*	*SD*
PI	7	1.35	0.50	6.35	1.04
TI	7	1.48	1.18	6.50	1.25

Table 8.4 Means and standard deviations for production task (pre-test and post-test) for learners aged 15–17

The statistical analysis showed that there is no significant main effect for Instruction (F (1, 13) = 10.493, p = .379; a significant main effect for Time (F (1, 13) = 54.239, p = .000); and no significant interaction between Instruction and Time (F (1, 13) = 9.458, p = .147). These results demonstrate that the processing instruction group and the traditional instruction group (aged 15–17) made statistically equal gains in their ability to produce sentences containing English third person singular present simple tense forms.

Comparison of the Processing Instruction Groups in the Two Experiments

In both experiments the two PI groups made similar improvements in the interpretation tasks. A one-way ANOVA was conducted on the pre-tests and revealed no significant differences among the groups' means (F (1, 16) = 12.348, p = .143). As seen in Tables 8.1 and 8.3 their gains were between 55% and 59% from the pre-test to the post-test. We then directly compared the performance of the two different age groups. A repeated measured ANOVA was conducted on the raw scores of the interpretation task (pre-test and post-test). Age Group (8–10 vs. 15–17) was the between-subjects factor, whereas Time (pre-test vs. post-test) was the within-subjects repeated measure. The results from the statistical analysis revealed a significant main effect for Time (F (1, 16) = 53.458, p = .000); no significant main effect for Age Group (F (1, 16) = 21.528, p = .458); and no significant interaction between Age Group and Time (F (1, 16) = 71.347, p = .156). These results indicate that both age groups made equal improvement from pre-test to post-test on the interpretation task.

In both experiments the two PI groups also made equal improvements in the written production task. A one-way ANOVA was conducted on the pre-tests and revealed no significant differences among the groups' means (F (1, 16) = 21.269, p = .121). As seen in Tables 8.2 and 8.4 their gains were 50% in both PI groups. A repeated measured ANOVA was conducted on the raw scores of the written production task. Age Group (8–10 vs. 15–17) was the between-subjects factor, whereas Time (pre-test vs. post-test) was the within-subjects repeated measure. The statistical analysis show a significant main effect for Time (F (1, 16) = 45.368, p = .000); no significant main effect for Age Group (F (1, 16) = 14.244, p = .453); and no significant interaction between Age Group and Time (F (1, 28) = 12.037, p = .249). These results indicate that both age groups made equal improvements from pre-test to post-test on the production written task.

Discussion and Conclusion

The present study specifically investigated the effects of two instructional approaches to grammar instruction on the acquisition of English third person singular present simple tense. The results of previous studies suggest that PI is a more effective and beneficial approach to grammar instruction than traditional instruction (VanPatten and Cadierno, 1993; Cadierno, 1995; Cheng, 1995; Benati, 2001; Benati, 2005). The two first questions of this study were answered positively in favour of the PI treatment. The results from both experiments confirmed the findings of previous research as the PI groups significantly outperformed the TI groups in the interpretation tasks.

The participants in the TI group were engaged in highly mechanical activities that required a focus on using the target structure to produce some sort of meaningless utterance. Because there is no message to be communicated there is an absence of meaning. This kind of practice is claimed to be ineffective and does not promote acquisition. PI provided participants with the opportunity to process the target form efficiently and appropriately. PI was successful at altering the way learners from different age groups process verbal morphology that is subject to the Lexical Preference Principle. The findings from the written production task indicated that the PI and TI groups made equal gains in their ability to produce the target form. Again, these findings support the main results of previous research on PI. This input-based approach to grammar instruction not only positively affects learners' ability to interpret the target form, but also their ability to produce it. As VanPatten claimed (1996: 96), 'apparently the intake data made available to the developing system as a result of input processing had an impact on the system such that learners were able to access the new knowledge and use it during production'. These findings are particularly important as participants of the PI group did not produce the grammatical feature at any time during instruction.

Regarding the third question of the study, it was found that processing instruction is of equal benefit to different school-aged learners, pre-puberty and post-puberty. The findings support the results obtained by most previous research and confirm the effectiveness of PI in improving learners' performance on both interpretation and production tasks no matter the age of the learners. Further, the results of the experiment stress the important role of structured input activities. Through this kind of practice learners are pushed to process input in order to make form-meaning connections. As a result, the developing system grows stronger via richer intake so that, in turn, learners can comprehend the message via processing the target form and also produce the target linguistic forms.

There are a number of limitations of the present study. Firstly, the size of participant pools in both experiments was small. Due to a number of practical factors it was difficult for a larger number of participants to be involved in the two studies. Therefore, a replication of the two studies including a larger number of participants is necessary to generalize these findings. Secondly, it was not possible to administer a delayed post-test to measure the long-term effects of the treatments.

Further research needs to be carried out to investigate these limitations to measure the effectiveness of PI on age differences. So far the outcomes of the present study clearly indicate that PI is equally effective among school-age learners of different ages. Learners who receive PI significantly improve in their ability to interpret and produce linguistic forms, whereas learners who receive traditional instruction improve only in their ability to produce the form.

References

Benati, A. (2001). A comparative study of the effects of processing instruction and output-based instruction on the acquisition of the Italian future tense. *Language Teaching Research*, 5, 95–127.

Benati, A. (2005). The effects of processing instruction, traditional instruction and meaning-output instruction on the acquisition of the English past simple tense. *Language Teaching Research*, 9, 87–113.

Benati, A., Lee, J. F., and Houghton, S. (2008). Chapter 4: From processing instruction on the acquisition of English past tense to secondary transfer-of-training effects on English third person singular present tense. In Benati, A. and Lee, J. F., *Grammar Acquisition and Processing Instruction: Secondary and Cumulative Effects* (pp. 88–120). Bristol: Multilingual Matters.

Cadierno, T. (1995). Formal instruction from a processing prospective: an investigation into the Spanish past tense. *Modern Language Journal*, 79, 179–93.

Cheng, A. C. (1995). Grammar instruction and input processing: the acquisition of Spanish ser and estar. Doctoral dissertation. University of Illinois at Urbana-Champaign. Dissertation Abstracts International, 56, 3485A–3486A.

Lee, J., and VanPatten, B. (2003) [1995]. *Making Communicative Language Teaching Happen*, 2nd ed. New York: McGraw-Hill.

VanPatten, B. (1996). *Input Processing and Grammar Instruction: Theory and Research.* Norwood, NJ: Ablex.

VanPatten, B. (2004). Input processing in SLA. In VanPatten, B. (ed.), *Processing Instruction: Theory, Research and Commentary* (pp. 5–31). Mahwah, NJ: Erlbaum.

VanPatten, B. (2007). Input processing in adult SLA. In VanPatten, B., and Williams, J. (eds), *Theories in SLA: An Introduction* (pp. 115–35). Mahwah, NJ: Lawrence Erlbaum.

VanPatten, B., and Cadierno, T. (1993). Explicit instruction and input processing. *Studies in Second Language Acquisition*, 15, 225–43.

VanPatten, B., and Oikennon, S. (1996). Explanation vs. structured input in processing instruction. *Studies in Second Language Acquisition*, 18, 495–510.

VanPatten, B., and Wong, W. (2004). Processing instruction and the French causative: another replication. In VanPatten, B. (ed.), *Processing Instruction: Theory, Research, and Commentary* (pp. 97–118). Mahwah, NJ: Erlbaum.

Appendix A

Instructional Material for Processing Instruction (sample)

Explicit Information (Teacher's notes)

- We use the present simple tense to talk about things in general. We use it to say that something happens all the time or repeatedly,or that something is true in general,but simple present tense verbs have a special form for the **third person singular** where the verb ends in –**s** or –**es**. For example [*write on board*]:
  I get up at 8 o'clock every morning. = first person singular.
  She get**s** up at 8 o'clock every morning. = third person singular.
- The third person singular forms are represented by the pronouns **he, she, it or special names.**
  For example [*write on board*]:
  She sleep**s** eight hours a day or Jennifer sleep**s** eight hours a day.
- Can anybody tell me which sentence is correct?
  I likes cheddar cheese (b) He like cheddar cheese (c) She likes cheddar cheese.

  [*Brainstorm some sentences then write them on board*]
  She walks everyday, he plays football every afternoon, John watches TV every night.

VERY IMPORTANT!

- **Do not rely on pronouns or explicit subjects (names) to understand who is doing the action or to whom the verb is referring. Sometimes you will hear a sentence without explicit subjects (names) or pronouns.**
- **You must pay attention to the verb ending to understand who is doing the action or to whom the verb is referring.**
- **In this case of describing who is doing the action or to whom the verb is referring, pay attention to the verb: –s or –es.** [the teacher circles and underlines –**s** and –**es** in the examples]

Activity 1 (Referential)

Patty

Listen to the following statements taken from a magazine article about the life of a TV star Patty and indicate with an 'X' whether you agree or disagree with each statement.

- **Step 1**

I agree…	I disagree…	[*Sentences heard by students*]
_____	_____	1… sings very well.
_____	_____	2… earns a lot of money.
_____	_____	3… plays the piano.
_____	_____	4… writes a lot of songs.
_____	_____	5… dances at parties.
_____	_____	6… makes video-clips.
_____	_____	7… gives concerts all over the world.
_____	_____	8… wears funny glasses.
_____	_____	9… wears different clothes.
_____	_____	10… eats a lot.

- **Step 2**
  Now compare your answers with your partner. Do you think Patty is a famous TV star? Why?

Activity 2 (Referential)

Your best friend's weekend

- **Step 1**
  Read the following statements about the things your best friend usually does on Sundays and decide if they are true or not true.

My best friend …	TRUE	NOT TRUE
1… sleeps until midday.	☐	☐
2… drinks coffee.	☐	☐
3… eats lunch at 2pm.	☐	☐
4… watches television.	☐	☐
5… phones his/her friends for a chat.	☐	☐
6… reads comic magazines.	☐	☐
7… plays Playstation.	☐	☐
8… skateboards.	☐	☐
9… listens to his/her MP3 player.	☐	☐
10… goes to bed around 11pm.	☐	☐

- **Step 2**
  Now decide in pairs whether your best friend's weekends are normally active or lazy.

Activity 3 (Referential)

- **Step 1 Leonardo's profile**
  Look at the information given for each person in the chart and tick the correct sentences about Leonardo.

	Country	**City**	**Job**	**Languages**	**Hobbies**
Robert	England	London	Doctor	English and Spanish	Running and reading
Leonardo	Italy	Venice	Footballer	Italian	Playing football, listening to pop music, swimming
Sarah	Australia	Sydney	Teacher	English and Turkish	Walking, watching TV
Angelina	American	New York	Actress	English and French	Travelling and dancing

1… comes from England. ☐
2… works as a footballer. ☐
3… likes listening to pop music. ☐
4… travels a lot. ☐
5… walks every morning. ☐
6… loves playing football. ☐
7… speaks English and Turkish. ☐
8… lives in Venice. ☐
9… reads a lot. ☐
10… comes from Italy. ☐

- **Step 2**
  Now check your answers with your partner.

Activity 4 (Affective)

Jennifer's summer holidays

- **Step 1**
  Read the following statements about Jennifer's school holidays and indicate whether you do the same or different things on your school holidays.

  Jennifer ...

	Yes	No
1… travels abroad.	☐	☐
2… visits museums.	☐	☐
3… meets her friends.	☐	☐
4… gets up late in the mornings.	☐	☐
5… sleeps over at a friend's house.	☐	☐
6… goes swimming.	☐	☐
7… reads a lot.	☐	☐
8… invites her friends around.	☐	☐
9… watches her favourite movies.	☐	☐
10… rides her bike.	☐	☐

- **Step 2**
  Compare your results with your partner. How many similar things do you do on your school holidays?

Activity 5 (Affective)

Julia's New Year celebrations

- **Step 1**
  Listen to the following statements that describe what Julia usually does to celebrate the New Year and decide whether you do or do not do the same things at New Year.

	I do	I don't	[*Sentences heard by learners*]
Julia…			
1	☐	☐	… receives presents from her family
2	☐	☐	… visits her cousins.
3	☐	☐	… eats lots of chocolate.
4	☐	☐	… buys presents for her friends.
5	☐	☐	… invites her best friend for dinner.
6	☐	☐	… cleans her room.
7	☐	☐	… drinks lots of cola.

8	☐	☐	… dances with her family.
9	☐	☐	… sings carols.
10	☐	☐	…. plays cards

- **Step 2**
  Now compare your answers with your partner. Who does mostly the same things as Julia?

Activity 6 (Affective)

What's right?

- **Step 1**
  Read each sentence, then decide which ones apply to your class teacher. Indicate your answer with an 'X'.

  My teacher….

  1… arrives to school early. ___
  2… wears colourful clothes. ___
  3… drinks coffee before every lesson. ___
  4… eats lunch at the school canteen. ___
  5… makes lessons fun. ___
  6… walks to school. ___
  7… smiles a lot. ___
  8… gives stickers to good students. ___
  9… knows everyone's name by heart. ___
  10… helps students after school. ___

- **Step 2**
  Do you think your teacher is much different from other teachers in your school? Why?

Appendix B

Instructional Material for Traditional Instruction

Explicit Information (Teacher's notes)

- We use the present simple tense to talk about things in general. We use it to talk about habits, permanent situations or about general truths. Very often it is used with the adverbs of frequency (always, usually, often, rarely, never) or other time expressions (every day, in the morning, at the weekends, once a month etc.). But the present tense verbs have a special form for the third person singular where the verb ends in –s or –**e**s.
- A verb in the present simple tense is inflected as follows [*write on board*]:

I visit	I watch
You visit	You watch
He visit**s**	He watch**es**
She visit**s**	She watch**es**
It visit**s**	It watch**es**
We visit	We watch
You visit	You watch
They visit	They watch

- **Spelling rules for he, she, it**
  In verbs ending with –**ss, -ch, -sh, -x** and –**o** we add the suffix –**es**. Pay attention to the following examples [*write on board*]:

  ki**ss**→ kiss**es**
  cat**ch**→ catch**es**
  g**o**→ go**es**
  pu**sh**→ push**es**
  mi**x**→ mix**es**

- Now tell me some sentences that are true for you or a person you know using the present simple, as in the example [*write on board*]:

  I ride my bike every Saturday.
  My sister reads her favourite magazine in the afternoon.
  [*Elicit answers from the students and write some on the board*]

Activity 1

Write the verbs in the present simple for ***he/she/it***.
catch, drive, stay, go, push, teach, walk, mix, sleep, eat

-s	-es

Activity 2

Circle the correct word.

Every day my family and I (1) **wake/wakes** up at 7.30 am. We (2) **eat/eats** breakfast at 8 o'clock. Mum (3) **prepare/prepares** eggs. My sister (4) **cut/cuts** the bread and I (5) **set/sets** the table. Dad sometimes (6) **go/goes** to the shop to buy milk. We all (7) **leave/leaves** the house at 9 o'clock. Mum always (8) **kiss/kisses** us before we (9) **take/takes** the bus to school and Dad (10) **drive/drives** to work.

Activity 3

Fill in the blanks with the present simple form of the verbs in brackets.

1. I never ………….. (drink) coffee.
2. We often ………….. (eat) in the office.
3. He ………….. (meet) his friend every day.
4. Our cat ………….. (watch) birds.
5. Andy always ………….. (invite) his friends around.
6. Victor and I ………….. (speak) English at home.
7. Teachers sometimes ………….. (help) students after school.
8. Cathy sometimes ………….. (dance) at parties.
9. She ………….. (play) tennis twice a week.
10. Monkeys ………….. (love) eating bananas.

Activity 4

Tick (√) what is true for you and what is true for your friend. Then write sentences using the chart below.

	I	My friend
take photos		
watch TV		
listen to music		
wear sunglasses		
do homework		
eat pizza		
play computer games		

I	My friend
1. ………………………………	1. ………………………………
2. ……………………………...	2.………………………………..
3. ………………………………	3. ………………………………
4. ………………………………	4. ………………………………
5. ………………………………	5. ………………………………

Activity 5

Read Tina's letter to her new pen friend. Complete with the present simple form of the verbs below.

eat/play/go/wash/work/do/live/teach/like/water

Dear Christine,
My name is Tina and I am your new pen friend. I (1) ……………….. in Scotland. My father (2) ………………….. in a factory and my mother (3) ……………. English at my school. I have got a brother and a sister.
At the weekends my brother and I usually (4)………………. football. My sister doesn't like football. She (5)………………riding her bike instead. My mother and father sometimes (6) ……………… to the cinema. Every Saturday my father (7) ……………..the car and my mother (8) ……………… the flowers in the garden. On Sundays we often (9) …………… in a restaurant.
What do you and your family (10)…………….. at the weekend?
Your friend,
Tina

Appendix C

Assessment Tasks

(Interpretation task)

- Listen to the following sentences and decide whether or not each sentence is referring to Patrick or his school friends.

	Patrick	school friends	not sure	[*Sentences heard by students*]
(1)	_____	______	_____	plays basketball every day.
(2)	_____	______	_____	read a lot of comics.
(3)	_____	______	_____	hates popcorn.
(4)	_____	______	_____	lives in London.
(5)	_____	______	_____	speak good English.
(6)	_____	______	_____	drinks lots of orange juice.
(7)	_____	______	_____	eat a sandwich for school lunch.
(8)	____	______	_____	walk to school every day.
(9)	_____	______	_____	goes to school by car.
(10)	_____	______	_____	love green apples.
(11)	_____	______	_____	gets up at 7 am every morning.
(12)	_____	______	_____	wake up at 8 o'clock.
(13)	_____	______	_____	take a shower every day.
(14)	_____	______	_____	runs every afternoon.
(15)	_____	______	_____	watches a film every night.
(16)	_____	______	_____	buy lots of books.
(17)	_____	______	_____	listens to an MP3 player.
(18)	_____	______	_____	know Italian.
(19)	_____	______	_____	goes to bed at 11 pm.
(20)	_____	______	_____	visit friends after school.

Test 1 (production task)

- Fill in the gap with the correct form of the verb.

Every Sunday Tim 1 _______(get) up before 7 am. Before eating his breakfast, he always 2 _______(drink) a cup of coffee. Tim 3_______(stay) at home at weekends as he 4 ______(want) to have a rest. He 5______(read) his book, 6_____(look) at magazines and 7______(watch) TV most of the day. If the weather is good Tim 8_____(walk) in the local park. He usually 9_____(eat) his dinner at his friend's house and 10______(arrive) home at around 7 pm.

Version B (Interpretation task)

- You will hear 20 sentences. For each sentence you hear, decide who is doing the action or to whom the verb is referring – to Michael or his cousins.

Michael	**his cousins**	**not sure**	
[*Sentences heard by students*]			
(1) _____	______	_____	plays the piano every day.
(2) _____	______	_____	visit the zoo three days a week.
(3) _____	______	_____	hates Coca Cola.
(4) _____	______	_____	lives in France.
(5) _____	______	_____	speak Italian and Spanish.
(6) _____	______	_____	drinks lots of coffee.
(7) _____	______	_____	eat pizza every Saturday.
(8) _____	______	_____	walk to school on Fridays.
(9) _____	______	_____	arrives at school on time.
(10) _____	______	_____	love green apples.
(11) _____	______	_____	wants to go to England.
(12) _____	______	_____	wake up at 6 o'clock.
(13) _____	______	_____	takes a shower every day.
(14) _____	______	_____	eat ice-cream every afternoon.
(15) _____	______	_____	watches a DVD every night.
(16) _____	______	_____	hate hot weather.
(17) _____	______	_____	listens to the radio.
(18) _____	______	_____	know how to play volleyball.
(19) _____	______	_____	swims every Sunday.
(20) _____	______	_____	enjoy school work.

Test 2 (production task)

Put the verbs in brackets in the correct form.

Sarah is a teacher. She 1_____(work) in the local primary school. She 2____ (live) five miles away from the school so she 3_____(get) up at 8 am, 4____ (eat) her breakfast, 5____ (get) dressed and 6____(walk) to school. Sarah 7_____(arrive) at school around 8.45am and 8____(drink) coffee before her lessons. At 9.15am she_____(start) her first lesson and 10____(finish) at 10 am.

9 Individual Differences and Processing Instruction

James F. Lee, University of New South Wales (Australia)*

The research presented in this volume adds considerably to a previously little researched aspect of the effects of processing instruction, that of individual differences. In Lee (2004: 318) I posed two questions: 'What are the characteristics of the learners who benefit the most from PI? What are the characteristics of the learners who benefit the least, if indeed there are learners who make no significant improvement after instruction?' At the time, the results of processing instruction research had only been presented in aggregate terms. No consideration of individual differences had yet emerged in the processing instruction research and so the proposed individual difference hypothesis was based on a logical assumption and was vaguely worded: some learners benefit more from PI than do others (Lee, 2004: 318; Benati and Lee, 2008: 172). In this chapter I consider the differential benefits to learners of receiving processing instruction as we move closer to identifying the characteristics of the 'some learners' I referred to. I begin with the research published before this volume emerged (Part I) and then move to consider the findings presented in this volume of research (Part II). Finally, I suggest avenues for future investigation (Where to Now?).

* **James Lee** is Deputy Head of the School of Humanities and Languages at the University of New South Wales, Sydney, Australia where he teaches Spanish area studies and second language acquisition. His main research interest is second language input processing and, with Alessandro Benati, has co-authored several books on processing instruction. His most recent work is with Paul Malovrh, *The Developmental Dimension in Instructed Second Language Learning: The L2 Acquisition of Object Pronouns in Spanish* (Bloomsbury, 2013).

Part I: What are the Differential Benefits of PI?

We have only a handful of investigations that have examined the role of individual differences in the results of processing instruction prior to the works collected in this volume. These are the works I treat here in Part I. The individual differences noted in the published literature include the following. First, some learners benefit from instruction more than others and, indeed, some learners do not benefit from instruction at all. Second, while the research strives to create homogeneous groups of participants such that all are, for expample, native speakers of English, some research has confronted the issue of the learners' language background. Finally, a body of work has emerged examing the role of grammatical sensitivity, a component of language aptitude, and the role of explicit information in the effects of processing instruction.

Lee and Benati with Aguilar-Sánchez and McNulty (2007) compared the performance of 25 learners of Spanish to whom processing instruction was delivered in three different modes: classroom delivery to the entire class of learners, individual delivery in a computer laboratory, and a hybrid mode of providing individuals in a classroom the screen printouts of the computer delivery mode and having them carry out the activities individually. The targets of instruction were past aspectual distinction and negative informal commands in Spanish. The aggregate results showed equally positive effects for processing instruction in the three modes, on both linguistic targets and with full retention of the effects after a two-week period. Lee *et al.* did, however, note some inconsistencies in the learners' performance while conducting the data analyses and decided to probe the data further.

They found that although the majority of learners benefited significantly from instruction, not all learners did. The learners' performance on the immediate post-test showed that nine learners (36% of the participants) did not benefit from instruction on aspectual distinction while three (12%) did not on the negative commands. The twenty-five learners they examined participated in the instruction of both linguistic targets. They found that the majority of the learners' performance on the immediate post-test across the two linguistic targets vacillated (n = 19 or 76%). Specifically, only six learners significantly improved on both targets and the same six's performance remained constant from the immediate to the delayed post-test. They did not gather background information on the participants that would have allowed them to analyse which characteristics this group of six possessed that contributed to their performance. But clearly, this subgroup of six benefited the most. The researchers simply noted the pattern in performance and left it to future investigation.

Participant screening in processing instruction research involves testing learners' pre-existing knowledge of the target structure. Learners whose knowledge exceeds a particular level, typically about 60% accuracy on the target structure, are not included in the study. Lee *et al.*'s participants all scored less than 60% on the pre-tests for both linguistic structures but the range of scores allowed them to classify the participants' pre-test scores as high, medium or low for both target structures. Interestingly, their analyses revealed that the learners with high pre-test scores (56% for aspectual distinction and 20% for negative informal commands) did not significantly improve their scores on the immediate post-test. Only the learners who were rated to have had medium or low pre-test scores significantly improved their scores on the immediate post-test. Why would this be the case? They speculated that perhaps the learners with some knowledge of the target structure did not put the same effort into learning in an experimental setting as the learners with less knowledge of the target structure did. Yet, the results presented by Benati (2001) and VanPatten and Wong (2004) suggest that previous knowledge is not a critical factor in performance. While Lee *et al.*'s results need to be replicated and further corroborated, they do suggest that I may have to refine one of my hypotheses about the effects of processing instruction: 'PI will be equally effective as an intervention for establishing initial form-meaning connections as it is for improving learners' performance' (Lee, 2004: 322). A direct comparison of +/– previous knowledge groups would begin to address this issue.

Lee and Benati with Aguilar-Sánchez and McNulty (2007) faced the issue of the role of language background in their investigation of the effects of processing instruction. One of the strengths of their research design was that they explored the performance of one group of learners who were taught two linguistic structures and participated in immediate and delayed post-testing on both items. The attrition rate of participants in their study was a noteworthy 87% due in part to learners not being present for all the data collections. Their desire to have native speakers of English for whom Spanish was their only second language yielded a small participant pool of 19. They did, however, find a group of six learners who had met the participation requirements but had studied a language in addition to Spanish. They statistically compared this group's performance (from pre-tests to post-tests) to that of the English + Spanish only group and found no significant differences. Therefore, they simply incorporated those learners into the study and did not treat language background as a separate variable.

Benati and Lee with McNulty (2010) did, however, treat language background as a variable in their research on the effects of processing instruction on the Spanish subjunctive after the adverb *cuando*. They examined native speakers of English who had studied only Spanish as a second language, native speakers of English who were studying Spanish as a third or subsequent language, and non-native speakers of English studying Spanish as a third or subsequent language. The pre-test scores of the three groups of learners showed no statistically significant differences across the groups for accurate sentence interpretation, accurate form production in sentences, and accurate form production in a guided composition. There were no apparent advantages of plurilingualism for a form and function they did not know. After receiving processing instruction, the three groups improved significantly and equally. That is, there were no statistically significant differences in post-test scores across the three groups. Language background did not affect the outcome as measured by accuracy. The plurilinguals did not learn more than the bilinguals.

One aspect of the performance of the non-native speakers of English on the guided composition pre-test did, however, distinguish the plurilinguals. Specifically, this group generated significantly more contexts in their guided compositions in which a subjunctive form after *cuando* should have been used than the other two groups did. The forms they used were not any more accurate than the forms the other two groups used but there was a difference between the groups going into instruction. This difference, however, disappeared after instruction. There was no statistically significant difference between the groups' performance on the post-test composition in the number of contexts generated for using the subjunctive forms. These results indicate that the groups benefited from instruction differently. That is, the two groups of native speakers of English benefited from instruction in that they learned the forms and they learned to create contexts in which to use the forms. The non-native speakers of English benefited from instruction in that they learned to use the correct forms in contexts that they were already generating. What appeared to be an advantage prior to instruction was equalized through instruction. Benati *et al.* concluded that all the learners benefited from processing instruction but that given one's language background there may be different benefits to be gained.

VanPatten and colleagues have undertaken several studies in which they measured learners' grammatical sensitivity, a component of language aptitude, using a section of the Modern Language Aptitude Test (Carroll and Sapon, 1959) and related it to the effects of explicit information in processing instruction. The subsection of the test that measures grammatical sensitivity requires the learners to identify words that perform similar functions in two different sentences. A summary of the results related to significant correlations involving grammatical sensitivity are presented in Table 9.1. VanPatten and colleagues correlated the learners' scores for grammatical sensitivity with two different measures: trials to criterion and final outcome. Criterion is a benchmark the researchers set to indicate when learners began to correctly process consistently. Trials to criterion is the number of practice items that the learners completed during the treatment phase before they achieved the criterion. The final outcome is a measure of overall processing accuracy. Final outcome in these studies is the number of items answered correctly in the last ten items of the treatment materials. The studies involve linguistic structures in Spanish, German, Russian and French that are all affected by learners' use of the first noun strategy to identify the agent.

The results for a significant correlation between grammatical sensitivity and trials to criterion show an overall significant correlation between the two for German accusative case definite articles in OVS word order patterns (VanPatten and Borst, 2012a; VanPatten *et al.*, 2013). The significant correlation in both experiments was isolated to the group of learners who had received explicit information (+EI) as part of the treatment. VanPatten and colleagues point out that the correlations are weak and that they account for very little of the variance in the learners' trial to criterion scores. These results indicate that for this grammatical form, grammatical sensitivity is a factor affecting performance but appears to be more in the background of events rather than the foreground.

The significant correlations between learners' scores for grammatical and the final outcome of learning show a more varied picture. There was a significant correlation between the two for German case markings on definite articles (VanPatten and Borst, 2012a; VanPatten *et al.*, 2013) and Russian case markings on nouns (VanPatten *et al.*, 2013). Even so, the correlations were weak, accounted for little of the variance in final outcome scores, and did not apply to the +/–EI groups separately. No significant correlations were found for Spanish object pronouns (VanPatten and Borst, 2012b; VanPatten *et al.*, 2013) and for French causative constructions (VanPatten *et al.*, 2013). These results show that for certain grammatical forms grammatical sensitivity is not even a background factor in accounting for learners' performance. VanPatten *et al.* (2013: 521) conclude that the lack of a strong relationship between grammatical sensitivity and processing instruction is 'because processing-defined as connecting meaning to form during real time comprehension-is not related to any traditional aptitude measures'. Traditional aptitude measures may be related to rule learning more than to correct sentence processing.

Study	Comparison	Trials to criterion	Final outcome
VanPatten and Borst (2012a) German case markings on definite articles in OVS sentence patterns	Overall	yes	yes
	+EI only	yes	no
	–EI only	no	no
VanPatten and Borst (2012b) Spanish object pronoun in OVS sentence patterns	Overall	no	no
	+EI only	no	not done
	–EI only	no	not done
VanPatten *et al.* (2013) Spanish object pronoun in OVS sentence patterns	Overall	no	no
	+EI only	no	not done
	–EI only	no	not done
VanPatten *et al.* (2013) German case markings on definite articles in OVS sentence patterns	Overall	yes	yes
	+EI only	yes	no
	–EI only	no	no
VanPatten *et al.* (2013) Russian case markings on nouns	Overall	no	yes
	+EI only	no	no
	–EI only	no	no
VanPatten *et al.* (2013) French causative construction	Overall	no	no
	+EI only	no	no
	–EI only	no	no

Table 9.1. Significant correlations between grammatical sensitivity and trials to criterion and final outcome

Part II: What are the Differential Benefits of PI?

Language Background

The research presented in this volume has added considerably to our understanding of the role of individual differences in the results of processing instruction. This part of the present chapter will highlight the insights gained from the research presented here.

Lee and McNulty, in Chapter 3, extended their previous investigation of the role of language background on the effects of processing instruction (Benati and Lee with McNulty, 2010). In the present volume, they examined the performance of three groups of learners: native speakers of English who had studied only Spanish as a second language, native speakers of

English who were studying Spanish as a third or subsequent language, and non-native speakers of English studying Spanish as a third or subsequent language. They provided learners instruction on the subjunctive/indicative contrast after the adverb *cuando*. They analysed performance on indicative as well as subjunctive contexts and provided greater detail of the learners' performance on the component parts of the production assessment task that they had analysed in aggregate terms in Benati and Lee with McNulty (2010). The consideration of the indicative contexts speaks to the issue of the overgeneralization of instruction, that is, the use of a newly taught form in inappropriate contexts. Because the use of the subjunctive after *cuando* entails the semantic concepts of [+futurity, +uncertainty], they analysed the forms learners used to express these concepts both before and after they received instruction.

The three language background groups showed no statistically significant differences in performance on the pre-tests: interpretation test, fill-in-the-blank form production test, sentence-fragment form production test, form production in a discourse-level guided composition, and the number of contexts generated to use the subjunctive after *cuando* in the discourse-level guided composition. There was, however, a trend towards significance ($p = .0526$) with regard to the number of contexts learners generated for using a subjunctive form after *cuando*. They explored this further to find that the non-native speakers of English generated significantly more contexts than the other two groups thus corroborating the findings in Benati and Lee with McNulty (2010). They then provided learners with processing instruction, the effects of which were very consistent. They found a significant effect for Time (pre-test/post-test), no effect for Language Background and no significant interaction of the two on an interpretation task, a fill-in-the-blank form-production task, a sentence fragment form-production task, accurate form production in a guided composition, and the number of contexts generated in which to use a subjunctive form after *cuando*. All learners improved significantly and improved equally.

Their analyses revealed only four learners who overgeneralized instruction on the subjunctive into indicative contexts and they did so in all test items. These four learners represent each of the language backgrounds. They concluded that overgeneralization was not a widespread phenomenon in the context of their study and that those who appeared to be overgeneralizing were using a test-taking strategy of 'use the new form'. Finally, they found that learners used a variety of forms to express the concept [+future, +uncertainty] prior to instruction, but that the use of the present indicative dominated, ranging from 48% to 64% of the forms across the three production tasks. They concluded that learners were not processing the [+future] meaning in the sentences on the pre-tests. The forms that dominated after the learners received processing instruction were the subjunctive forms, ranging from 79% to 92% across the three production tasks. They concluded that learners not only acquired the formal feature of the subjunctive morphology but also processed the [+future] meaning of the sentences. That the instruction was extremely effective across all three language backgrounds provides convincing support for the Native Language Hypothesis: 'PI will be effective for instilling target-language specific processing strategies, no matter the native language of the learners' (Benati and Lee, 2008: 173). While a linguistically homogeneous subject population is desirable in terms of research design, it may not be a necessity when assessing the effects of processing instruction which could look more heavily at pre-test scores. Language background may not be an individual difference that researchers need to concern themselves about. Certainly in terms of classroom applications, teachers may feel confident when using processing instruction that all the students are benefiting.

Age

This volume contains four empirical examinations of the role of the learners' age in the results of processing instruction. In Chapter 4, Benati compares the performance of children and adults who received processing instruction on the English passive construction. The participants were all native speakers of Turkish; the children were enrolled in secondary school and the adults in university. Identical materials were used with both groups. Benati measured performance with an interpretation task and sentence completion form-production test. He carried these out as a pre-test, immediate post-test and a three-week delayed post-test. The two groups' performance on the pre-test showed no statistically significant differences in scores indicating that the two groups began the treatment with equivalent knowledge of the English passive. The results after instruction were extremely consistent. Benati found that there was a significant effect for Time, no effect for Age Group and no interaction between the two on either the interpretation or production test. Moreover, learners retained the benefits of instruction over the three week period. Both groups improved significantly and equally as a result of receiving processing instruction.

Laval (Chapter 5, this volume) expands on her work with the transfer-of-training effects found in Benati, Lee with Laval (2008). In this chapter, she replicates the study carried out with university-age adults by carrying it out with 9–10-year-old native speakers of English. She made minor changes in the materials to make the age-appropriate. The present study offers us an indirect comparison with the 2008 findings. The children performed almost the same as the adults did in that five out of six statistical comparisons yielded the same results for this group of children and the adults investigated previously. The results for the primary effects of processing instruction on the French past imperfect indicated that the processing instruction group improved significantly on both the interpretation and production tasks whereas the control group did not. The results for the secondary effects of processing instruction on the French subjunctive verb morphology indicated that the processing instruction group improved significantly on the interpretation task but not on the production tasks (the post-test score was 0); this finding contrasts with that of Benati, Lee with Laval (2008) who found that the 10% increase in performance yielded a statistically significant effect. The control group did not improve on either task. The results for the cumulative effects of processing instruction on the French causative construction showed that the processing instruction group improved significantly on both the interpretation and production tasks whereas the control group did not. Laval's research adds further support to two hypotheses.

> *The Secondary Transfer-of-Training Hypothesis*: learners who receive training on one type of processing strategy for one specific form will appropriately transfer the use of that strategy to other forms without further instruction in PI.

> *The Secondary Transfer-of-Training Hypothesis:* learners who receive training on one type of processing strategy will begin to work differently with primary linguistic data (Benati and Lee, 2008: 174).

Laval's work, along with that of Benati, Lee with Houghton (2008), have demonstrated primary and transfer-of-training effects with children. Substantiating the findings with children demonstrates the power of processing instruction to alter the way learners process primary linguistic data.

Angelovska and Benati (Chapter 6, this volume) directly compared the performance of children and adults who received processing instruction on the English simple past tense. The participants were all native speakers of German enrolled in either a high school or language centre; the children were, on average, aged 10.5 years old and the adults, 26. Angelovska and Benati performed two separate comparisons, although they provided all groups the same instructional materials, because they used two different interpretation tasks to measure performance. One interpretation task was typical for processing instruction, indeed it was used in Benati (2005). Learners heard a sentence and identified the temporal framework. The second task was developed because of the way simple past and the present perfect function in German, the learners' L1, which prefers the present perfect in colloquial speech to express past. Statistical analyses revealed that both age groups had equivalent knowledge on both tests prior to treatment. The results of their statistical analyses indicated that there was a significant effect for Time, no effect for Age Group and no interaction between the two on the interpretation test. Both age groups improved significantly and equally. Additionally, both groups retained the benefits of instruction through two weeks after instruction. These results corroborated Benati's (2005) so that we can affirm that processing instruction is effective for Greek-, Chinese- and German-speaking children as well as extending those results to affirm that it is equally effective for German-speaking children and adults.

The results on the second interpretation test were quite different. They found a significant main effect for Time, a significant main effect for Age Group and a significant interaction between the two. The significant interaction was due to the fact that the children did not improve from pre-test to the post-tests. Only the adults improved significantly from pre-test to post-test and retained their level of performance on the delayed post-test. On the one hand, Angelovka and Benati found in favour of the Age Hypothesis (Benati and Lee, 2008), but, on the other, they obtained a result contrary to it. The results that support the Age Hypothesis were derived from an interpretation task that required learners to identify a temporal framework as 'last year' or 'right now', based on the distinction between the simple past and the simple present. Both adults and children improved significantly and equally through to the delayed post-test. Only the adult group, however, improved on the interpretation task that tested the difference between the simple past (i.e., an action completed in the past) and present perfect (an action begun in the past but still relevant to the present time). The instructional materials associated the lexical adverbs 'now' and 'still' with the present perfect. The challenge for the learners, especially the children, is that both the simple past and regular past participles of the present perfect in English end in *–ed*. The children may have focused on the end of the verb while not attending to the auxiliary. Angelovska and Benati could pursue their results by comparing the two groups' performance on the instructional materials. Did the children perform well or poorly on the practice items using the present perfect? What did the two groups score for trials to criterion on the practices using the present perfect compared to the practices with present/past?

Another consideration is whether there are cognitive maturational factors to consider in the children's performance. To that end, I gave my three 11-year-old children, who are monolingual speakers of English, the six items from Angelovka and Benati's activity (step 3 of the referential activity 3 in Appendix B). They were to decide whether the sentences were true, false, or that they couldn't tell. After they responded to the items in writing, I had them do a retrospection. Item 5, the sentence about visiting Mexico, is the only item to which all three responded the same and in this instance they responded correctly, indicating that the second sentence was true.

5) *I visited Mexico.*
   ⇨ Now I am not in Mexico T/F/C

The children stated the following in their retrospections.

1. It's past tense. I visited Mexico last year, not I visited Mexico I'm there now.
2 It's speaking in past tense. He had visited Mexico. So he's back.
3. It's like [item] 2. It's past tense. I visited Mexico. Now I'm not in Mexico. That makes sense. It's past tense.

Interestingly, all three children gave a metalinguistic rationale for their response to item 5 (it's past tense) but none of them consistently applied that rationale to other items. For example, two of them responded incorrectly to item 2 about the chopped finger.

2) *John chopped his finger with a knife.*
   ⇨ He is in pain now. T/F/C

They stated the following in their retrospections.

1. If you chop your finger with a knife, it's going to hurt.
2. If you chop you feel pain.

Although item 2 is structurally similar to item 5, the two children's incorrect responses are based on their world view of cause and effect relationships.

Their responses to the sentences with the present perfect all referred to the truth value of the statements.

1) *Mary has received a new bike.*
   ⇨ Her bike (the only one she has) is new now. T/F/C

Their responses follow. The first two indicated that the sentence was true and the third that the sentence was false.

1. She got a new bike so it's new.
2. New [pointing to the word in the first sentence]. New [pointing to the word in the second sentence]. Mary has just received a new bike.
3. It's as if she had one before. You can't buy one and have it be new.

Their responses are not metalinguistic but rather lexically driven. They are expressing their views on what the word 'new' means.

Angelovska and Benati's findings regarding the children's performance on past versus present perfect, plus my informal results with native speaking children, suggest that there are maturational constraints on the Age Hypothesis. Therefore, I propose the following reiteration of the Age Hypothesis.

> *The Age Hypothesis.* PI will be just as effective as an intervention with younger learners as it is with older learners for grammatical structures and concepts within their cognitive maturational level.

Agiasophiti (Chapter 7, this volume) conducted an investigation of the effects of colour enhancement and the learners' biological gender on the effects of processing instruction on German case-marked definite articles in OVS sentence patterns. She used a different font colour to highlight and hence draw learners' attention to the different cases of the definite articles in the input and compared that to unenhanced (typographically neutral) processing instruction. The results for enhancement were mixed whereas the results for biological gender were consistent. Males and females benefited equally from enhanced and unenhanced processing instruction. There was no effect for enhancement on learners' performance on the interpretation task on either the immediate or delayed post-test and both processing instruction groups outperformed the control group. There was, however, a positive effect for colour enhanced input on the immediate form-production post-test but that effect disappeared by the delayed post-test at which time the scores of the two processing instruction groups showed no statistical differences between them and, again, both groups outperformed the control group.

Mavrantoni and Benati (Chapter 8, this volume) also explored the effect of age on the results of processing instruction and traditional instruction by examining the performance of two differently aged groups of children (pre- and post-puberty). The target of instruction was the English simple past tense. The participants were all native speakers of Greek. Identical materials were used with both groups. Mavrantoni and Benati measured performance with an interpretation and a form-production test. Their first analyses focused on the differential effects of instruction type. They analysed the performance of the two age groups in separate statistical analyses; the results were, however, the same. The processing instruction groups significantly outperformed the traditional instruction groups on the interpretation task. The two different instructional groups both improved significantly and equally on the production task. Mavrantoni and Benati then directly compared the performance of the two age groups that received processing instruction. They found a significant effect for Time, no effect for Age Group and no interaction between the two on either the interpretation or production test. These results indicated that both age groups that received processing instruction improved significantly and equally. There was no effect for puberty in their results.

I proposed the Age Hypothesis in 2004 based only on the results of VanPatten and Oikennon (1996). Benati and I reiterated the Age Hypothesis in 2008 based on the results of Benati (2005), Benati, Lee with Houghton (2008) and Marsden (2006). The research presented in this volume, however, provides the necessary direct comparisons of different age groups to affirm the fundamental claim of the Age Hypothesis that processing instruction is effective across a range of age groups.

Where to Now?

I developed the Individual Difference Hypothesis in 2004 and Benati and I reiterated it in 2008. '*The Individual Difference Hypothesis*: some learners benefit more from PI than do others' (Benati and Lee, 2008: 172). At both points in time I had not considered the characteristics of the 'some learners' to whom I had referred, and I had only considered the idea of 'benefit more' in terms of outcomes on interpretation and production tests, the dominant measures used in processing instruction research. The first point to make about individual differences is that they are not widespread. The vast majority of learners benefit significantly from processing insruction so that the 'some learners' referred to in the hypothesis must be seen as a small handful of learners who are, nonetheless, important to understand. The research that has emerged in the literature and in this volume allows us to characterize the 'some learners' based on their previous knowledge of the target structure (e.g., Lee and Benati with Águilar-Sánchez and McNulty, 2007) and grammatical sensitivity (e.g., VanPatten and Borst, 2012a; 2012b; VanPatten *et al.*, 2013) but not in terms of their language background (e.g., Benati and

Lee with McNulty, 2010; Lee and McNulty, Chapter 3, this volume), age (e.g., Angelovska and Benati, Chapter 6; Benati, Chapter 4; Laval, Chapter 5; Mavrantoni and Benati, Chapter 8, all in this volume) nor gender (Agiasophiti, Chapter 7, this volume). The benefits, or lack thereof, have been documented in terms of outcomes on interpretation and production tests, that is, we look for group differences on the outcome scores (e.g., Agiasophiti, Chapter 7; Angelovka and Benati, Chapter 6; Benati; Chapter 4; Laval, Chapter 5; Mavrantoni and Benati, Chapter 8, all in this volume). But we have also documented the benefits, or lack thereof, by examining learning gains, that is, the outcome or the end point in relation to the starting point, such as high or low level of previous knowledge and contexts generated in which to use the target form (Benati and Lee with McNulty, 2010; Lee and Benati with Águilar-Sánchez and McNulty, 2007; Lee and McNulty, Chapter 3, this volume). And we have sought to find differences in terms of a process measure, i.e., trials to criterion or learning rate (e.g., Fernández, 2008; VanPatten and Borst, 2012a, 2012b).

An important question for future research to consider is, How do we reveal the different ways in which processing instruction is differentially beneficial? To date we have measured the effects of individual differences via outcomes, gains and learning rate but have done so on a limited number of tasks. The research by Mavrantoni and Benati (Chapter 8, this volume) and Lee and McNulty (Chapter 3, this volume) demonstrate that individual differences manifest themselves in tasks that are not directly reflected in the instruction learners received. Future research on individual differences could pursue the relationship between tasks and the results of processing instruction by using tasks such as video retellings (e.g., Sanz, 2004) and other discourse-level oral tasks, guided compositions (e.g., Cheng, 2002), and grammaticality judgment tasks (e.g., Toth, 2006). Discourse-level production tasks provide the opportunity to examine learning gains by comparing, not just outcomes, but the number of contexts learners generate for the target form before and after instruction. Benati (Chapter 4, this volume) and Angelovska and Benati (Chapter 6, this volume) included delayed post-tests up to three weeks after instruction and found no effects based on a learner's age during this time period. Future work on individual differences could address retention over a longer period of time and not just with learners' age but other individual differences as well, for example, language background and grammatical sensitivity.

We have very good evidence that processing instruction is effective with secondary- and university-level learners; they achieve the same outcome. There are two avenues of future research to pursue with regard to the role of a learner's age and processing instruction. First, we could pursue the extremes of the age spectrum by providing processing instruction to very young primary school-aged children and to more mature learners whose age may have slowed their processing mechanisms. The research on learners' age presented in this volume compared learning outcomes. The findings of the work presented in this volume showed no significant differences among the age groups on pre-test scores and none on post-test scores including a delayed post-test up to three weeks later (Benati, Chapter 4, this volume; Angelovska and Benati, Chapter 6, this volume). So, the second line of future research to pursue is to examine the effects of age on learning rate (trials to criterion). Do adults begin to accurately process more quickly than children do?

The questions I posed related to the Individual Difference Hypothesis include the phrase '*if* indeed there are learners who make no significant improvement after instruction' (Lee, 2004: 318; emphasis added). This phrase reflected my obvious optimism about the power of processing instruction to alter learners' ineffective or inefficient processing strategies. Trials to criterion is a process-oriented measure and indicates the amount of practice a learner needs to be successful. Fernández (2008), Henry, Culman and VanPatten (2009) and VanPatten and Borst (2012b) all indicated that there were learners who did not meet the criterion of answering correctly three target items and a distracter in a row. Given these results I see two areas for further investigation. First, what are the characteristics of the learners in Fernández (2008), Henry, Culman and VanPatten (2009) and VanPatten and Borst (2012b) who did not reach the criterion? Second, the number of practice items used in the studies varied, 30 in Culman *et al.* and Fernández but 50 in VanPatten and Borst. I note that VanPatten and Cadierno (1993) used over 100 items and Sanz (2004) used 56. All these studies, except Henry *et al.*, examined the same target structure, object pronouns in Spanish in the OVS sentence pattern. Future research could systematically vary the number of practice items to determine its role in processing instruction with both process and outcome measures as suggested by Henry *et al.* (2009: 573). What are the characteristics of learners who require only a few practice items to succeed and those who require many?

The critical variable in Fernández (2008), Henry, Culman and VanPatten (2009), VanPatten and Borst (2012a; 2012b) and VanPatten *et al.* (2013) is the role of explicit information in the results of processing instruction. Their results suggest that an area of future research could examine the role of individual differences in the way learners use or do not use explicit information in processing instruction. Trials to criterion is one indication but future research might approach the question another way, specifically, with learners doing an introspection (think aloud) as they carry out the practice items, a technique that has successfully revealed learners' input processing strategies (e.g., Lee, 1999; Rossomondo, 2007). The technique could be applied to processing instruction research to reveal how different learners interact with the different components of explicit informtion (explanation and information about processing strategies) and reveal the learning mechanism(s) used by successful learners as well as those used by unsuccessful learners. In this way we may be able to provide evidence to support the following: 'Our conclusion is that not all EI [explicit information] is the same, not all structures are the same, and the interaction of EI, structure, and processing problem may yield different results in different studies' (Henry *et al.* 2009: 573).

Another avenue for further investigation is in the area of transfer-of-training effects. Benati and Lee (2008) demonstrated positive transfer-of-training effects for processing instruction on both interpretation and production tasks. Laval (Chapter 5, this volume) adds to this research base. Admittedly, the effect sizes are small which leads me to believe that certain individuals are more prone to transfer-of-training effects than others. What are their characteristics?

Conclusion

Who benefits the most from processing instruction? Who benefits the least? These questions are still worth investigating. We may, however, wish to ask more nuanced questions. Who benefits the most from processing instruction, on which linguistic structures and under what contextual conditions? Who benefits the least from processing instruction, on which linguistic structures and under what contextual conditions? We may also wish to take a more nuanced approach to individual differences by examining aptitude complexes (Robinson, 2001) thereby compiling an inventory of individual differences, for example, grammatical sensitivity + working memory capacity or grammatical sensitivity + age. There is much work left to do in the area of the role of individual differences on the effects of processing instruction.

References

Benati, A. (2001). A comparative study of the effects of processing instruction and output-based instruction on the acquisition of the Italian future tense. *Language Teaching Research*, 5, 95–127.

Benati, A. (2005). The effects of PI, TI and MOI in the acquisition of English simple past tense. *Language Teaching Research*, 9, 67–113.

Benati, A., and Lee, J. F. (2008). *Grammar Acquisition and Processing Instruction: Secondary and Cumulative Effects*. Bristol: Multilingual Matters.

Benati, A., Lee, J. F., with Houghton, S. (2008). Chapter 4: From processing instruction on the acquisition of English past tense to secondary transfer-of-training effects on English third person singular present tense. In Benati, A. and Lee, J. F., *Grammar Acquisition and Processing Instruction: Secondary and Cumulative Effects* (pp. 88–120). Bristol: Multilingual Matters.

Benati, A., Lee, J. F., with Laval, C. (2008). Chapter 5: From processing instruction on the acquisition of French *imparfait* to secondary transfer-of-training effects on French subjunctive and to cumulative transfer-of-training effects with French causative constructions. In Benati, A. and Lee, J. F., *Grammar Acquisition and Processing Instruction: Secondary and Cumulative Effects* (pp. 121–57). Bristol: Multilingual Matters.

Benati, A., Lee, J. F., with McNulty, E. (2010). Chapter 4: Exploring the effects of processing instruction on a discourse-level guided composition with the Spanish subjunctive after the adverb *cuando*. In Benati, A. and Lee, J. F., *Processing Instruction and Discourse* (pp. 97–147). London: Continuum.

Carroll, J. B., and Sapon, S. (1959). *Modern Language Aptitude Test*. San Antonio, TX: The Psychological Corporation.

Cheng, A. (2002). The effects of processing instruction on the acquisition of *ser* and *estar*. *Hispania*, 85, 308–323.

Fernández, C. (2008). Reexamining the role of explicit information in processing instruction. *Studies in Second Language Acquisition*, 30, 277–305.

Henry, N., Culman, H., and VanPatten, B. (2009). More on the effects of explicit information in instructed SLA: a partial replication and a response to Fernández (2008). *Studies in Second Language Acquisition*, 31, 559–75.

Lee, J. F. (1999). On levels of processing and levels of comprehension. In Gutiérrez-Rexach, J. and Martínez-Gil, F. (eds), *Advances in Hispanic Linguistics*, 42–59. Somerville, MA: Cascadilla Press.

Lee, J. F. (2004). On the generalizability, limits, and potential future directions of processing instruction research. In VanPatten, B. (ed.). *Processing Instruction: Theory, Research, and Commentary* (pp. 311–23). Mahwah, NJ: Erlbaum.

Lee, J. F., and Benati, A., with Aguilar-Sánchez, J. and McNulty, E. M. (2007). Chapter 4: Comparing three modes of delivering processing instruction on preterite/imperfect distinction and negative informal commands in Spanish. In Lee, J. F. and Benati, A., *Delivering Processing Instruction in Classrooms and Virtual Contexts: Research and Practice* (pp. 73–98). London: Equinox.

Marsden, E. (2006). Exploring input processing in the classroom: an experimental comparison of processing instruction and enriched input. *Language Learning*, 56, 507–566.

Robinson, P. (2001). Individual differences, cognitive abilities, aptitude complexes and learning conditions in second language acquisition. *Second Language Research*, 17, 368–92.

Rossomondo, A. E. (2007). The role of lexical temporal indicators and text interaction format on the incidental acquisition of Spanish future tense morphology. *Studies in Second Language Acquisition*, 29, 39–66.

Sanz, C. (2004). Computer delivered implicit versus explicit feedback in processing instruction. In VanPatten, B. (ed.). *Processing Instruction: Theory, Research, and Commentary* (pp. 241–55). Mahwah, NJ: Erlbaum.

Toth, P. D. (2006). Processing instruction and a role for output in second language acquisition. *Language Learning*, 56, 319–85.

VanPatten, B., and Borst, S. (2012a). The roles of explicit information and grammatical sensitivity in processing instruction: nominative-accusative case marking and word order in German L2. *Foreign Language Annals*, 45, 92–109.

VanPatten, B., and Borst, S. (2012b). The roles of explicit information and grammatical sensitivity in the processing of clitic object pronouns and word order in L2 Spanish. *Hispania*, 95, 270–84.

VanPatten, B., Collopy, E., Price, J., Borst, S., and Qualin, A. (2013). Explicit information, grammatice sensitivity, and the First-Noun Principle: a cross-linguistic study in processing instruction. *The Modern Language Journal*, 97, 504-525.

VanPatten, B., and Cadierno, T. (1993). Explicit instruction and input processing. *Studies in Second Language Acquisition*, 15, 225–43.

VanPatten, B., and Oikennon, S. (1996). Explanation vs. structured input in processing instruction. *Studies in Second Language Acquisition*, 18, 495–510.

VanPatten, B., and Wong, W. (2004). Processing instruction and the French causative: another replication. In VanPatten, B. (ed.), *Processing Instruction: Theory, Research, and Commentary* (pp. 97–118). Mahwah, NJ: Erlbaum.

Index

CPSIA information can be obtained
at www.ICGtesting.com
Printed in the USA
BVHW040717041218
534607BV00008B/103/P